Keeping Women in
Their Digital Place

Keeping Women in Their Digital Place

The Maintenance of Jewish Gender Norms Online

Ruth Tsuria

The Pennsylvania State University Press
University Park, Pennsylvania

Library of Congress Cataloging-in-
Publication Data

Names: Tsuria, Ruth, author.
Title: Keeping women in their digital place :
the maintenance of Jewish gender norms
online / Ruth Tsuria.
Description: University Park, Pennsylvania
: The Pennsylvania State University
Press, [2024] | Includes bibliographical
references and index.
Summary: "Examines the web of tensions
found in online Jewish spaces, including
websites, forums, and social media
debates, and explores how Orthodox
Jewish women negotiate gender and
sexual norms by both pushing the
boundaries of accepted norms and
enforcing traditional behaviors"—
Provided by publisher.
Identifiers: LCCN 2024008489 | ISBN
9780271097183 (hardback) | ISBN
9780271097190 (paper)
Subjects: LCSH: Jewish women—Conduct
of life. | Gender identity—Religious
aspects—Judaism. | Digital media—
Religious aspects—Judaism. |
Internet—Religious aspects—Judaism.
Classification: LCC HQ1172 .T78 2024 | DDC
305.48/8924—dc23/eng/20240320
LC record available at https://lccn.loc.gov
/2024008489

Copyright © 2024 Ruth Tsuria
All rights reserved
Printed in the United States of America
Published by The Pennsylvania
State University Press,
University Park, PA 16802–1003

No portion of this book may be reproduced,
stored, or transmitted in any format—
including uploading to websites, databases,
language-learning models, and other
repository, retrieval, or artificial intelligence
systems—without prior written permission
by the publisher. Inquiries may be directed
to Penn State University Press, USB II, Suite
112, 22 University Drive, University Park, PA
16802 or rights@psupress.org.

The Pennsylvania State University Press is
a member of the Association of University
Presses.

It is the policy of The Pennsylvania State
University Press to use acid-free paper.
Publications on uncoated stock satisfy
the minimum requirements of American
National Standard for Information
Sciences—Permanence of Paper for Printed
Library Material, ANSI Z39.48–1992.

GPSR Authorized Representative: Logos
Europe, 9 rue Nicolas Poussin, 17000 La
Rochelle, France, contact@logoseurope.eu.

*To my mother and father,
Who taught me about the weaving of
Feminism and technology.*

To my love, my most careful reader.

And to you, my daughter, a future Jewish woman.

Contents

Acknowledgments ix

Introduction
1

1 Exploring Digital Judaism as a Discourse
20

2 Getting Married
43

INTERLUDE 1: Window Installation—Technological Affordances
68

3 Being Intimate
71

INTERLUDE 2: Looking Through Windows—The Power of Everybody
99

4 Becoming a Mother
102

INTERLUDE 3: Breaking Mirrors—Using the Internet for Resistance
124

5 Dealing with Feminism
127

Conclusions
151

Notes 169

Bibliography 180

Index 188

Acknowledgments

No book is an individual project, even if it is a manuscript. A project like this, which spans over many years, requires collaboration with readers, editors, peers, and the constant support of family and friends. In this acknowledgment section, I wish to thank those people who supported me and this project during the writing, thinking, editing, and finalizing of this book.

First, I'd like to thank my mentor and friend Dr. Heidi Campbell, whose work inspired me to explore digital religion and who endlessly gave me direction and encouragement. To the first readers of the early version of this book, Dr. Cara Wallis, Dr. Tasha Dubriwny, Dr. Claire Katz—many thanks for your feedback and support. Thank you to my colleague and mentor at Seton Hall University, Dr. Renee Robinson, without whom I would have been lost navigating the life of an academic. And to my peers and friends, Dr. Aya Yadlin and Dr. Apryl Williams, who helped me move into a more stable "station" in life, thank you.

Thank you to my dear family, who love me and always celebrate my victories and struggles, my parents Anat and Yossi, and my siblings, Shira Clara, Jonathan, Daniel, and Avigail—the best team anyone could have; to my friends and teachers Denise and Karl, who helped me breathe; to my partner, Nick Marshall, whose love and critical eye always has me looking for more. And to my daughter, who was born during the writing of this book, thank you for making me a better person.

Last, I'd like to thank the editorial team at Penn State University Press—first, Kathryn Yahner, who saw the potential of this book long before I could. Thank you to Maddie Caso, who shepherded me through the revisions, and to Tristan Bates, whose friendly communication style made the last stages of allowing this book to be born easy.

And to you, the reader, who are braving through trying to understand how digital media impacts our life—thank you.

Introduction

It's May 1993 and tomorrow is my bat mitzvah. I can't sleep. I stare into an illuminated screen of a computer that is printing copies of my speech for tomorrow and of the family newspaper that we made. I carefully caress each copy and staple it. In these pages, a joy is discovered for me. Tomorrow, according to Jewish law, I become a woman. I have no idea what that means, but if it is anything like being a girl, I don't really care for it. In fact, for my first *Purim* (Jewish costume-based holiday), I asked to dress up as a boy. Just a year before, the night of my eleventh birthday, I cried into my pillow because I was growing up and now Peter Pan would not take me. I was interested not in dolls but in Lego, and the things that girls my age liked seemed silly to me. But there were some things I was enjoying as a result of being a young adult: covering more complicated texts and topics at school and studying religious texts with my dad on Sabbath days.

In the pages of my bat mitzvah speech and newspaper, my new joy was revealed: the joy of studying, of writing, of creating (not babies but content). For me, my bat mitzvah meant that I would get to take an active part in my Judaism, to study Torah, Talmud, and philosophical texts, and eventually (although this thought was just a seed in my mind at that point), I would get to teach those texts to others as a Rabbi. Boy, was I in for a disappointment.

In 1993, at the edges of Jerusalem, these were radical thoughts for an Orthodox girl. And they were strange. No one else (aside from my parents) talked or thought this way about Jewish women, and it left this almost-twelve-year-old girl very lonely. It was also 1993, and in a few months something else magical would happen in my life: I would have my first encounter with the internet. Looking back at this girl staring at a screen, I wonder if she would have been more or less lonely if that screen was connected to other screens.

Would she find like-minded Jews? Would she have known more about what awaits her as a Jewish woman and, as a result, abandon her quest for a rabbinical title? What would have been her ideas about womanhood if she had access to the World Wide Web?

This book attempts to answer these questions, albeit retroactively and from an academic, not religious, perspective. In this book, I explore the ways in which the internet is used to construct and make sense of Jewish womanhood. As we will see, the internet is not a neutral tool here—it has the power to amplify and mirror certain opinions, and, as a result, I argue, concretize certain social norms. In other words, the internet is a powerful tool for the normalization of social norms, and, in the context of religion, it is mostly used to reify traditional, even fundamental, attitudes toward women. The internet is theorized in this book as a reflector—a mirror or window into society—which we contribute to and learn from at the same time. By participating in online discourse, we both construct our society and learn how we are expected to behave in our society. Using this theoretical mindset, this book helps us make sense of the processes through which we normalize our behaviors as readers, researchers, and members of a given society.

The book is structured around four themes or stages in a Jewish woman's life: dating and getting married, being intimate, becoming a mother, and dealing with feminism. The source material examined in this book—"the internet"—refers, of course, not to the entire internet, since that would be a useless and impossible task. Instead, I have carefully selected online material from which most religious Jews in Hebrew- and English-speaking countries receive their information. This includes the three most popular Jewish websites, Chabad, Aish, and Kipa, as well as popular social media outlets (Facebook pages dedicated to Jewish women, the Chabad Instagram account, etc.), some popular blogs and forums, and some dating applications and similar sources.

This exploration is important for a couple of reasons. First, as a feminist, I argue that it is pivotal to expose the construction of gender and sex and the power structures that enforce, maintain, and recreate them. This approach also answers a need to address issues of intersectionality (race, ethnicity, gender, sexuality, etc.) in the study of religion and digital media. Second, sexuality and gender are key concepts in the construction of religious traditions[1] and are important for Jewish practices and the conceptualization of peoplehood. If we want to understand digital Judaism, we must observe how these relatively new communication technologies are being used by, and how they influence, religious individuals as they negotiate their understanding of gender identity and sexual practices. That is, we need to explore how the digital is entering into the Jewish bedroom. After all, as the Talmud (Jewish canonic text) reminds us, sexual intercourse is Torah, and one must study it.[2] Last, as I argue throughout this book, the exploration of the online hegemonic discourse—religious or otherwise—highlights the ways in which digital technologies are used to resist and enforce power. It shows that this online negotiation creates a discourse with a tendency toward the strict, or the extreme. It further contributes to the study of Digital Religion by suggesting a theoretical and methodological approach that views the digital as a discourse while at the same time considering the religious worldviews and technological affordances that inform this discourse. To better understand the world this book portrays and examines, the rest of this introduction provides the reader with some context about contemporary Judaism, especially a survey of Jewish approaches to gender, sexuality, and digital media, before presenting more specific communities within the Jewish religion and their particular uses of digital media. This introductory focus on Judaism, as opposed to media studies, is intentional. If the reader is generally familiar with Judaism and wishes to skip directly to a more media-focused account, you are welcome to skip ahead to chapter 2.

Understanding Contemporary Judaism

There is an old joke, whose origins are lost to time, and which appears in a variety of different versions. In one version, the joke goes that there were once two Jews who were shipwrecked on an island. Many years later, they are rescued and as they are sailing away from the island, the captain of the ship notes there are three synagogues on the island. He asks why the two Jews needed three synagogues. One of the Jews answers, saying, "The one on the right is my Orthodox synagogue. The one on the left is his reform synagogue. And the one in the middle is the one we would both never attend." Although Judaism is by no means unique among the world religions in its denominational diversity and variety, it may nonetheless be true that Judaism has a special degree of self-awareness to this variety. The history of Judaism is rife with examples and events that testify to the diversity of interpretation and expression that the Jewish religion has permitted. Even though some groups excommunicate each other, there persists the notion that all these expressions are somehow "Jewish," and that the synagogue one never enters should nonetheless have its place on the island. What follows is therefore merely an approximate description of the varieties of

Judaism, and it concerns only those expressions of contemporary Judaism that this book deals with.

Contemporary Judaism has its roots in the rabbinical (Pharisees) tradition, which highlighted daily and communal praxis over temple or messianic worship. Exiled from Israel during early and late antiquity, Judaism has been, for most of history, a diasporic religion. Therefore, Jewry can be split between the *Ashkenazim* (European-descent) and *Sephardi* (Arab- descent) denominations. *Ashkenazim* in turn was split between two major groups, the *Chassidim* (the Pious), a charismatic sect that structured much of Jewish religious life around the reverence of rabbinical authority, and the *Mitnagdim*, a group that defined itself mostly in terms of their devotion to Torah study and their opposition to the perceived innovations of the *Chassidim* (*Mitnagdim* literally means "those who protest"). During the nineteenth century, Judaism underwent a massive change in response to the political, social, scientific, and spiritual upheavals engendered by the European Enlightenment. Jews in Europe responded in one of three ways, thus creating three major divisions of Judaism as they exist today. One of the reactions to the Enlightenment was to fully embrace secularism and with it a host of contemporary European ideas, including nationalism—ideas that would later lead to the creation of the State of Israel. This reaction led to what we now know as secular or cultural Judaism. Other Jews responded to the Enlightenment by strengthening their commitment to their traditions and rejecting many of the ideas of secularity. This denomination, known as Orthodoxy and ultra-Orthodoxy, centers its worldview on the importance of the Halacha (religious-legal code), which is considered divinely inspired. Aside from these two extremes there were also a loosely connected series of movements that sought to maintain some of the religious beliefs and customs of Judaism while rejecting many of the legal practices. These are the Conservative (*Masorati*), Reform, and Reconstructionist denominations.[3]

Contemporary Judaism has two main geographical centers: the United States and Israel. There are Jewish communities in Europe, Canada, Australia, South America, Africa, and Asia, but these communities are less notable in the religious and political scene. As a result, scholars in the field of contemporary Jewish studies tend to focus on communities in the United States and Israel. It is important to note that not all Jewish individuals are religious. Because Judaism can be thought of as a religion, ethnicity, culture, or some combination of these three, Jews might feel connected to Judaism, or describe themselves as Jewish, yet not practice the religious aspects of Judaism. In Israel, where Judaism is the majority national religion, most Israeli

Jews identify as either secular (43 percent of the Jewish population) or traditional (23 percent). Twenty-five percent self-identify as religious, and 9 percent label themselves as ultra-Orthodox.[4] According to Pew research, one in five Jews in the USA define themselves as slightly-to-not religious.[5] Ten percent of Jews living in the USA define themselves as Orthodox, 35 percent as Reform, and 18 percent as Conservative.[6] While Orthodoxy still represents a minority in both the Israeli and US Jewish populations, it is a rapidly growing sector. According to the Pew research, "Though Orthodox Jews constitute the smallest of the three major denominational movements, they are much younger, on average, and tend to have much larger families than the overall Jewish population. This suggests that their share of the Jewish population will grow."[7] Similarly, in Israel, the Orthodox sector is predicted to double each decade.[8] Thus, trends and norms in these communities are bound to be influential on the general Jewish population. This book research focuses on the more religiously observant portions of the Jewish population, namely those within the Orthodox and ultra-Orthodox denominations.

The Orthodox denominations are mostly understood as more traditional and strict denominations. Probably the most important difference between Orthodoxy and other Jewish religious denominations is that Orthodox communities are (fairly strictly) committed to a Halachic way of life (to at least some degree); they consider the Torah and Halacha as divinely inspired and as the main pillars of Judaism.[9] Orthodox Judaism has also developed into several different offshoots, which may be distinguished predominantly by their religious observance and the degree to which they include modern values. One side of the spectrum can be labeled as Modern Orthodox. Members of Modern Orthodoxy adhere to Orthodox religious belief and praxis but have, for the most part, accepted many modern values such as the use of technology, liberal ideals, and nationalism. For example, the National Religious (Dati Leumi) group in Israel (established in the late nineteenth century), while Orthodox in its approach to the Halachic way of life, has embraced modern concepts of the nation and sees its main value in combining Torah with *Avoda* (literally "work," meaning the work of maintaining a state in Israel, having employment even within the secular society, and working to better the world). On the other side of the spectrum, there are several groups that may be subsumed under the general category of "ultra-Orthodox" (*Haredim*). The groups that have the strictest interpretation of Halacha tend to be self-isolating and reject modern values. However, even within ultra-Orthodoxy there is a varying degree of exclusion, with some groups, like the *Gur* sect, who live in isolated villages and neighborhoods, and some sects, like *Satmar* or *Neturi Karta*, who object to and reject the State of Israel. Other ultra-Orthodox groups are more inclusive, like the Chabad sect that seeks interactions with the secular world and uses digital communication technology. Generally, most Orthodox individuals fall between Modern Orthodox and extreme ultra-Orthodox, constantly having to negotiate their adherence to Halacha and tradition within their daily work and life in a modern society.

It is within this group of Orthodoxy that I grew up and, like many in this community, tried to make sense of my identity in a complex world. To better understand the main issues of this book, it's important we dive specifically into issues of gender on the one hand and technology on the other. Therefore, the next two sections review the general Orthodox attitudes toward gender and sex and Orthodox adoption and negotiation of media.

Jewish Attitudes Toward Gender and Sexuality

As in other religious traditions, gender is pivotal in the structure of Jewish life, worldview, and praxis. As Mia Lövheim argues, "Gender is . . . a fundamental source for structuring identities, traditions, values and rituals within religious traditions."[10] In the case of Judaism, which is a praxis-based religion, gender and sexuality norms are defined and corrected through Halachic practice. Halacha is the Jewish legal code that constructs and determines Jewish life. It informs daily and ritualistic behaviors from prayers and holidays to financial and personal relationships. When it comes to gender and sexuality, Halachic code dictates how men and women should behave toward one another, which roles they can take in the community and in the household, and how they understand and practice their sexuality. Halachic code, however, is not stable but constantly adaptable to historical and social contexts—to Jewish lived experience.[11] The negotiation of Halacha and Jewish life has thus far taken place through texts or lived experience. The digital offers a sort of combination of both. Online, researchers can see how lived communicative behaviors (users asking questions, commenting, sharing on social media) inform religious lives and meaning. For users too, like myself at twelve and even today, we use digital media to understand our gendered identity. But any interaction online is also based on our offline ideologies and practices, and it is therefore necessary to review the general Jewish mindset regarding these issues.

Gender and sexuality are central to the structure of Jewish life, worldview, and praxis. The perceived differences between men and women inform both daily practices and long-held issues of identity pivotal for Judaism.

Gender differentiation plays an important role in Jewish ritual life. For example, in Orthodox Jewish synagogues, men and women are separated by a barrier (*mechitzah*). Supposedly, this is because prayer demands absolute focus on the divine, and women would be inherently distracting to men. Furthermore, in Jewish communal prayer, there is an explicit requirement of ten Jewish men to form a *minyan* (quorum)—boys under the age of thirteen, men who are mentally disabled, and women do not count toward the completion of a *minyan*.

Orthodox daily life consists of the need to fulfill *mitzvoth* (commandments). Many of these *mitzvoth* are icons of Jewish identity that are only performable by men, for example, circumcision. Such *mitzvoth* also include the wearing of *tzitzit* (tassels on the corners of one's clothing), the binding of *Tefillin* (phylacteries containing parchment scrolls) on the forehead and on the arm, and praying the required three times a day. In contrast, women primarily have three commandments unique to them: they must light candles on Friday evenings (*Shabbat*) and on festivals, they must prepare *challah* (ceremonial bread), and they must obey the laws of family purity (*Niddah*). The last two commandments are vague and can be (and have been) further interpreted to include the obligation to keep and promote a kosher home (as *challah* would be invalid if not prepared in a kosher home) and to avoid intimate contact with one's husband while menstruating (i.e., to obey the laws of *Niddah*), or more generally maintain "correct" sexuality. As can be seen, it is through the *mitzvoth* that "correct" gender relations and sexual relations are constituted.

As in most traditions, gender in Judaism is based on the dichotomous distinction of male and female, man and woman.[12] Throughout Jewish history, women were ascribed to the house and prohibited from obtaining public responsibilities, such as explicit community leadership. At the same time, Judaism is matriarchically concerned, as the ethnicity of being Jewish is inscribed only through the mother (that is, the child of a Jewish man and a non-Jewish woman is considered not Jewish). In this way, the Jewish woman plays an important role in Jewish history, as a mother and an educator. And it is one of Judaism's cornerstones that each man and woman should "build a house in Israel"—that is, get married and have children.

When considering gender from a Jewish perspective, it is important to note that the masculine-feminine distinctions in Judaism are not based on physical power but on intellectual access.[13] The Jewish male, according to Daneil Boyarin, is constructed as feminine and learned, which, while in contrast to the European ideal man, is the Jewish ideal of appealing masculinity:

"The East European Jewish ideal of the gentle, timid, and studious male—Edelkayt—moreover, does have origins that are deeply rooted in traditional Jewish culture. . . . These characteristics, however, were not supposed to render the male even slightly unappealing . . . indeed, he is represented as the paramount desiring male subject and object of female desire."[14] The positioning of masculinity in Torah studies has de facto made religious and scholarly spaces and actions a segregated space from which women were excluded. Boyarin, following other feminist thinkers, shows how in Jewish tradition, patriarchy was not a violent but a "kinder, gentler patriarchy," which can also be called "soft patriarchy." Nevertheless, this cultural system still controlled women's bodies, property, habits, intellectual rights, and occupational options.[15] Boyarin argues that the exclusion of women from studying Torah was not motivated by possible contamination of the holy scrolls or even the fear of erotic tension in the process of studying. If this were the case, separate areas for Torah study for men and women would have been created. Instead, the exclusion was based on the perceived inherent masculinity of Torah study: "If study defined the rabbinic male, then the exclusion of women was the practice that constructed gendered differentiation and hierarchy within that society."[16] Indeed, one can see that as the gender boundaries are bent in contemporary Jewish society, women studying Torah (either in segregated or coed spaces) becomes a more common practice.

Excluding women from Torah and Halacha study also reflects how this Jewish religious-legal discourse was used to maintain patriarchal gender structures. In her book *Women and Jewish Law*, Rachel Biale explores how the Jewish legal system constructed and regulated gender roles and women's lives. For example, in the first chapter, Biale begins by unpacking the biblical commandments addressed to a certain gender or sex (such as circumcision, which is addressed only to men). She continued by presenting the rabbinical logic of categorizing the *mitzvoth* according to positive or negative and time bound or not time bound. Halachic texts suggest women are exempt from positive time-bound *mitzvoth*, but through further analysis of the law, Biale shows how the logical presentation is inconsistent. A more accurate model is that women are exempt from practices that might interfere with their domestic duties: "The principle that women are exempt from all time-bound positive mitzvoth [. . .] was probably an after-the-fact attempt to explain and systemize the reality that women did not perform all the mitzvoth equally with men. Therefore it is not at all surprising that there are a good many exceptions to the rule [. . .] the common thread uniting them [the practices that women are exempt from] is that they are all obligations outside the realm of women's domestic role."[17] Thus, it seems the Jewish religious attitudes concerning gender and sexuality were mostly concerned with separating the domestic (female) and the public (male). These attitudes take place and derive power through the Halachic discourse. As a result, the question of combining Orthodox Jewish life, which is based on Halacha, with feminist ideas has been taken up by scholars of Jewish feminism, as made clear by the prominent feminist Jewish scholar Rachel Adler: "Whether gender justice is possible within halakhah and whether a feminist Judaism requires a halakhah at all are foundational questions for feminist Jewish theology that have no parallel in Christian feminist theology. . . . Appropriating the terms and method of halakhah itself, many feminists concluded, drew them into a game they could not win. . . . Halakhah became the feminists' elephant in the living room."[18] As a result, some Jewish feminists reject Halacha. But from an Orthodox perspective, that is not an option. Therefore, Orthodoxy has to negotiate both feminism and Halacha. According to Ronit Irshai, that is not an obstacle but rather a necessity or even opportunity.[19] Irshai considers Halachic discourse as a discourse in a Foucauldian sense, meaning as a site of struggle, one that has the potential to change and shift. That is, she suggests that all people participating in Halachic discourse have the option to resist, construct, and take part in the discourse. We will see that this is exactly what is happening online within the digital communal discourse. Irshai does not think that this is a game in which feminists "could not win" but rather one they have to play wisely: "I suggested at the outset that, in the manner suggested by Foucault and Fish, the halakhic community functions as a player in the game and already has the power to influence the shaping of the hegemonic halakhic narrative. But that is not the full picture; for one who is empowered must know as well how to deploy that power wisely. Only in that way will it be possible to achieve any sort of consensus."[20] In other words, and as will be seen throughout this book, Orthodox women and feminists cannot abandon Halacha—instead, they employ the study and interpretation of Torah and its rules (Halacha) in the discourse in which gender and sexuality were and are constructed and negotiated in Judaism. Biale, in her epilogue, reviews current Jewish reactions to feminist thought.[21] For some, there is no need to reconcile Halacha with feminism, since they reject either Halacha or feminism. But for Jews who want to live a religious and feminist life, the need for reconciliation is grave. Biale provides several examples for different ways to combine Jewish law and feminist thought—from a (perhaps postfeminist) position of equal but different to a radical call for new legal leadership within Judaism. As will be seen throughout this book, the digital discourse creates another avenue for the negotiation of gender and sexuality. However, while the medium might be new, the discourse is still concerned with practice and meaning through the interpretation of Torah and Halacha.

Understandings of gender are also inherently tied to attitudes toward sexuality. Sexuality is a complex topic in Jewish religious theology, as it is subjected to both negative and positive attitudes. As a general rule, sexual intercourse is not only permitted but encouraged. A healthy sexual relationship is both a virtue and a duty for married couples. Marital sexual relations are governed by two *mitzvoth*: the obligation to "be fruitful and multiply"[22] and the husband's obligation to give his wife her conjugal rights, which are understood as regular sexual relations (at least once a week, according to some Jewish sources). If a husband refuses or is incapable, this can be a legitimate reason for the woman to seek a divorce.[23] In short, Jewish law and thought understand sex not as an unclean or sinful activity but rather as the core upon which a healthy Jewish lifestyle must be based.

However, this positive attitude toward sex is applicable only to highly regulated sexual behavior. In his book *Kosher Sex: A Recipe for Passion and Intimacy*, Rabbi Shmuel Boteach celebrates the following Halachic (legal) restrictions: First, sex outside of marriage is strictly forbidden. This includes both adultery and sexual relationships between two single people. For Boteach, monogamy is an idealized sexual lifestyle that stabilizes society. He also explains how sexual relations should occur—in the missionary position and, preferably, in the dark. Second, Halacha forbids coitus or any physical contact during the woman's menstruation and for seven days after. Of course, homosexuality in all its forms is strictly forbidden. Last, male masturbation is prohibited, and female masturbation is strongly discouraged.

Although earlier rabbinical texts permitted greater flexibility during coitus (for example, Maimonides allowed for oral sex[24]), Boteach represents an authoritative contemporary rabbi,[25] as well as the general rabbinical movement toward a more restrictive view of sexuality.[26] In an attempt to explore current trends within the Orthodox and ultra-Orthodox community, Nurit Stadler interviewed contemporary (postmillennial) Israeli ultra-Orthodox students and surveyed the handbooks, audio, and visual materials the students received regarding intimacy. She found the rabbinical material focused on overcoming one's bodily needs, counting sexual desires as one of the most dangerous needs.[27] Yakir Englander and Avi Sagi point to similar trends in the National Religious community, which tends to be more open about issues of sexuality.[28] According to Englander and Sagi, in the last twenty-five years, this religious community has started to have a stricter attitude toward modesty, for example, by segregating schools and youth movements by gender. Englander and Sagi, Stadler, and Simon Theobald all agree that this growing panic about sexual "purity" is most likely a response to the sexual "promiscuity" of the modern, liberal world.[29] Stadler goes one step further and describes how in Israel, the ultra-Orthodox discourse about sexual modesty has become militant in its presentation of sexual purity as a battle against "the evil inclination."[30] This increasingly militant attitude against sexuality does not represent all Orthodox communities, but it does stem from a similar general attitude that resists the open, promiscuous sexuality usually associated with modern Western society. This resistance, I argue, colors the way in which Orthodox communities and individuals interact with modern media as well. This is true concerning old media (television, newspapers, etc.) and digital media. Indeed, a few Orthodox communities choose to create their own media content in which they can censor offensive sexual images or external ideas.[31]

As can be seen from this context, Orthodox Jewish attitudes toward gender and sexuality tend to be traditionalist, but at the same time, they are constantly negotiated through people's lived experience. While *some* ultra-Orthodox shy away from modernity, most Orthodox communities embrace modernity to some level and, as a result, also have to negotiate modern attitudes toward sexuality and gender, such as feminism and changing ideas around the LGBTQI community and premarital intimacy. This is especially true for the types of Orthodox groups that are not in opposition to modern or digital media, as these media make a variety of attitudes and worldviews accessible to users and allow religious users to more easily communicate their needs and disagreements. That is, interaction with digital media has the potential to reshape communal norms concerning sexuality and gender. It is exactly this negotiation of gender and sexual norms that this book highlights—the space in which modernity and tradition are negotiated when it comes to gender/sex norms. This negotiation and construction, I suggest, can be accessed by researchers and users alike through the Orthodox digital discourse. In order to understand more fully why and how Jewish Orthodox groups use digital media, the following section provides a review of general Orthodox attitudes toward digital media.

Digital Media and Judaism

The study of Judaism and digital media should be thought of as a continuation of the more general study of Judaism and media, which has focused on the representation of Judaism in general media as well as on the reaction, adoption, and use of mass media by Jewish communities. This scholarship includes studies of mass media such as television, radio, and newspapers,[32] as well as community produced media, such as books and audio cassettes.[33] Research on both old media and new media tends to consider what role the media play in communal and religious norms construction and how these religious communities negotiate their relationship with media. This role is especially noted in the reaction to digital media, a medium that is more open and less easily restricted. The lack of communal and rabbinical regulation of digital media poses threats to the Orthodox communities, for which regulated communal life is pivotal.[34] Especially considering negotiation and gender issues, scholars have portrayed the internet as an avenue for resistance or transgression.[35] Most of the scholarly study of Jewish interaction with digital media has been focused on the ultra-Orthodox reactions against new media,[36] or the impact of new media on Jewish authority or institutions.[37] In her book *Digital Judaism*, Heidi Campbell called upon scholars to search for more "interpretive categories for describing these [strategies and responses to digital technologies]."[38] This book hopes to answer this call and contribute to the overarching field of research by examining the existence of power and resistance in the digital discourse itself, thus providing another interpretive approach to the study of "digital Judaism." That is, in this project, I expand current scholarship on digital Judaism by offering a more explicitly feminist perspective on the relationship between Judaism and new media. By "feminist," I mean to capture the unique contribution of scholarship influenced by the concerns and attitudes of the women's liberation movement. These concerns have led scholars to consider more carefully the instrumental issues of gender and power in cultural studies. That is, the feminist perspective demands that we examine the cultural institutions and discourses that maintain patriarchal power. In the case of digital media, the medium enables new forms of power and resistance, which are explored in this book.

Although there seems to be a general rejection of digital media by ultra-Orthodox and Orthodox Jews, Heidi Campbell and other scholars have argued that this is not a complete rejection but rather a complicated negotiation. Campbell maintains that many Jewish religious communities negotiate new media in various ways.[39] For example, the Chabad sect, which has a missionary vocation within Judaism, embraced the internet fairly early on for outreach purposes. Since the internet supplies business opportunities, especially for women who could utilize the internet for work while staying home, ultra-Orthodox communities had to shape tools to allow access to the internet while maintaining community boundaries and the authority of the religious leaders.[40] In 2008, the ultra-Orthodox leaders officially allowed community members to use the internet for work. As Karine Barzilai-Nahon and Gad Barzilai argue, this process is best understood as "cultured technology," where specific communities localize the internet for their needs instead of simply rejecting or accepting it.[41] One way in which the technology of the internet is being cultured is by restricting certain content online. This can be done, for example, via the use of a specific internet filtering program, Internet Rimon.[42] This program filters internet content and provides access only to "kosher" content, that is, clean of sexual or heretical content. Another way in which Jewish communities negotiate their relationship with digital media is by creating "local" spaces—blogs, web pages, or web-portals—specifically for their communities. These digital enclaves,[43] like the Kipa site (for the Israeli Orthodox community) or *Behederi Haredim* blog portal (for the Israeli ultra-Orthodox community), are where religious communities create a safe haven online for their religious denominations. It is these religious digital enclaves that are explored in this book.

In this book, I am interested not in the cases of total rejection of digital media but rather in the Orthodox communities that embraced it early on and use it for religious purposes. The Orthodox communities examined in this project embraced the missionizing tools and communal resources the internet offers. Among these religious entrepreneurs, three websites stand out in their early adoption of internet technology and their current breadth of materials: Chabad, Aish, and Kipa. These websites provided a starting point for religious Jews to interact with the internet in a "safe environment," which Heidi Campbell and Oren Golan describe as "digital enclaves."[44] Therefore, I suggest that it is via these websites, in which a purposeful religious use of digital media occurs, that we can examine how this everyday use of digital media shapes Jewish religious common sense and mainstream concepts of gender and sexuality. That is, Jewish religious websites and web spaces that normalize religious use of the internet and use it to negotiate and construct religious ideological issues are seen as building blocks of the "Orthodox Digital Discourse." The next section provides more detailed information about the specific websites I study, and the communities they serve.

Approaching Orthodox Digital Discourse: The Material in Focus

While a variety of online material is used in this book, the main focus is on three websites that can be thought of as forming an Orthodox digital discourse. Alongside these three websites, various other online sources are peppered throughout the book: forums (like Supartova, Imamother, OKclarity), blogs (JewishMOM), websites of Jewish organizations (JOFA, LeOran), and some references to social media pages and groups (the Facebook group "Jewish Women Talk about Anything," Chabad's Instagram account, etc.). These sources are supplemental to the three main websites and together represent the mainstream online sources for Orthodox Jews.

The three websites in focus—Chabad, Aish, and Kipa—were all established early and serve as centers of knowledge for Jewish information in the United States and Israel. That is, these websites were early innovators regarding Jewish content online[45] and are currently leading in terms of Jewish-related online traffic.[46] Some context about each website, and the community it serves, is important for understanding how they come together in this book and how they are used to negotiate digital media.

The Chabad Movement and Chabad.org

Chabad.org is a website that was created by the Chabad Orthodox community during the late 1990s. The Chabadnikim, or Lubavitchers as they are sometimes called, are the largest Chassidim Jewish group in the world, thanks primarily to the efforts of the last rabbi in the Chassidim lineage, Menachem Mendel Schneerson, known to the Lubavitchers simply as "the Rebbe" (the Rabbi). The Chabad movement was founded in the eighteenth century in Europe by rabbi Schneur Zalman of Liadi, as a Chassidim movement established on kabbalistic (mystical) thinking. The Chabad sect, like most Chassidim sects, is centered on the worship of a specific rabbi and his linage, operating in ways not so different from a regal court. A descendant of Schneur Zalman, rabbi Menachem Mendel Schneerson (1902–1994), was the most influential rabbi in the Chabad movement and perhaps one of the most influential rabbis in the world. The Rebbe, who lived in New York, saw the goal of the Chabad movement as bettering the world and maintaining and growing the reach and stability of Judaism, Jewish culture, and Jewish peoplehood, especially in light of the Holocaust. He acted politically and religiously to spread Judaism and promote Jewish, and general, education, using any available tools. For example, he created "Education Day" in the United States, and it is to this day celebrated on his birthday. He met with world leaders and took an active position concerning both Israel and maintaining peace between the United States and Russia during the Cold War. His Jewish outreach inspired Chabad to create outposts in every country and to utilize media to connect secular Jews with Judaism. Chabad is famous for its practice of establishing Chabad Houses throughout the world, especially in tourist destinations and in US colleges and universities. These Chabad Houses are missionizing outposts where any Jew can receive the comfort of a kosher Shabbat meal. For some, this is their first contact with Judaism.

This missionizing ideology takes place online as well as offline, and Chabad as a movement perceives all media as ways of proselytizing. Chabad's attitude toward media in general, and digital media specifically, is welcoming.[47] According to Tsuriel Rashi and Maxwell McCombs, the Rebbe "recognized the media's tremendous inherent power and refused to shy away from using it to advance his religious views simply because it was generally associated with concepts alien to a Jewish religious lifestyle. Although he completely forbade reading secular newspapers and viewing secular television, he did issue a call to his followers to exploit media technology in order to popularize Jewish thought."[48] One of his followers, Yosef Yitzchak Kazen, answered this call and already in the early 1990s was exploring the internet as a tool for missionizing. He became the creator of Chabad.org. According to the Chabad.org narrative, "'I asked the Rebbe if it would be worthwhile to look into going on the Internet,' Kazen said in 1997. 'And the Rebbe said to go ahead with it—absolutely pursue it.'"[49]

Chabad embraces and uses digital media as tools to proselytize and define Judaism. While a distinction between outward and inward communal use exists, community members also use the internet in their private lives for religious purposes and community connectivity. In short, Chabad's website reflects the sect's goals both as a space for maintaining a strong community, and, maybe even more importantly, as a tool for spreading the Rebbe's vision and wisdom.

Aish HaTorah Organization and Aish

Another Orthodox Jewish organization and religious sect that embraced the internet early on is Aish HaTorah (in Hebrew, "Fire of the Torah"), an organization that, like Chabad, has a missionizing aim. Whereas Chabad's doctrines and practices are in some conflict with the less Chassidic streams of Judaism stemming from the *Mitnagdim*, the mission statement of Aish HaTorah includes an explicit intent to blend Chassidic and *Mitnagdic* streams of Judaism. Aish HaTorah is considered a new religious movement with a transnational orientation.[50] Established in 1974 by Rabbi Noah Weinberg (1930–2009), an American-born Jew who moved to Israel in the 1960s, the organization's main goal is *kiruv* (outreach to secular Jews). Aish HaTorah is also very involved and concerned about the State of Israel and sees bringing

Jews to Israel as part of their mission. This translates to their use of online media: for example, their website features a Western Wall camera, so that one can access this holy site from anywhere in the world. The organization also created a program that brings American university students to Israel for a two-week intensive study trip, offers Jerusalem Fellowships, and takes part in *Hasbara* (the Israeli Foreign Ministry's program for presenting and explaining Israel's actions). They encourage a transnational connection between Jews in the diaspora and Jews in the State of Israel and see it as a way of advancing their goal of giving all Jews access to their heritage.

Weinberg saw bringing as many Jews "back to the flock" as possible as his main mission. To achieve this, he first created *yeshivas* (religious higher education institutions) that would educate "*kiruv*-soldiers." The organization grew and established various schools and centers in Israel and the United States,[51] conducted seminars and programs throughout the world, and embraced media, including digital media, for outreach purposes. They understand the internet as a place in which they can reach people who are interested in Judaism but are not ready to commit. In an interview conducted by Heidi Campbell and Wendi Bellar, one Aish web editor explained, "People are often curious about their Jewish roots, but don't know what is available to them. They trust us because of what they see and read on our site. [. . .] The online contact helps them get over the hurdle to explore Judaism more offline."[52] While the outward use of digital media is acceptable for Aish members, personal or inward communal use is deemed more problematic.[53] At the same time, Aish as an organization invests resources in creating a web space that not only promotes Judaism but also caters to Jewish religious needs, providing news, Torah portions, calendar information, recipes, dating resources, Hebrew lessons, and a Judaica store. Thus, the website becomes a valuable source for both religious and unaffiliated Jews. In sum, Aish uses the internet mostly for missionary purposes within Judaism by creating a website that is a "one-stop-shop" for various religious needs that also highlights their religious commitment to Israel and to Jewish law.

National Religious Sect and Kipa

The Israeli Orthodox group that was quickest to embrace digital technologies was the "National Religious" (Dati Leumi) or "Religious Zionists" (Dati Tzioni) group. This group, as the name suggests, has embraced the modern ideology of nationalism and they are strong proponents of the existence of a Jewish State. This community believes in many modern values, the most prominent of which is nationalism, but they are also more open to other values such as socialism (for some subgroups), capitalism (for other groups), scientific and technological progress, and, to some degree, feminism or a degree of gender equality. While keeping their own religious values and norms, they also view integration with general Israeli secular society as a positive value, as well as the use and advancement of science and technology.[54] This community has a more egalitarian approach toward rabbinical authority. Although rabbis still represent the religious institutions and knowledge, each (male) person is encouraged to study Halacha and be the master of his own religious life and home.

The National Religious community in Israel makes up about 10–20 percent of the general population.[55] While the majority of National Religious members are united in their conception of Zionism, they differ slightly in thinking about gender, technology, and other modern values. For example, only a minority of families encourage girls to join the Israeli military and take leadership roles, while most families encourage girls to take on more domestic jobs, such as teacher or social worker.

Kipa was created for this community as a resource. Boaz Nechstern, Kipa's founder, started it as a website intended solely for the *mitzvah* of selling leftover bread before Passover. The website was so popular it was clear that there is a need for a religious "cyberspace" in which various in-group communications could occur. Kipa was the first Israeli site for the religious community, established as early as 2000. It is, to this day, one of the leading Israeli Jewish religious websites, with news, shopping, multiple forums, and a tablet application version of the website. The website is not an outreach website per se but rather a website for this religious community. The website represents the National Religious tendency to combine Torah and technology, tradition and modernity. The National Religious community, by and large, accepts modern media in a negotiated fashion—for example, they have constant online access, but it's restricted through religious internet filters. As Michele Rosenthal and Rivka Ribak explain, "The internet is embraced, but not as a free market of ideas that early entrepreneurs of the web envisioned, but rather a restrained and domesticated version that does not transverse the invisible yet articulated cultural boundaries."[56] One of the struggles of Kipa as a website is maintaining these cultural boundaries while at the same time supporting the variety of opinions in the National Religious community and creating interesting conversations on their website. According to Golan and Campbell, "Rather than silencing discussions of potentially controversial issues, [Kipa's CEO] encourages their proliferation because they yield increased web traffic."[57] This guiding strategy adopted by the website editors allows for the negotiation of communal and religious terms, including gender and sexuality. Material from Kipa has been collected from 2016 to 2020. In 2019, however, Kipa redesigned their website, and many of the comments to various articles were lost. If interested, those comments can be found using websites like WebArchive or by contacting the author. In sum, Kipa as a website mostly serves communal and religious needs and is less structured for missioning. Instead, it operates as a source of knowledge, culture, and commerce related to the National Religious community.

The inward negotiation and outward representation of Judaism that happens on these three websites, and on various accompanying sites (social media, organizations' websites, blogs, etc.), includes negotiating and representing Jewish attitudes toward gender and sexual norms. Thus, these websites are fertile ground for the cultivation of an Orthodox digital discourse on gender and sexuality, in which power (the established traditional, patriarchal, views of gender and sexuality) and resistance (the opposition and questioning of these norms) coexist. It is this negotiation and construction of gender and sexuality that this book presents. But how does it present this information? The last section in this introduction describes the book's structure so that you, the reader, can more easily navigate it.

Book Structure

After introducing the reader to the world and study of online Judaism in this chapter, the next chapter answers the question, how does one make sense of this world? In the next chapter, various theories from the study of digital religion and from feminist studies are examined. Through the combination of media theories and feminist theories, the internet here is seen not as a substitute for the synagogue or the rabbi; instead, it operates as the street, the market, the dinner table—spaces in which social norms are crystallized and policed. The internet is imagined as a window to our society and mirror of ourselves. Arguing for a Foucauldian understanding of the internet, chapter 1 theorizes why and how the internet is used and experienced and what that means for the process of understanding our own society and ourselves.

The chapters that follow each dig deep into a different theme related to gender and sexuality in online Jewish discourse: dating and marriage (chapter 2), modesty and intimacy (chapter 3), motherhood (chapter 4), and reacting to modern, feminist notions about gender and sexuality (chapter 5). This can be imagined as a journey of a young Jewish woman, from dating all the way to maturely assessing one's role in society, based in the inherent tensions between the traditional society in which she was raised and the modern tools (the internet) and ideologies (feminism, for example) she encounters. Of course, this journey is imaginary, and most Jewish women's lives are far messier and less linear. But, for the purposes of narrative, this structure is useful to lead the reader—and myself—through these various issues and their online negotiation.

In between these chapters are three short interludes, which are specifically focused on the digital media aspects of the discourse. These would be hard to understand without reading the main chapters, but they are very informative and meant to be thought provoking. They help us ask the big questions about digital media uses and how negotiation happens in those spaces.

The book's final chapter, the conclusion, is more of an open end to the story than a conclusive one. The book's goal, as is my goal in almost anything I write, is to ask questions and to broaden perspectives so that we might look at things differently. To that end, the last chapter attempts to highlight the main argument in the book: that this negotiation is complex. Religious women speak online in their own voices about their bodies, their aspirations, their experiences. At the same time, these narratives are constructed through traditional understandings of gender and power, de facto strengthening patriarchal religious authority. Digital tools—through their anonymity, participatory affordances, and general logic—allow silenced voices to be heard and shift the weight of authority. However, as this book shows, most of those participating in the religious discourse use the ability to post, comment, and share to support and reinforce traditional norms. As a result, women's voices, minority voices, and liberal and modern voices at large are heard and then *shut down* actively in these online spaces. In these ways, new communication tools help maintain and even create fundamental viewpoints within Judaism. The book leaves the reader with the question: who is really empowered in this online participatory religious discourse?

Chapter 1

Exploring Digital Judaism as a Discourse

From a young age, I was always interested in theory. Of course, it wasn't until my academic education that I knew I was interested in it, but I have always looked for the "why" of how things—especially humans and cultures—operate. More specifically, I was interested in why humans conform to the rules of society around us: why do we listen to the rules? And who made the rules, anyway? While on the outside I was being a "good girl," inside I was always asking "Why are we doing this?" This approach got me into some trouble with confronting teachers, but I also recall a young philosophy teacher in my high school encouraging me to always keep asking. And I did.

This chapter is all about theory. It contextualizes the theoretical approaches and key ideas that are dealt with throughout this book. While the introduction chapter provided context for Orthodox Judaism and its attitudes toward media and gender, this chapter reviews and contextualizes theories of gender, religion, and digital media. In other words, it answers these questions: How do we understand online religious discourse and its relation to gender negotiation and construction? What is the relationship between religion and digital media? What is the relationship between gender/sexual norms and digital media? And more generally, how do we actually use digital media to make sense of our world? This last question ties back to my adolescent questions, those I asked while trying to figure out the role of digital media in power structures and normalization processes.

Put simply, I argue that online media can be theorized as a type of discourse or a tool that enables discourses in various communities. By understanding communication technology as a tool for power and resistance, we can think of the digital as a "space" in which people negotiate social practices—specifically, in this book, in which they negotiate religious, gender, and sexual norms. We can think of digital media as a *window* and a *mirror*. It's a window in that we use digital media to "see" the world: to read the news, learn how to fix a leak, and see what people are saying about a certain topic. But it also functions as a mirror in that we use digital media to understand and "see" ourselves: our profile, our friendships, our values and identity. We use digital media to engage with "everybody" and learn how to behave based on their behavior. *I* use digital media to know if I'm normal (full disclosure: I'm not; I suspect no one is).

We also contribute to what is considered an accepted perspective or behavior by liking, sharing, and expressing our own worldview (informed both by offline and online interactions). Thus, we partake in the push and pull of social norms through our online interactions. As I've written elsewhere, "I suggest conceptualizing digital media as a Foucauldian Discourse, or, for a lack of a better analog: the street, the marketplace. What I mean by Foucauldian discourse is the systematic ways in which communication shapes our social norms. This happens online because, while we use digital media individually, we are taking part in a social space. Online media includes the multiplicity of opinions experienced through an individual's lenses."[1] In this chapter, I offer an understanding of digital media as a space of resistance *and* coercion, a sort of *Foucauldian discourse*, a "site of struggle."[2] This chapter outlines cyber-feminist and cultural studies theories that inform this study and are used to explain what is meant by discourse. Furthermore, after reviewing Digital Religion scholarship, I suggest that online texts as discourse can only be fully understood through an examination of both the technological tools and the cultural-religious worldviews informing the users.

In order to understand Jewish online texts concerning gender and sexuality as a discourse in which both technology and religion matter, this chapter reviews some of the major scholarship related to digital religion and media studies, especially the research of Judaism online from a feminist perspective. First, I consider how to approach digital media by reviewing media studies, and more specifically, feminist media studies and its understanding of media as a tool of power and resistance. The discussion in this section informs my discursive approach, as it explains how gender and sexuality are constantly constructed and negotiated via media and technology, particularly through the power structures that media technologies support. Second, I discuss how to approach the digital as a space in which religious norms are negotiated. The review of Digital Religion studies supplies the scholarly background to theorizing religion and media technology. Two theoretical approaches inform this study: religious social shaping of technology (RSST), from which I draw the importance of understanding the religious context and how religion informs the discourse, and mediatization of religion, from which I draw the importance of paying attention to technological affordances and how socio-technological context shapes the discourse. Finally, I summarize the major takeaways from the review of the scholarship and point to how the scholarship informs the rest of this book.

Media Studies: Understanding the Digital as a Discourse

Are you a dog online? In the early phases of the internet anyone could pretend to be anything online. However, as digital media became more pervasive in everyday life and identity, it seems that offline identity markers inform online representation and interactions more and more. In the early days of Facebook, I made a fake Facebook page for my pet snake, my alter ego, and so on. Today, it's much harder to do that for various reasons. In other words, most people present themselves online and on social media using their real name, photo, and identity markers.[3] This means that important identity markers— for example, religion or gender—are presented, constructed, and negotiated online.[4] It is an ongoing process on a personal and societal level, as people constantly change who they are and how they act online. For example, in my first social media interactions on Twitter, I put my personal photo. But later, as I became more professionally oriented in my use of Twitter, I replaced it with a photo of a book I edited. It is this process that I suggest we need to understand as a *discourse* in which power and resistance play, and by understanding communication technology as a tool for power and resistance, we can think of the digital world as a "space" in which people negotiate gender and sexual norms. This discourse can only be fully understood, I argue, by analyzing the "support mechanisms"[5]—technological affordances and religious worldviews. This section explains theorizing digital communication as a discourse while the next section expands on understanding religion and media.

In the last forty years, technological advancement has accelerated at a pace so overwhelming, developments have been called revolutionary almost every other year. The digital revolution, information revolution, mobile revaluation, and other advancements in communication technologies have been broadly titled "new media" or "digital media." Digital media in this book are defined as modes of communication accessed through electronic and digital computers, especially communication online—that is, via the internet—but can also refer to any other digital media communication technologies. Digital media tend to include diverse and malleable media (from e-books to Vines);

thus, digital media can be thought of as a "meta-medium."[6] One basic and important characteristic of this medium is that it "integrate[s] the storage capacities of print media with the transmission speed of electronic media."[7] The electronic and storage capacities for digital media allow for asynchronous and constant communication. Furthermore, in the digital media age, creation is considered more participatory and interactive and, therefore, more democratic. It is more democratic and participatory because the internet is open; any user can create and upload content, interact with other users and companies, blog, react, post, and repost. This means people have more avenues in which to voice their opinions and more access to participate in the creation and distribution of media, which naturally destabilizes existing power structures of media production and distribution and grants more power to individuals and communities.[8]

However, even in this participatory culture, traditional power and authority structures are still present and influential. Specifically, patriarchal and religious power structures, I argue, operate through digital media to maintain their status. The interaction between feminist studies and internet studies explores how digital media's characteristics influence and are influenced by gender politics.

Gender and Digital Media

When computer technologies, cyberspace, and Web 1.0 first emerged, feminist scholars wondered if this virtual space might be the place where identity could become flexible and playful, where gender norms could be bent, where hegemonic patriarchal power structures could be resisted. Sadie Plant considered the digital revolution a moment of a genderquake—a revolution of sexual and gender relations in which "all the old expectations, stereotypes, senses of identity and security faced challenges."[9] According to Plant, the advances in computer technology have been, from the beginning, signs of the sexual revolution; thus, feminist progress and technological progress can be seen as interconnected. Technology and media have changed the structure of traditional gender relations by, for example, representing women on television in a multiplicity of ways; they have also impacted sexual norms with, for example, the development of contraception and the wide access to pornography. As Joshual Meyrowitz argues, electronic media have profoundly changed notions of masculinity and femininity and the spheres in which they interact.[10] Donna Haraway similarly suggests that new technologies could bend gender binaries: "Certain dualisms have been persistent in Western traditions; they have all been systematic to the logics and practices of domination of women, people of color, nature, workers, animals . . . chief among these troubling dualisms are self/other, mind/body, culture/ nature . . . *High-tech culture challenges these dualisms in intriguing ways.*"[11] However, the reality of power in digital media is far more complicated, and although some power structures have fractured, it is worth noting many traditional power structures have survived. Digital media have also been presented as tools used to intensify gender normativity and regulate "correct" sexual behavior.[12] A funny example of this from my own personal experience is that when I was young and still learning English, I started chatting on old ICQ chat forums. I was chatting with a nice person and wanted to know if they are male or female, so I typed, "are you a gay?" (meaning, of course, to ask if they are a guy). They got very insulted and left the chat. It was only much later that I understood my mistake. But this funny example showcases how even in the early days of the internet, knowing a person's gender and sexuality was pivotal, and blurring those categories (for example, asking someone if they are "a gay") was punished in implicit and explicit ways.

According to Anne Balsamo, "Technologies of the body not only manipulate alterity, but also reproduce it. Sexual differences are both the input and the output of the technological production of the gendered bodies."[13] In other words, Balsamo states that technology is created in line with current social norms regarding gender, and therefore, technology is used to replicate and enforce those norms. Although Balsamo accepts that technology has an impact on society, she limits that impact to only what the designers of the technology—the shapers—intended that output to be. In Balsamo's understanding of the relationship between society and technology, it is existing societal norms that shape technology and not the other way around. On this account, it seems that the same new technologies that have the potential to break the binary are just as likely to empower it. As Jodi O'Brien shows in her study of gender in online chats: "Gender is a dominant, shared social construction that constitutes a primary symbolic form around which we organize interaction. Despite the hype of cyberspace as 'unmarked' territory, we are nonetheless mapping this frontier with the same social categories of distinction that we have used to chart modern reality—which we tend to code as based in a state of nature."[14] That is, even in moments and places where the technology allows for an escape from gender norms, the construction of gender is so pivotal to our understanding of ourselves, others, and society at large, that we (re)enforce it—as in my example above. Even when modern tools are provided, "they do not necessarily disrupt 'traditional' notions of gender."[15]

The important assumption made here, and reaffirmed throughout scholarship on media technology and gender, is that "technology is never neutral and always works as a form of knowledge and power."[16] Furthermore, Web 2.0 and especially virtual and social online gaming have become spaces of extreme sexism and chauvinism. I suggest this is mostly because digital media are not just tools for change, experimentation, and resistance; online engagement is concurrently used by and large to maintain and intensify hegemonic power.[17] Thus, it is the work of feminist scholars of media and digital media to explore how these technologies impact and are impacted by gender roles and sexual norms. We need to question and illuminate the power structures these technologies support and explain them. In sum, gender studies scholarship views media as a force that influences society's understanding of gender and sexual norms. Media can be used to resist *or* to enforce traditional gender norms. One theoretical way to understand "resistance and power" is to conceptualize digital media as a form of Foucauldian discourse.

The Digital as a Discourse

As can be seen from this chapter so far, media at large and digital media specifically play an important part in feminist thought, both as perpetrators of hegemonic gender behavior and as places and tools for resistance. Given their participatory affordances, digital media especially have been theorized as tools useful for liberation and negotiation of gender and sexual norms and narratives. However, digital media have also been presented as tools used to intensify gender normativity and regulate "correct" sexual behavior. I would argue it is precisely this tension between liberation and regulation that can be thought of as a tangible version of Foucauldian discourse.

What do I mean by Foucauldian discourse? Not every form of conversation can be classified as Foucauldian discourse; rather, Foucauldian discourse requires *systematic statements and practices that aim to define, produce, or regulate a certain term or structure*. According to Christian Pentzold and Sebastian Seidenglanz, "discursive practices are delimiting the field of objects, defining a legitimate perspective and fixing the norms for the elaboration of concepts."[18] That is, discourse is understood as an epistemological power structure that works to maintain, for example, traditional gender and sexual norms. Discourses are "ways of constituting knowledge,"[19] and they allow for both domination and resistance.

Therefore, the tension present in the discourse highlights the negotiation and construction of gender and sexuality. Furthermore, I suggest that digital media allow the creation of a *tangible* discourse, because in the case of digital technology the discourse is public and archived, stored, and quickly transmitted, thus making it possible for the feminist researcher (or anyone, really) to closely examine and analyze the negotiation and construction of gender norms that takes place in online communication.

Understanding digital media as discourse means theorizing digital communication—in this book, it means theorizing Jewish Orthodox online communication as a set of systematic statements and online practices that create, construct, and negotiate Jewish gender and sexual norms. Digital communication technology is theorized in many different ways: as participatory culture;[20] as a social network;[21] as a communal space;[22] and as a tool, place, or environment.[23] What is unique in conceptualizing the internet as discourse is that this lens does not view the digital only from the perspective of the individual (how one uses it to create social relations or collect information) but also examines the digital as a structure, an "institution" to which users contribute and in which they partake. A mirror and a window. It also differs from viewing the digital as a networked society,[24] because while that theory pays attention to society as a whole, its main foci are on the organizational and material aspects of how networked societies function because of the digital (such as businesses or social networking sites), and less on the cultural discourses the digital creates and maintains. The usefulness of Foucault and his notion of discourse has been recognized in digital media studies and used to investigate the construction of online identity,[25] information systems,[26] Wikipedia's knowledge structures,[27] internet archaeology and genealogy,[28] and even "e-religion."[29] While these studies use Foucault in various ways, the common underlying assumption is that through the digital, knowledge and power are constructed, negotiated, and maintained. This is a helpful approach for the aim of this book, which is focused on the negotiation of norms.

More specifically for our purposes, theorizing the internet as discourse is helpful in analyzing patriarchy from a cultural perspective. As Syliva Walby argues, "Patriarchal culture is best analyzed as a set of discourses which are institutionally-rooted. [. . .] Religions have historically been very important patriarchal discourses, laying down correct forms for men and for women. [. . .] Discourses on femininity and masculinity are institutionalized in all sites of social life, not only in those institutions such as religions, media and education, which have cultural production as a central goal."[30] As Walby observes, both religion and media are institutions that produce and maintain gender discourses. However, this is not just a historical phenomenon, it's one currently taking place through digital media. By theorizing religious digital media as a discourse in which patriarchal structures are maintained and resisted, we can explore this current phenomenon in depth. To summarize, while there are various ways of theorizing digital media (as a network, as a space, etc.), in this book, I suggest conceptualizing digital media as a Foucauldian discourse, as a site of struggle in which power and resistance operate. The next subsection briefly reviews power in the context of technology, religion, and gender.

Power, Authority, Gender, and Digital Media

Power can be understood in many ways, including access to wealth and decision-making; the ability to force and control; or the ability to lead, impose, or resist social norms. Power, and specifically patriarchal power and the hegemony's power to correct gender behaviors, has been a feminist focus of study.[31] For centuries, the social structures in our societies have been created and controlled by men. Take for example the Christian church, which gave privileges and authority to men as leaders, as religious clergy, and even as heads of their households.[32] But power also works in subtle ways. Growing up Modern Orthodox (or, more specifically, Dati Leumi, National Religious), it was often emphasized to us as a point of pride that this denomination is unique in its hierarchal structure—unlike ultra-Orthodox, who have clear leadership and communal roles (and punishments), the Dati Leumi community didn't have agreed-upon authority figures; each of us had to be proficient in Halacha and make our own decisions. However, the social roles and punishments were still there and felt—they were just more implicit. For example, I myself, and women like me who were interested in feminism, heard more than once that "you will have a hard time getting married"—thus, while traditional gender roles weren't enforced, they were other, more subtle ways in which they were kept.

This process is also true in general secular society in the West; in the last two centuries, social and technological changes have shifted the sources of power and authority at least to a certain extent. However, patriarchal structures still exist and are, in many ways, dominant. One of the ways patriarchal structures maintain their power is through normalizing discourses, a process that takes place in social institutions (such as school or church), in daily conversations (like telling religious feminist they will have a hard time getting married), and through the media.

Power in this book is understood as operating through discourse—that is, power is theorized in the Foucauldian sense of power rather than the Weberian one. Broadly speaking, Max Weber understands power as the ability to coerce, either forcefully or through psychic coercion.[33] However, according to Foucault, power operates not only via brute force, coercion, or state-enforced ideology but also through a mainstream discourse and the creation of a mental panopticon.[34] Within the creation and maintenance of the discourse, each individual has a certain amount of agency and power, but centralized social institutions (such as schools, churches, or the media) tend to enjoy the highest level of influence because they are understood as sources of authority.

These institutions and structures of power were conceptualized further in Foucault's later writings as "governmentality": a way to understand power and authority in liberal modern societies. Foucault suggests that modern societies are governed by the creation of institutions, procedures, and mental strategies that construct specific types of actions.[35] For example, instead of banning or taxing cigarettes, a psychological campaign in the media and schools is used to make individuals adopt mental structures that refuse smoking. It becomes a personal choice rather than one enforced by the government. Governmentality examines how various authoritative actors work to shape societal choices, needs, and aspirations. In other words, governmentality explores how "power is productively and diffusely harnessed in the governance of others and the self."[36]

There are various ways in which governmentality operates in micro- and macroprocesses of power, but the aspect that is most useful for the exploration taken in this book is its role in creating a "subjective self" that maintains the existing religious gender and sexual norms. By crafting people's subjectivity in specific ways, state and nonstate actors encourage individuals to behave in ways that reflect that subjectivity. Nikolas Rose explains, "The self is to be a subjective being, [. . .] to interpret its reality and destiny as a matter of individual responsibility, [. . .] to find meaning in existence by shaping its life through acts of choice."[37] These acts of choice, however, are not dependent on individual autonomy but are instead part of the structures of power. Rose goes on to explain how Foucault ties "practices bearing on the self" to a "form of power" through the concept of governmentality: "Foucault conceives of power as that which traverses all practices—from the 'macro' to the 'micro'—through which persons are ruled, mastered, held in check, administered, steered, guided, by means of which they are led by others or have come to direct or regulate their own actions."[38] Governmentality thus brings into the notion of power not only explicitly defined "macro" institutions but also "the diverse techniques that are deployed to produce subjects."[39] In Judaism, for example, the macro level of Rabbinical Courts and Halachic textual authority represent institutional power. A study that concentrated solely on this power would explore how gender and sexuality are enforced top-down. However, as I argue in this book in accord with the insights of Foucault, power can also be observed to operate through the micro level by, for example, creating the discursive strategies that produce subjects who understand themselves as "divine" females or by framing housework as joyful and empowering. This book examines how power (in the shape of gender and sexual norms) operates, is enforced, and is negotiated through technologies of the self as mediated by digital technologies.

Governmentality works through encouraging internalization and surveillance.[40] Foucault uses the architectural metaphor of a prison panopticon to provide a visual image of his theory on how power relations and surveillance work. Instead of prison guards constantly checking on each prisoner by walking between the cells, prisons can build a panopticon. Through this central tower, the guards can randomly observe in whichever direction they choose and are able to watch each prisoner without that prisoner's knowledge. The prisoner, then, under the fear of being constantly watched, begins internalizing this type of surveillance, monitoring their own behavior without being forced to do so. Therefore, using the metaphorical concept of the panopticon, Foucault argues that power can be internalized by the regulated individuals who then take an "active" part in their own surveillance.

This understanding of power through self-regulation is important when examining examples of online religious discourse dealing with issues of gender and sexuality. It suggests an examination of the construction of gender and sexuality via discourse. According to Dmitri Williams et al., "Gender roles are shared cultural expectations that are placed on individuals on the basis of their socially defined gender."[41] Gender roles and expectations are formed and regulated through social and cultural practices, representations, and narratives. Feminist research uncovers these forms of gender regulation via hegemonic discourse. For example, Sandra Lee Bartky suggests that "in modern societies [...] power now seeks to transform the minds of those individuals who might be tempted to resist it, not merely to punish or imprison their bodies. [...] Women have their own experience of the modernization of power, one which begins later but follows in many respects the course outlined by Foucault. [...] The disciplinary power that is increasingly charged with the production of a properly embodied Femininity is dispersed and anonymous [...] invested in everyone and in no one in particular."[42] Bartky used Foucauldian notions of power to show how the female body is surveilled and made docile, subordinate to the male. She goes on to show in her work how media, specifically magazines, act as a disciplinary force in the discourse of gender and sexuality. This conception of disciplinary power as "invested in everyone and in no one in particular" is how, I suggest, we can view digital media as well.

In summary, in the context of religion and gender, power in this book is understood to work through discourse. The discourse becomes more tangible, visual, and constantly available through digital media. Thus, examining the negotiation and construction of gender and sexual norms on digital media is to examine how (Foucauldian) power operates in this religious digital context.

This review highlights the positioning of communication technology as a tool or space in which our understanding of gender and sexuality is shaped. That is, as subjects, we use the internet as a site of information seeking to understand social norms—a window into what our community considers as a "right" or "wrong" behavior. And if we as researchers theorize the digital as a "tangible" or "fossilized" discourse, it can be used to track and examine the "archaeology of now"[43]—that is, the ways in which current trends and behaviors become normalized. In the case of digital media and religion, technology plays an instrumental part by expanding the reach and access of religious communities. By doing so, digital media allow conceptions of gender to be explored and questioned. That is, a religious individual could use digital media conduits to search for sexual or gender interpretations differing from those within their religious community, or they could use religious digital media spaces to anonymously question religious authority and raise issues for communal discussion.

Digital media can also (re)affirm traditional views on gender and sexuality. Through online religious spaces, or various religious mobile applications, religious individuals, communities, and institutions can encourage traditional behaviors. For example, a mobile application like JDate allows people to date online within the Jewish ethnicity/religion. A website like AskTheRabbi allows individuals anonymous, ongoing access to rabbis, and allows rabbis to constantly and publicly confirm their religious norms. These seemingly binary possibilities of digital media—to liberate and regulate, to defy and affirm authority—are in fact part of the construction of the religious discourse on gender and sexuality. As noted above, a Foucauldian approach to power considers how individuals and institutions negotiate and manifest their positions through an ongoing discourse. I therefore expand on a Foucauldian-based understanding of power as it translates into "real" technologies and technologies of the self. In other words, in this book, I explore the ways individuals use technologies that shape their perspectives on gender and sexuality, and I identify ways individuals engage with these technologies to change, maintain, and negotiate these perspectives. Understanding digital media as a site of struggle, we must further consider what elements constitute this discourse. I suggest that in the case of an online religious discourse, we need to examine all three words that make up this phrase—the online (technology), the religious, and the discourse. So far, I have reviewed how to understand the online as a discourse; the next section explores how to understand the relationship between religion and communication technology.

Digital Religion: Understanding Discourse in Terms of Technology and Religion

Many years after my bat mitzvah, I have become secular, and I was studying religion from a secular perspective in one of the most secular countries in the world—Denmark. I was working on my MA in religious studies in Denmark in 2010, just as the world was becoming aware of the political power of social media (remember the "Arab Spring"?). Denmark was a secular country, but as I was studying religion in a secularist hub, I noticed very quickly the various ways religion still plays a role in this society, especially when it came to identity. To be "Danish" meant to be White, of Danish descent, and, well, culturally Christian. As one of my Danish friends put it, "You have to love drinking beer and eating pork"—something most Muslim immigrants to the Scandinavian countries could generally not participate in. On the surface, it felt welcoming and nonreligious. But online, I noted, there was a quiet battle between Christianity and Islam and an alarming growth of Islamophobic messages. I decided to write my master's thesis on online Islamophobia, which led me to investigate the relationship between new media and religion.

Religious traditions adjust to and exist in the material affordances and limitations of the world around them. Technology has always been a powerful force in the development of religions. Communications technologies in particular have been used to spread religious ideas, negotiate religious authority, and construct religious worldviews and concepts. Think of the technology of writing, or printing, and what it has done to Christianity, for example. With the emergence of the internet and digital media technologies, scholars began to study the relationship between this new communication technology and religion.

This section provides a brief overview of the development of the study of religion online, focusing on the theoretical tools developed in this field and how they contribute to this book. The focus of this section is on two theories within digital religion studies—religious social shaping of technology (RSST) and mediatization of religion—which provide helpful perspectives for studying the negotiation of religious gender norms online in this study. They offer ways to understand how religious individuals use the media for religious purposes as well as how the media allow for specific media logics and affordances. This is important because the ways media are used for the construction of religious gender norms and meanings is informed, I argue, both by religious cultural background and by media affordances. Therefore, in order to understand gender and sexuality as religious norms constructed and negotiated online, the analysis must also consider the religious and technological contexts they operate in.

The Study of Digital Religion

As the internet became more widely used in the Western world through the late 1980s and the 1990s, scholars began to ask themselves about the impact of this new technology on religious individuals and institutions. This field of study is known as "digital religion," and it explores the "evolution of religious practices online which are linked to online and offline contexts simultaneously."[44] The study of religion and digital media has taken a few twists and turns,[45] evolving alongside the development of the internet itself and the many uses of the internet. In the early days of the internet, there was a fascination with how this new technology could facilitate new approaches to religion or maybe even give birth to new religious movements. As the internet became more commonplace, there was a growing focus on understanding it and the religious uses of digital media. As the internet became less of a "cyberspace" and more of a mundane medium, scholars began observing the ways religious groups and individuals negotiate their relationship with these new media. Most recently, scholars of digital religion are more focused on exploring the daily religious use of digital technology, for example, studying religious iTunes applications,[46] religious games or religious symbolism in video games,[47] or religious internet memes.[48] As can be seen from these examples, more nuanced attention is being given to the specific medium, its affordances, and how it is used by religious individuals. This current wave also displays an array of intersectional studies, which combine the study of digital religion with questions of race, ethnicity, sexuality, gender, and nationality.

Theories of Digital Religion

The literature on religion and digital media deals not only with phenomenology, or describing religious uses of media, but also with theory, or explaining the relationship between digital media and religion. Knut Lundby provides a detailed review of the main theoretical stances in the study of digital religion. According to Lundby, five main theoretical stances can be found in the study of religion and media: technological determinism, mediatization of religion, mediation of religion, mediation of sacred forms, and RSST.[49] For the purposes of this book, I focus only on mediatization and RSST, as they provide what I consider to be the most helpful tools for understanding how religious negotiation through online discourse. That is, both mediatization and RSST are helpful because they consider the complicated socio-technological contexts in which digital religion takes place and are concerned with religious communities and institutions. In contrast, mediation of religion and mediation of sacred forms are helpful when trying to understand personal spiritual consumption, representation of religion via the media, or the ways media and religion are interconnected. For the purposes of this book, it is more important to understand the "religious" and the "technological" as two forces that together inform the online discourse on Jewish gender and sexuality.

Mediatization is a nuanced version of technological determinism explicitly articulated in Stig Hjarvard's book *The Mediatization of Culture and Society*. Unlike technological determinism, which sees every technology as a determining force, Hjarvard's mediatization theory focuses on the influence of media in the twentieth and twenty-first centuries, in societies that live in highly technological, highly modern surroundings. Hjarvard claims that in those societies, media industries operate as social institutions. That is, media industries are organizations that inform or establish norms of social behavior. Furthermore, media as social institutions are increasingly gaining power. His theory about the mediatization of religion, therefore, suggests that these media institutions are replacing religious institutions or that existing religious institutions begin to function using "media logics." According to Hjarvard, "The overall outcome of the mediatization of religion is not a new kind of religion as such but rather a new social condition in which the power to define and practice religion has changed."[50]

The way we understand religion, according to Hjarvard, is preconditioned by media logics. Media logics are the scripts and ways of behavior that media create and promote (for example, online media logic "invites" interactivity). According to Hjarvard, media logic can be "understood as a conceptual shorthand for the various institutional, aesthetic, and technological *modus operandi* of the media, including the ways in which the media distribute material and symbolical resources, and operate with the help of formal and informal rules."[51] Another useful term from this perspective is the concept of technological affordances. Hjarvard suggests we consider James Gibson's concept of affordance to understand how a technology's structure might determine its possible uses; Hjarvard states that "the affordances of any given object make certain actions possible, they exclude others and structure the interaction between the actor and user."[52] Digital media, like other communication technologies, have both certain media logics and technological affordances. Technological affordances are defined as ways in which the design features of the websites request, demand, allow, encourage, discourage, and refuse users' interactions and engagement.[53] Technological affordances can inform media logics—for example, hyperlinks might create a media logic that is ahistorical or context-free[54] or, as discussed later in this book, anonymity online can lead to a greater tendency to ask about taboo issues.[55]

The second theory informing the analysis in this book is Heidi Campbell's RSST. Campbell suggests that we should pay attention to the way society shapes technology, rather than the other way around. Coming from the tradition of information communication technology studies, social shaping of technology is a theory adapted by Campbell to address religious users and uses. Within the theory of social shaping of technology (SST), "technology is seen as a social process, and the possibility is recognized that social groups may shape technologies towards their own ends, rather than the character of the technology determining use and outcomes."[56] SST considers how technologies are created, shaped, used, and negotiated in the societies that make and employ them. This process happens during the invention, creation, application, and appropriation of the technology by the human individuals involved. SST further stresses "the negotiability of technology and highlighting the scope for particular groups and forces to shape technologies to their ends."[57] Campbell combined SST with religious studies to highlight the specificity of how religious groups negotiate technology, a process she called religious social shaping of technology. According to Campbell, this theory "takes into account the factors informing a religious community's responses to new media—their relationship to community, authority, and text—and combines it with a social shaping approach that highlights the practices surrounding technology evaluation."[58] This theoretical approach offers an in-depth exploration of both religion and technology and views their interactions as processes of combining social factors instead of combating ones.

RSST is a theoretical approach and method for collecting and analyzing information. It urges researchers to ask questions "about how technologies are conceived of, as well as used, in light of a religious community's beliefs, moral codes, and historical tradition of engagement with other forms of media technology."[59] While this book does not fully employ RSST as a method, it does consider specific religious context as highly important for understanding the online negotiation of gender and sexuality norms. In each of the following chapters, I provide some religious context before analyzing the digital discourse. That is, RSST contributes to this book by insisting on the investigation of traditional Jewish beliefs and moral codes concerning both gender and technology as part of the aspects that construct this discourse.

In order to answer the research question of this book, which is focused on negotiating gender through online religious discourse, both the religious worldviews and the technological affordances that allow this negotiation must be carefully considered. I suggest that combining RSST with mediatization of religion allows for a theoretical framework that considers both religious worldviews and technological and media "logics." This combination, I argue, helps one conduct nuanced research, and is especially useful in the case of researching the complicated topics of gender and sexuality. Mia Lövheim argues that "a focus on gender brings out how mediatization of religion is a contextualized process, where the outcomes of the general tendencies suggested by Hjarvard vary depending on the interplay between *the particular form of media* and the *religious setting*."[60] Lövheim suggests that an exploration of gender negotiation demands that we pay attention to both the form of media and the religious setting. Therefore, although these two approaches are in opposition regarding, for example, the shaping of technology development—where RSST argues that religious communities shape technology and mediatization claims that technology as a social institution shapes society—I argue that combining these views creates a holistic approach. To be more concrete, each of these approaches helps in theorizing the Orthodox digital discourse: RSST calls attention to the religious cultural context used in the discourse while mediatization of religion, in contrast, draws attention to the technological affordances and media logics and the types of discourse they enable. RSST thus informs the analysis of the religious cultural context, and mediatization of religion the analysis of the technological affordances. We need to consider both processes: the religious cultural context and how it informs religious uses of technology as well as the logics and affordances of the media and how these logics and affordances impact religious uses of technology. I suggest we think about this as an ecosystem in which media/

technology and religion/culture are two forces that, in different ways, shape our lives, our worldviews, the ways we use technology, and the ways we understand our religion.

Throughout this book these approaches inform my analysis of the data: I consider, on the one hand, the religious history, traditions, and norms informing a certain religious discussion or behavior and, on the other hand, the affordances and logics of the specific medium being used. This discussion includes two approaches. First, it requires reviewing and considering the religious and cultural aspects related to a topic. What are the religious norms regarding discussions and arguments? What are the historical attitudes toward a specific sexual behavior? What are the social norms regarding this topic? Second, it requires examining certain media for the affordances they have. Can the users react? Comment? Share? Are there audio or visual aspects to the discourse? I believe these two theories in conjunction can help us explore how Jewish religious individuals, informed by their religious traditions, authority, and community structures, use digital media and how that interaction, based on the affordances of the medium, might construct their religious concepts and behaviors.

Thus, I suggest a theoretical approach that begins by conceptualizing the internet as a discourse, then insists this discourse exists in a technological medium and is informed by cultural and religious worldviews. By considering all three—discourse, medium, and religion—we are better set to understand the construction and negotiation of gender and sexuality in Jewish online texts. The next section reviews previous scholarly approaches related to Jewish gender and sexuality online and problematizes some of the assumptions made in this literature.

Jewish Sexuality and Gender Online: Problematizing the "Liberating" Assumptions

When I began my research of Jewish communities online, I was also still thinking about that twelve-year-old Ruth I mentioned in the introduction. There was a part of me that hoped that if she had access to the internet, she would have the space to formulate her feminist identity with others—to not feel so alone. I had hoped that through my research, I would discover the power of online discourse, the power to break away from old traditions and oppressive practices, and I would see that the internet has, indeed, "liberated" religious Jewish women. (I write liberated in quotation marks, because who am I to decided what is liberation?) I was not alone in these feelings, as this next section discusses; other scholars have tried to argue that the internet does in fact allow for religious Jewish women to oppose patriarchal structures. However, my own research has shown me, as I hope to show you, that things are much more nuanced and complex.

While the introduction to this book supplied context about Jewish Orthodox attitudes toward media and sexuality in general, this section reviews scholarly literature that examines issues of gender, Judaism, and digital media. I begin by briefly outlining the themes brought up in this scholarship, showing their various contributions, and that, while these themes are diverse, they have a common thread—that most of these the research on Jewish gender and sexuality online shows the liberating abilities of the internet. That is, previous scholarship tends to understand power through a Weberian authority instead of a Foucauldian one, and thus digital media are viewed as tools for liberation and empowerment, instead of as a discourse, in which power, regulation, and resistance operate. I then conclude by suggesting the uniqueness of this study, and how it contributes to our understanding of Orthodox Judaism online, specifically by arguing that the internet is not only a "liberating tool" but also one in which power and religious enforcement are enacted.

The study of gender, Judaism, and digital media can be divided into a few themes: attitudes toward female use of digital technology, digital technology as a tool for female empowerment, and digital technology as a space to voice and explore divergent sexualities. More specifically, when looking at how Orthodox women use the internet, scholars show how women use it for empowerment and negotiation.[61] Some scholars particularly explore instances in which ultra-Orthodox women use the internet out of necessity (for work), in which case, the women tend to provide an apologetic perspective.[62] Other studies look at how epistemic rabbinical authority is challenged by women using digital media tools.[63] Last, a few studies examine sexual deviance explored in ultra-Orthodox forums.[64] As can be seen from this list, many of the previous studies examine what women do once they are online and how they negotiate their use of digital media. These studies deal with the issue of religious authority within the community. In this book, instead of asking how religious women negotiate authority, I ask how they negotiate their understanding of *what it means to be a Jewish woman*. My investigation is about the construction and negotiation of gender and sexual norms through the use of digital media tools and spaces. Simon Theobald comes the closest to asking similar questions, but his work focuses only on sexuality.[65] He also examines online places of deviance (homosexuality, "diverse sexual practices")—forums used by individuals on the periphery of these communities. In contrast, this book examines typical issues of gender and sexuality (heterosexual relationships) and their construction in the online *mainstream* discourse. I propose we look at digital media not only as a space in which women can negotiate authority and where peripheral religious individuals can find their voice but also as a tool for constructing, negotiating, and (re)enforcing communal religious understandings of correct sexualities and normalized gender behavior.

While the media's ability to reinforce traditional gender norms in Judaism has been discussed in relation to electronic media such as film[66] or audio cassettes,[67] most research regarding digital, networked media, tends to highlight the liberating, democratizing abilities of the medium. In order to argue for a challenge to authority via digital media, many of these studies highlight the liberating possibilities afforded by internet use. For example, Avi Lev-On and Rivka Shahar carefully show how the use of even a closed forum for only ultra-Orthodox women might allow for an opening of views and the creation of empowering relationships: "Ultra-Orthodox women form online relationships, but most of them are only with other ultra-Orthodox women. [. . .] Even if many of these relationships are work-oriented and legitimate unto themselves, the participants still have here a novel opening to acquainting the non-ultra-Orthodox world."[68] This citation demonstrates the scholarly conclusion that internet use facilitates liberating discussions, allowing ultra-Orthodox women to connect with others and to acquire access to non-ultra-Orthodox society. Lev-On and Shahar ask, how do religious women negotiate internet use in their lives, and what possible changes for the ultra-Orthodox society could this use facilitate? Their research makes positive assumptions about the use of digital media as a place of interactivity and participation, focusing on challenging authority and creating access to information for ultra-Orthodox women through internet use.

This notion of the internet as a liberating tool is also highlighted in Theobald's work. In his study, Theobald shares a case in point of Orthodox individuals using the internet to negotiate sexuality. In his research of LGBTQI websites and online support groups, he claims that "Orthodox community members have used digital technologies to step outside the narrow confines of communal control and create 'safe spaces' for the exploration of non-hegemonic sexual practices and sexualities."[69] Theobald shows how the internet is used by Jewish community members for experimentation with sexual identity by openly asking questions and imagining scenarios, while maintaining community boundaries by staying in digital enclaves limited by language (Yiddish) and content (Jewish terminologies and community topics).

Looking at a similarly restricted digital enclave, Judith Baumel-Schwartz examines ultra-Orthodox women's forums.[70] Her research focuses not on the technological affordances of digital media but rather on the historical and cultural trends scholars can extract from this material. However, she does offer some thoughts about the potential role these forums play in shaping communal trends related to gender:

> It appears that the Internet forums of OJW [Orthodox Jewish Women] serve a dual purpose. On the one hand, they echo and mirror major social, educational and religious trends affecting the Orthodox and Haredi Jewish communities today. On the other hand, they play a role in shaping and reshaping these trends. . . . By allowing dissenting voices to be heard, albeit anonymously, they act as a safe arena in which posters can express their true personal and gendered selves. . . . On the individual level, these factors have a dynamic potential impact on the development of the Orthodox Jewish female self. On the communal level, they have the potential of slowly changing the form and nature of the Orthodox Jewish world.[71]

In a later article, she continues to research these forums as ways of learning about the world of Orthodox women, and specifically how they use these forums to "reinvent" tradition.[72] According to Baumel-Schwartz, although the creators and users of these forums think of them as places where one can learn how to act correctly, "these fascinating discussions are indicative of how each and every member is at one and the same time participant and observer, *partners in the social production* of Jewish religious boundaries, belief, and praxis in the contemporary Jewish world."[73] That is, Baumel-Schwartz sees these women as active prosumers (producers and consumers) of religious content and ideology. Similarly, Michelle Pitkowsky shows the possibility of liberating Jewish religious women through their use of online Q&A. In her 2011 article, Pitkowsky reviews questions sent to rabbis in the twentieth century and compares offline questions to online ones: "I argue that the Internet has in a sense changed the rules of the game by allowing women almost unbridled access to rabbinic authority."[74] She is aware that gatekeepers still exist (they are, after all, asking male rabbis), but claims that this gatekeeping is reduced due to the participatory nature and easy access allowed by new media technologies. Pitkowsky's praise of the liberating power of the internet is clear throughout her article.

The dominant approach in previous scholarship is that the online Jewish discourse related to gender and sexuality is challenging traditional structures and positively empowering female resistance. Online Jewish religious Q&As, forums, and other spaces in which discourse on sexuality and gender occurs have generally been conceived in academic scholarship as liberating spaces. In this book, I hope to problematize these assumptions by highlighting the regulatory uses in these digital media spaces and the negotiation processes of power and resistance. This book thus expands the understanding of the negotiation of authority by developing a concept of authority and power that includes self-regulation and normative speech. The theoretical framework discussed in this chapter helps explain the construction and negotiation of gender and sexuality online as it offers a way of thinking of the digital as *discourse*, as a place of power and resistance. Examining the material from a feminist media studies perspective, this book also complicates current scholarly conclusions by asking questions related to shifting terminologies and how gender and sexuality as terms and norms are (re)negotiated and constructed online.

Summary

This chapter provides a worldview from which to understand online Jewish negotiation of gender and sexuality. It does so by reviewing of both religious studies and feminist approaches to communication technology. Through the lenses of these two different fields, I examine how communication technologies are used to construct, inform, regulate, and destabilize cultural practices and worldviews. More specifically, this review informs the book project by understanding Orthodox digital discourse as a discourse in which religious gender and sexuality norms are regulated and resisted. That is, when thinking about communication technology—and specifically the internet—as a site of struggle, where discourses in which both power and resistance are enacted, we can begin to examine the social processes of negotiation and construction of sexual and gender norms through communication. This important assertion stands as the guiding principle of this book. As we examine how gender and sexuality are constructed and negotiated in online Jewish discourse, I suggest we keep in mind the following theoretical considerations.

First, inspired by critical and feminist media theories, and specifically the work of Michel Foucault, I consider the digital as a *discourse*, in which Orthodox gender and sexual norms are systematically defined, enforced, and resisted. That is, digital media are understood as a site of power and resistance in which norms and concepts are confirmed, rejected, and negotiated; therefore, I am not arguing for a clear binary but a complicated ongoing process of negotiation. Second, following the RSST approach, I consider specific religious context and user choices, focusing on lived religious experiences as they are communicated via digital technology. That is, I examine the material as a product of this specific religious tradition, supplying historical and sociological information about these communities and examining their media usage as part of their religious practice. Third, informed by mediatization theory, I pay close attention to media logics and affordances inherent in the websites—including, for example, the ability to comment, share, interact—and show how the media logics inform the various ways in which users communicate about their religious negotiation of gender and sexual norms.

These key ideas help construct and inform the analysis performed in this book. As can be noted from this literature review, I assume that the use of communication technology has the power to mirror and shape our perspectives of the world. However, that use is always already informed by the ideologies and cultural norms in which we live in.

Bringing these different scholarly approaches together, we can now consider how gendered religious discourse online can be understood. Research into gendered uses of the internet by religious Jews has tended to suggest that this use opens and challenges communal norms. I would like to problematize this by suggesting we consider digital media a force that pervasively acts as a regulatory force at the hands of patriarchal powers on the one hand, and acts as a tool for resistance and users' involvement in the negotiation of gender and sexuality on the other. By critically analyzing, and not only describing, Jewish online discourse on gender and sexuality, I highlight the ways in which this religious use of digital media works within a semidialectic tension between liberating and regulating sexual and gender norms. That is, I consider the digital as a discourse, a site of struggle, and I suggest examining this discourse through the lenses of gender/sex, religion, and the digital.

I propose a theoretical perspective that considers online texts as fossilized discourse, as sites of struggle. Moreover, I claim this discourse can only be fully appreciated in light of the cultural (religious) and technological elements composing it. Since this approach calls to attention various elements—discursive, cultural (religious), and technological—that make up this discourse, I call this a *layered approach to digital communication*. This approach allows researchers to consider the digital as a communicative tool, a space of public negotiation, and a public sphere or site of struggle, while at the same time forcing us to consider the technical aspects of the digital and the analog cultural elements individuals and groups bring into their use of the digital as discourse. In the rest of the book, these theories are weaved into the analysis in each chapter. Each chapter also highlights specific religious/cultural elements. In between the chapters, you will find "technological interludes" that examine more closely the media logics. Equipped with this type of theoretical thinking, we now embark on the imaginary life journey of a Jewish woman, from dating to mothering, navigating her identity and community with the internet as her mirror and window.

Chapter 2

Getting Married

I had received three marriage proposals before I turned thirty. The most dramatic time, the one that impressed me and made me reevaluate my society's attitude toward dating, was in a car, on a rainy Jerusalem winter, sometime in the mid-2000. I was about twenty-two, and my date was about twenty-four. He was the son of a liberal religious rabbi, a charming and intellectual guy, and we had been dating for . . . three weeks. In the car, he said that he really likes me, but we need to understand where this relationship is going. I was sure he was about to ask me to "go steady." But he meant we should either get engaged or break up. We broke up.

This was not a very unusual situation in the contemporary Orthodox context. Jewish Orthodox women and men marry relatively young (younger than twenty-four years old), according to a 2013 Pew Research Report.[1] And in Israel in 2018, 43 percent of ultra-Orthodox were married before the age of twenty-one.[2] Many of my high school peers got engaged while we were still in high school. One of my best friends got married after dating for three months. I cried in her wedding, and not only from joy—I was also afraid I was losing her for a more conservative life in which her creativity and self-expression would be diminished by her responsibilities as a wife and, later, mother. I also had friends that went on dates for many years but couldn't find "the one." They reached their mid- or late twenties feeling that something was inherently wrong with them. The pressure within these communities to marry, and to marry young, is enormous, for both men and women, although, at least in Israel, women tend to marry a little younger (around twenty-five) than men (age twenty-seven), according to Israeli Central Bureau of Statistics (2019).[3]

This pressure to marry translates also to how we dated. Obviously, like in most religious or traditional communities, dating was not for sexual encounters. Dating was also not "for fun"—it was always goal-oriented, with a relatively quick turn-around if we felt that the other person was not a good fit for marriage. I was one of the few among my friends who had a long-term relationship without the intention to marry. This relationship ended, much like the date in the car, exactly because my partner wanted us to "get serious"—and he did not mean sexually. He meant engaged. I was twenty-three, confused about my own sexuality, and in no shape to commit.

But I was the anomaly (which later, when I came out as lesbian and later bisexual, made sense). Most of my friends dated quickly or seriously. Seriously, meaning both parties know that they are on the path to marriage; or quickly, meaning both parties were trying to assess if the other person was "the one." Finding out if the other person was "the one" depended not only on feelings of love or attraction but also on calculated questions like: How religious are they? How many kids do they want to have? Where do they want to live? What profession do they have? What are their perspectives on feminism? Zionism? And so on. This tension that exists in the various Jewish religious Orthodox communities between what I call "romantic love" and "transactional partnership" is also evident in the online discourse. As noted in the introduction, we can see traditional, modern, and mixed worldviews throughout this online content. In this chapter, the traditionalist perspective calls for dating and marriage that is planned, transactional, and based on a clear understanding of the differences between men and women. The modern perspective encourages searching for romantic love and basing a marriage out of respect to the complexities of human experiences (not necessarily a gendered approach). The "mixed" perspective can be found in those who wish to hold both—have a romantic love that is based on traditional gendered relationship. Before we dive into the online material, the next section provides a short overview on Jewish attitudes on these topics.

Jewish Attitudes Toward Dating and Marriage

Marriage in Judaism is a cause for a great celebration and an important milestone in the life of religious Jews: both a party and a religious and social imperative. An allusion to the role of religion in bringing two people together is found in the sayings that a marriage is "made in Heaven" and that the couple is blessed that they have achieved the high goal of "building a Jewish Home in Israel." Marriage and childbearing are interrelated, and this is impressed on the young couple from an early age.

The traditional concept of marriage is that the man buys the woman from her family. The original Halachic source describing marriage reads,

"A woman is acquired in three ways, and she acquires herself [i.e., divorce] in two ways. She is acquired through money, document, and sexual intercourse, she acquires herself through a Get [divorce document] and through her husband's death."[4] As can be seen from this text, marriage is considered a purchasing contract, like other economic contracts. However, even in ancient Judaism, women had some rights in this contract, such as divorce, and the right to expect her husband to feed her, dress her, and provide safety to her. Furthermore, in the case of the husband's death or divorce, she is owed a certain sum of money to help her maintain a quality of life. These details are finalized in a wedding document known as a *Ketuva*, which, while it used to be strictly a legal document, has become in modern days an artistic souvenir from one's wedding, a souvenir many couples frame and display in their houses.

To this day, many Orthodox Jewish marriages are arranged marriages, with a varying degree of agency on the part of the future wife and husband. For example, in the National Religious community, it is customary for friends, friends of family, or a matchmaker (*Shadchanit*) to set up a date between two young people. However, once the date is set, it is completely up to the couple to decide whether they wish to continue dating. That is, while the date might be set up for them, the young couple have total agency. In more strictly religious communities, an engagement is at times agreed upon between two families, but the couple will still go on a date or two and can still veto the arrangement.[5] That is, in these strict communities, while the couple does have some agency, it is very limited, and most of the prewedding communication between them is handled through parents or the professional matchmaker.

Therefore, dating happens in a mindset that is focused on the purpose of marriage. Dates usually include questions like, "How many kids would you want?," "What kind of kosher style do you keep?," "Which synagogue do you go to?," and so on. These questions are meant to help the couple understand what their married life would be like but also to understand what kind of a person their date is, as answers to these questions tend to be tied with issues of religious identity and ideology. Dates are usually half-blind dates—dates that are set up through networks of friends, community, teachers, and parents. Since most young Orthodox Jews live in gender-segregated life, with different schools for boys and girls and gender-segregated youth activities, creating relationships with the opposite sex does not usually happen "naturally"—but it's not unheard of. I met the rabbi's son in the synagogue. Other friends met their dates and future husbands at work, in social gatherings, or in other activities.

With the advent of the internet, dating culture has shifted a little bit. While Orthodoxy by and large is suspicious of the internet, as discussed in the introduction, it is still widely used especially in the Modern Orthodox and National Religious denominations. Even more strict communities might use the internet, but using it for dating seems to be a more complicated matter. Yoel Cohen and I show that "in the case of online dating, this growing need within the religious Jewish Israeli community was met with overall acceptance from the religious leaders. In other words, this study shows how the needs of the community and the importance of the marriage trump the rabbinical hesitance to new media. Religiously adherent dating websites seem to be a small, but growing, niche, and rabbis seem to, by and large, support the use of new media for online dating and match-making, especially those websites which are tailored to the religious needs of the community."[6] It is clear that the internet is used by religious individuals to help them achieve what is one of the most important social-religious goals in Judaism: to get married. This is done in various ways. People use social media, for example, to "spy" and assess their dates. They use niche, religiously focused, online dating sites. They consult rabbis through online Q&As regarding the dating process. They confide in online forums and communities their dating struggles, and once married, they make sense of what it means to become a wife or husband through online material, advice columns, Q&As, and forums. Once engaged to be married, religious youth receive some guidance from a rabbi or religious leader, usually regarding sexual expectations. Because these communities do not have any sex education,[7] these short meetings just before the wedding are pivotal. But these meetings are a one-off, and very little advice is provided on marriage expectations, or *how to be married*. While divorce is not religiously banned, it is socially less acceptable, and religious leadership continuously seeks ways to lower divorce rates.[8] Online, there is a growing assortment of Jewish religious marriage advice, which might be used by couples in navigating relationships, with ease of access and anonymity. This chapter explores how digital media is used in the dating process and how digital sources frame a gendered understanding of marriage.

In order to explore that, various sources are used throughout the chapter: dating apps and websites, dedicated forums, and general advice columns and religious content on the three mainstream websites of Chabad, Aish, and Kipa. Regarding the dating websites, I examine only dating websites and applications that are targeted specifically at Jews, and by examining that niche market, we can see what makes Jewish online dating "Jewish."[9] Second, I sample data from various online forums in order to examine the role online community plays as it relates to dating. Three forms are observed, two in English (Supertova and OKclarity) and one in Hebrew (Kipa's *Lo Kala Derchenu*). These forums were selected not necessarily based on popularity (like in the case of the websites I selected) but based on specificity—I was looking for *Jewish* forums that explicitly discuss *dating*. The forums had to also be open, anonymous, and accessible to anyone with an internet connection. Like with the other online material examined throughout the book, the idea is to experience what a Jewish religious person, who was looking for communal advice or support regarding dating, would find. Last, articles from the three main websites discussed in the introduction (Aish, Chabad, and Kipa) were selected based on their topics. As noted before, three main perspectives on dating can be found throughout the online discourse: modern (love), mixed (divine), and traditional (transactional).

What Is Love? Modern Concepts of a Religious Partnership

Even though my friends might have dated "fast" and with a goal of marriage, we were all definitely looking for "the one"—inspired by Disney and romantic comedies, by content and ideology usually external to religious teachings but which never seemed in contradiction. Of course, things like premarital intercourse were a huge no-no, but falling in love? Yes, please. My friends and I dated through social circles like youth movements, after-schools activities (since schools were gender-segregated), and later, university clubs, singles sabbaths, or other social events. We also went on blind dates, usually organized through a friend. And much later, for those of us not married in their late twenties, online dating started to become a thing. Of course, it was not just my "older" friends who were online dating. As suggest by Cohen and I (2019), online dating is a pretty common activity among Jewish singles. Exploring online dating and dating apps reveals some of the norms, wishes, and guidelines Jews have when looking for "the one."

When people think of online Jewish dating, probably the first website that comes to mind is JDate. JDate, one of the first Jewish dating websites (created 1997), prides itself as being the leading Jewish dating site and claims to have facilitated "hundreds of thousands of romances, friendships, engagements and marriages."[10] This language indeed seems to align with a type of ideology that connects dating with romantic feelings. As I explore later in this chapter, not all online dating is so romantic. JDate profile building is relatively easy, and all profiles are screened before they are published. For example, all users must upload a picture when creating their profile, and those pictures are then examined by the website moderators. Then, users are asked to submit some personal information, and here, the Jewish, family-oriented focus of the website becomes clear. That is, through the profile building exercise, users must balance their quest for "love" with the more realistic and logistical aspects of dating within a (religious) Jewish mindset. For example, users need to select a specific relationship type, ranging from friends to marriage and kids. Out of the six first profile questions, two are related to family (have kids? want kids?) and every user must state their religious affiliation. JDate also allows for same-sex relationships.[11] However, homosexual Jews might feel more comfortable using a website that is specific for gay Jews, such as Yente Over the Rainbow.

Aside from dating online, digital media is also used by religious Jews to navigate the terrain of dating and, eventually, marriage. They use digital media to help them prepare for, and make sense of, dating. For example, Aish has an entire section in their website dedicated to "dating,"[12] which includes articles on how to deal with dating anxiety, what should be your dating criteria, how to have a successful date, how to know if you are ready for marriage, and more. There are also various forums that are dedicated to dating. These forums, while less popular than social media, tend to be more supportive in regard to the issue of dating and usually embrace the romantic perspective. Facebook Jewish singles groups, in comparison, mostly post events or allow people to introduce themselves, share pictures, and so on. In that way, the Facebook groups work more as "matchmaking" sites, while the forums are spaces where people share their fears and disappointments and get advice on how to behave on and in between dates. As one user wrote in the forum OKclarity, "It is like a community/support group, which I am grateful to have come upon, and fortunate to be a part of."[13]

I specifically selected three online communal spaces. The first forum I explore is Supertova, a Jewish dating website and forum platform, established in 2009. The forum has multiple categories, mostly focusing on dating (such as dating advice, internet dating experience, etc.), but which also has categories like "funny video section" or "interesting Torah lectures." In fact, the most popular thread is on uploading music videos. In that way, this forum works like a community that is focused on dating. The second forum is OKclarity, the forum section of a website dedicated to mental health within the Jewish society. Here, I selected only a few threads, those in which the topic of dating or being single were explicitly discussed. The third forum, in Hebrew, is Kipa's "Lo Kala De'rchenu" ("Ours Is Not an Easy Way," לא כלה דרכנו; a pun in Hebrew, as the word "easy" sounds like the word "bride").

This popular forum, which has more than 669,000 posts, operates as the hub for religious singles in Israel to discuss dating, religion, being single, and even issues of gender and sexuality more broadly. Together, these three forums supply ample examples for how religious ideas about dating, men, women, and marriage are negotiated and constructed online.

In some of these forum conversations, it is very clear to see the presence of the romantic perspective. Those who hold this more modern approach to dating can be more active in various modes of online dating because they are less restricted by traditional communal boundaries—they are not waiting for parental approval, for example. However, they also experience a lot of frustration with online dating, especially as they might feel that this process is not helping them find the one. For example, Supertova has dedicated a category for "Internet dating experience" in which users discuss experiences specific to the Supertova dating website, and to general online dating. For example, one user opens this topic up for general discussion by writing: "Internet dating experiences—I've had mixed reviews of it. What has yours been like?"[14] (note: this discussion is from 2012). Users react to this prompt with a variety of stories and complaints, mostly related to people being nonresponsive or rude online. One user writes, "Not great. I was talking to someone for a while . . . but then poof, she just stopped talking to me. Maybe it was something I said or didn't say . . . flirting over the computer is awkward for me."[15] Another says, "[I] am single and still wondering if the internet dating is for real." A third says, "Generally, I find that people are not honest about themselves through social networking sites and as such when you do eventually meet them, you are surprised and shocked as they don't live up to their own description of themselves."[16] These complaints are in line with what other research on online dating has shown—that deception, and as a result, disappointment, are common in online dating.[17] What is interesting in these forum discussions, however, is how people use these forums as a source of comfort, community, solidarity, and eventually, as communities tend to do, a source of correction and normalization.

This correction and normalization happen in various ways, most explicitly when it comes to dating behaviors. One constant question that comes up in various forms is "How should one behave in a date?" or, more negatively, "Did I screw this up?" Many forum users, new and avid daters, young and old, male and female, express either anxiety about their own behavior or frustration at the behaviors of their dates. They use the online forums to make sense of these behaviors, to learn from others, or to get advice. And they do. Users are quick to respond and give advice, thus de facto judging and correcting general behaviors. That is, these individualistic cases online feed into a general discourse that then works to construct what behaviors are right and wrong or, more specifically, attractive and unattractive. For example, a user on Supertova posed the following frustration: "I have tried to initiate by sending flirts, emails to men I thought would be suitable after reading their profiles. None have even bothered to OPEN the messages, let alone acknowledge them. What's the big deal? One would think oh, maybe she's a nice person, she thought enough of me to try, let me give a look."[18] While this was a personal question, based on one person's experience, this post opened up a debate on how one should behave in initial online conversation, with varying opinions. Most users support the author's statement, writing things like "People can be rude and not replying,"[19] thus equating nonresponsiveness with rudeness and setting the tone for correct online dating etiquette. Others offer a different type of etiquette: "I would rather get ignored than get a rude response. For example, a guy I sent a message to yesterday told me I was old for being 30 and I wasn't Jewish enough for him. If you don't have nothing nice to say, don't say it at all!"[20] This user takes her experience and creates a general rule from it: "If you don't have nothing nice to say, don't say it at all!" Similarly, a different thread on Supertova discusses the accuracy of dating profile photos. Can they be from two years ago? Five? The users in this forum debate and negotiate how online Jewish dating should happen rather than rely on the dating website's rules or lack thereof. In these ways, they try to normalize not only the online dating experience but also dating norms more generally—that Jewish dating should be based on accuracy and honesty but also on conversation, connection, and attraction.

The need for a romantic connection in dating is also clear when the date doesn't work out. Indeed, heart break seems to be a "hot topic" in these forums, and Supertova, for example, even dedicates an entire category to "breaking up/heart broken." While the forum is mostly filled with songs related to heartbreak, users also share their stories of rebounding, being dumped, being cheated on, or just being lonely, mostly while keeping themselves and their dates' details anonymous. These posts tend to generate sympathy and, alongside that sympathy, encouragement to continue dating or advice on how to date better. For example, in a poetic style, one user writes on Kipa:

Again I am captive . . .
Again in love for months with someone

> Again for every "hello" and smile she gives me I build mountains of hopes, and again for every distance she take I'm deeply hurt.
> Again she has a boyfriend, again I'm obsessive about her and think of her 95% of the time.
> Again I can't function because of a girl, again my semester is screwed up because of this enormous pain . . .
> . . . .
> Again, an endless ocean of pain, again [username] discovers he hasn't changed at all . . .[21]

The responses to this heartbreaking post seem focused on correcting this behavior, which is considered problematic, both in the author's words and in the way it is understood by the forum users. They offer various advice, like, "Forget about it and go hang out with friends," "You should not even think of her as an option," or, even more drastically, "I think you should consider getting treatment."[22] While this advice might read as crude, the underlining message is that searching for love is a difficult, but worthwhile, path.

In other cases, too, on Kipa, when people share stories of breaking up, most of the time the other users react by answering with a range of advice, even when the person clearly did not ask for it. For example, in a post titled "just venting" a user shares how bad he feels after breaking up with a person—like he is the "bad guy."[23] Users respond with various advice, ranging from "You are being too harsh on yourself"[24] to "Let it go."[25] In these examples we can see how the forum is used for social corrections—even in the sensitive cases of people sharing their deep emotions of distress. That is, through the practice of advising, users explain, dictate, and negotiate what they would consider proper dating behavior.

Not only is dating behavior negotiated, so is gendered behavior. Even for users who take a more progressive and modern stance regarding gender, the role of gendered behaviors is still evident. For example, in Kipa's forums, a lively discussion can be found on what constitutes being a real Jewish "man" or "woman." For example, a user shares a TV interview with a popular Israeli singer who says she can't be attracted to a man who helps around the house. The user does not attribute this to gendered, antiwomen, or patriarchal thinking, but rather asks more broadly, "What are your bizarre turn-offs?" The users reacting, however, immediately turn this to a gendered conversation, with the first response being "a man who knows how to cook is the sexiest."[26] Users go on to talk about how labor division is a historically based social construction, and how important it is to maintain equal partnership, especially when both people are working full time. This is not the only example, and discussions about gender roles and social constructions seem popular in this forum. However, not all users or discussions are so gender progressive. The forum is peppered with various stereotypical gendered statements like "girls only care about looks,"[27] and "men are slower to commit" or other generalizing statements. It is also worth noting that, even when gender is discussed as socially constructed, many users still point to ideal or preferred female and male behaviors. Thus, there is constantly a silent correction and realignment of gender norms, even as those are more egalitarian. Moreover, we can see how the romantic perspective is subtly present; by asking a question about "turn-offs," the users agree that dating needs to be based on attraction.

A successful date, as mentioned above, eventually leads to a wedding. But after the wedding, the young couple also needs to live with each other and to be married. This is not necessarily an easy task for anyone, and for these, usually young, people who grow up in gender-segregated societies, it can be especially challenging to learn how to live with the opposite sex. Luckily, they have sources, offline and online, that deal with maintaining marriage and understanding the roles of husband and wife. There are books, rabbis, counselors, workshops, lectures, and more. Accessing the offline sources, of course, demands a level of honesty and bravery, because you have to sign your name or show your face. In other words, the offline sources are visible. The online sources, on the other hand, can be accessed publicly and anonymously. As such, these online sources, forums, online articles, lectures, and so on, provide context and guidance to married people. However, online sources also allow for feedback, in the form of comments or other interactive features and as such, allow for pushback, resistance, negotiation of what it means to be a Jewish house, a Jewish husband and wife.

One of the themes that is communicated in online articles throughout the three Jewish websites of Chabad, Kipa, and Aish is that marriage can have struggles but should not be abandoned; it is something to work at, a process. This can sometimes be a surprise for those who sought marriage that is born out of love: if we love each other, why should we have struggles? But the romantic perspective also has avenues to keep romance between a married couple. For example, one of the articles on Kipa is written by a marriage counselor named Molli Grossman, who advises people to let go of the myths surrounding marriage, such as, for example, the idea that couples should solve all their issues without consulting an external person. His column, titled *Love at Second Glance* begins thus: "What's the problem with the stigmas that we believe in? That the moment we think 'It should be this way, this is my role as a wife, this is what is needed in marriage' then we have no flexibility. [. . .] The husband cannot work otherwise because it contradicts the 'husband role' as he sees it."[28] This is an interesting statement, as it both affirms that husbands and wives have roles in a marriage that are gender-specific, while at the same time, the author asks readers to expand and be more flexible regarding these roles. This expansion and negotiation of gender roles is not inspired by religious motivations or explained through religious sources or theology but rather is described in therapeutic terms. Namely, the writer's authority stems not from any religious position but from his knowledge and training as a marriage counselor. Furthermore, his text calls for better communication between the couple, for flexibility and for keeping an open mind in marriage—thus providing religious individuals with couching tactics that stem from therapeutic rather than religious context, supporting emotional, romantic, reasons to stay married, rather than (as seen later in this chapter) reasons like a sense of commitment or adherence to religious creed.

The author also calls for more preparation and open discussion of marital relations before marriage. It is custom in Orthodox communities that both the bride and the groom receive Halachic guidance before marriage, regarding how to engage in intimacy and how to keep family purity. The author of this article suggests that "it would be so good if alongside the *Halachic* preparation there will be relationship guidance that can save the couple much anguish in the beginning of their marriage"—that is, while not dismissing the religious (Halachic) duties of the newly wed, the emotional and relational aspects of the partnership are the ones being highlighted in this article.

These modern conceptions of marriage—that it should be based on love, connection, and emotional support—are becoming more popular, at least in the National Religious society in Israel, where there is also a growing trend of "late" bachelorhood.[29] A recent survey conducted by the website *MiShelch* (משלך), examines this trend. One of the interesting results of the survey is that 60 percent of the women who answered the survey said they prefer an equal marriage, and 40 percent answered in favor of a traditional one. Furthermore, 77 percent said that love is more important than marriage. The survey is not academic, nor does the website supply information about the methodology (how many people, what type of sampling), and thus, it should be taken with a grain of salt. However, it is very clear that the women surveyed are interested in romantic love and are even willing to delay their marriage in the hopes of finding "the one." This progressive approach toward relationships is still largely based on a semitraditional understanding of gender. For example, the author of the article explains, "the survey that was published this week asked all the hard questions about what actually are single religious women looking for in the men they date, how they want him to look and act and also what they don't want."[30] The question of what "women want" seems to be part of the way in which marriage and gender norms are tried and negotiated. And, of course, the goal of men and women's life is to be married, as highlighted by the survey producer: "If one guy will change something in his behavior [and so will get married]—we did our job."[31]

The romantic perspective tries to balance the religious creed of marriage with modern conception of personhood, psychology, and rights, by suggesting that marriage should be based on love and connection. This can be seen through the structure and technological affordances of some dating websites; through online communal negotiation and regulation in forums; and even more explicitly in edited materials published in religious websites. But this perspective is not the only way in which the online Jewish discourse presents dating and marriage; in fact, this attitude can even be at odds with the "official" or "traditional" Jewish attitude toward marriage, which, as will be explored later in this chapter, highlights responsibility and the religious commandments related to marriage. Navigating this tension between the traditional and the modern, some Jewish content suggests an "in-between" stance, which brings God (and a little bit of neoliberal thinking) into the mix. This is explored in the next section.

Three in My Marriage (Me, My Partner, and God): Combing Love and Religion

Online, religious Jews navigate dating as religious Jews—meaning, their religiosity plays a major role in how they approach dating and marriage. But this looks different for different Jewish communities and individuals, depending on their level of religiosity or the role religion plays in their life. For some, religion is about community. For others, it's about a deep relationship with the creator. Many of the online sources examined in this section operate from a worldview that marries (pun intended) God and their personal life. I recall my friends and I discussing this many times. Some of us didn't really subscribe to this level of personal attention from God, but some of my friends would pray and ask God for the smallest things, like doing well on an exam or not missing the bus. Many believed that God would help them find love. A common Yiddish term for this is *Bashert*, literally meaning "destiny" but often understood as "one's divinely predestined spouse or soulmate."[32] By adding love into the mix, the search for love becomes a religious issue, not one inspired by modernity.

This perspective is less explicit in dating websites or apps, because, well, no app developer could claim to involve God in their algorithm. But it can be seen in some of the descriptions for dating apps. For example, an app aptly named "Basheret—Jewish Dating" describe itself as "a traditional Jewish dating app. The app is based on a deep knowledge of the community, so there's no swiping, questions are targeted towards the interests of Jews, you can set up your friends. [. . .] Match or find your shidduch, there's no doubt you'll find love."[33] This description, much like other online sources taking this perspective, combines traditional attitudes with modern conceptions. In terms of tradition, there is "no swiping" and instead the app is based on an understanding of the community and Jewish values and allows for matchmaking of a couple by others (such as their friends or family). But the goal is still modern—finding love—and the tool is very new, algorithm-based, modernly designed, app.

In the Kipa forum, religiosity plays a different part. Every week or so, the forum manager of Lo Kala Derchenu publishes a snippet from the Torah reading of the week (a segment of the Bible) and the users discuss it, usually in relation to their lived experiences. For example, referring to the biblical commandment of sabbatical, the forum manager wrote, "The Pharash [bible portion] know that it is permitted and advisable, for time to time, to take a break"—hinting at the need, also expressed elsewhere in the forum, to rest from dating after a disappointing relationship or dates. Because the pressure to find a partner is so high, users feel that if they are not dating, they are "being lazy" or not being responsible for their future. Here, biblical texts are used to ease that stress and encourage each other to take those needed breaks. But religion also plays a more emotional part as a system that one can use to motivate and comfort themselves. For example, responding to a story of a seeing one's ex getting engaged, users on OKclarity encouraged the author by writing things like: "I believe you can find a lot of peace in telling yourself that it must be HaShem [God] has a better partner out there for you if He didn't let this work out."[34] And, "You will certainly have more heart to share with your true bashert [the one], whom Hashem [God] should help you should find very soon."[35] In these various ways, forum users balance a modern emphasis on love while centering religious texts and the place of God in dating and in relationships.

The balancing act between modern romantic conceptions and more traditional religious attitudes toward dating and marriage requires blending religious concepts with modern ones. In that way, the concept of *Bashert* or *Hasgaha Alyona* (providence) is mixed with the idea of "finding the one."

Similarly, for those holding this perspective, gender roles and gender difference are conceptualized in terms that blend the religious-traditional with modern self-empowerment. For example, in a Kipa article discussing marital difficulties, author Odelia Maimon explains that the reason for tensions between married couples is that "they might be in the same relationship, but from *different points of view*. From a different place. *He as a man. And she as a woman*. He is married to Soshi [female Hebrew name]. But she is married to Yuval [male Hebrew name]. And it is not always the same. More than that—*she has certain expectations from the relationship, and he has others*."[36] Here, the reason for marital tensions lies in the inherent differences between the genders—"He is a man," "He has a role as a husband." That is, the reason for tensions between the couple, according to Maimon, is that men and women have inherently different points of view of the world. Maimon, like Grossman, the marriage counselor in the previous section, claims that marriage needs to receive more attention in the religious community as something that one needs to work on and needs to feel safe and happy in—she acknowledges that relationship should be based in emotional connection. But for Maimon, that connection is based on a correct understanding of gender roles. Surprisingly, many of the readers commenting on this article disagree with this emphasis on relational well-being. One of the commenters writes, "This is an Egoistic analysis focused on 'me.' [...] This is not the way of Judaism."[37] Another commenter writes, "I disagree. If someone feels like the relationship is lacking (and let's be honest, in 99% of the cases it is the woman who wants more, and the man is content) then the problem is with them. S/He needs to search how to solve it, of course the partner can help and they should do so to be benevolent to their partner, but the problem is not relational."[38] What is being discussed and negotiated in these articles, I suggest, are marital norms and expectations of wives and husbands in the Israeli Orthodox religious context. Some of the users and authors in Kipa see marriage in a more traditional light, as a partnership between two people who have different roles, with the outcome of raising a family and building a "home in Israel" (the traditional blessing couples receive in the Jewish wedding ceremony). For people who have this mindset, there is no need to focus on personal well-being—that kind of attitude is "Egoistic." Those on the other side of the spectrum see marriage as a more romantic and emotional relationship between two people who find love and meaning in this relationship. They use the anonymity and interactivity of digital media to push back against these traditional views. These different views create tension and negotiation, and as a result, I suggest, users reacting to articles written on the topic of marriage tend to be more argumentative.

This negotiation is not one directional (website authors as more "therapeutic" or individualistic and websites readers as more traditional). Rather, Kipa as a website gives various authors a voice to present their perspectives and gives users who disagree with those perspectives—be they traditional or individualistic—a place to voice their disagreement. For example, in a different article in Kipa, author Merav Lavi, advises women who are frustrated with their husbands not doing enough at home to "give him a feeling that he is your hero—even if he is not."[39] She describes a situation where the wife is annoyed that her husband is not doing enough, but the husband feels that he is doing plenty that is not being appreciated. To solve this situation, Lavi offers women various kinds of advice, some of which includes expanding the definition of "doing things at home" to include actions that are outside the household duties, as well as allowing or giving him "time off" when he gets home from work:

> When your husband goes to work—He is helping at home! When he goes to study [Torah]—He is helping at home. [. . .] If you want to be not just a good person, but a good wife, you have the option not only to allow him [to rest] but to give it to him yourself. [. . .] Going forward, every evening when he gets back, smile at him warmly, tell him: 'I'm happy you are here . . . I'd like to hear how you are doing and tell you how I'm doing, but first, come, I made you the cake you love and your coffee is ready. Go to you room, drink, read your newspaper [. . .] I'll make sure the children won't bother you.[40]

Lavi uses the "feminist" liberal modern concept of partnership in marriage to maintain traditional division of labor. She tries to argue that when the man is working and the woman is taking care of the household, they are both equal partners "at home." This traditional ideal—of a devoted wife and a working husband—is quickly rejected by the readers. Users comment, for example, "You are stuck in the sixties!"[41] "I think you forgot that most mothers are also working!"[42] "We are also working outside the home!!"[43] These comments and discussion show how the topic of gender norms in marriage is constantly negotiated in Kipa—that readers and authors try to balance religious and modern concepts of marriage through the push and pull of online discourse.

Negotiating gender norms, religion, and modernity as they relate to marriage is not limited to the Israeli context or Kipa website; it is present in the US Jewish Orthodox context too. The relationship between men and women in marriage is defined through gender, and gender is the key to understanding oneself in this relationship. In the Chabad article "The Role of Women in Judaism," Sara Esther Crispe tries to answer the question "What does it mean to be a Jewish woman?" and suggests that it has to do with females' unique abilities and their meaning for the Jewish community and spirituality.[44] In her words:

> *Both men and women have masculine and feminine traits.* [. . .] The differences between the masculine and feminine are great. [. . .] The differences are psychological, emotional, physical, spiritual and intellectual. And, while we may be a combination of both these masculine and feminine traits, *at the end of the day we are either a man or a woman.* [. . .]
>
> A woman need not be in the home. *A woman is the home.* [. . .] Therefore, unlike the masculine, which is the side of our self that is external, which can be viewed by others and is not private, *the feminine is the polar opposite—completely internal,* involving no one else and entrusted to the individual alone. [. . .] The true meaning of this expression, then, is that when a woman is using her potential in the proper way, she is able to connect to her spouse and help rectify him. *Through her ability to develop, she can take his ideas, his talents, his potential, and internalize them, becoming impregnated with them, until they are ready to be birthed in a public, external way.* [. . .] When our concern is not about what we are obligated to do, but on how we can help another fulfill his or her obligations, this is when *we shine forth and reveal our true power.*[45]

This text suggests a different meaning of what it is to be a man or woman and a different concept of marriage from the one presented thus far; it suggests a divinely inspired gendered difference, meant to empower the individual. While gender seems to be complex in this text—"we may be a combination of both these masculine and feminine traits"—eventually, the author takes a decisive and binary gender approach, one that claims that men are men, and women are women: "At the end of the day we are either a man or a woman." The ideal relationship depicted in this text is one that contains spiritual meanings. According to the author, by being in a correct marital relationship, one's true power is revealed. Furthermore, ideal relationships are structured by meaning derived from biblical sources, and an ideal woman is conceptualized through the religious concept of *eizer kenegdo*. In other words, being married is key to being a woman—but only so far as it is part of the feminine qualities of giving and creating. The female—that is, the woman—is born to help others fulfill their obligations. Her path is that of a guide or a helper, and this is a sign of her superior role and spiritual closeness to the divine. Following a traditional, feminine, path leads one closer to God. This does not *have to* happen through marriage or childbearing, any way of creating and helping works, but being a mother and wife seems to be the ideal. As one comment goes, "Woman, Daughter, Bride, Wife . . . the role of the woman brought me to our standing with G-d. As a unit both man and female (treasured people) formed to be the helpmate of Hashem [God]."[46]

The user seems to agree with the content, like most of the users commenting on this article (fifty comments supporting the article out of eighty-three comments total), and takes the idea of "fulfilling our role" to mean not just as part of society or in a marriage but our role in our relationship with God. Here, gender roles take on a deep theological and spiritual meaning. This gendered spiritual approach seems to follow neoliberal logic, one that is self-focused and individualistic. According to this gendered spiritual discourse, behaving in a religiously traditional gendered way is not just a way to maintain social order and keep the family safe but also—and more importantly—a way to connect to God and to reveal your "true power," your spiritual path. This article suggests that to be a good woman is to understand oneself as an internal, wise, generous helpmate who guides her husband and children in their external and internal paths, and by doing so, she herself becomes closer to God. There are three in her marriage (and dating): her, her husband, and God.

Many of the readers find this concept not only acceptable but also empowering and liberating. A few of the supportive comments start off with the saying "I AM A WOMAN" and go on to express how "this article is beautifully written" and to thank the author for an "excellent article." For example, one user writes, "I like it! This is *very liberating*! It makes so much sense, yeah!"[47] For Chabad readers, being a woman is not just about being married—being a woman is a special spiritual talent, which can be expressed through giving, ideally in marriage. This perspective, for many of the readers, is "liberating" and "empowering," both discursive strategies used in this online discourse to reframe traditional gender roles into a matter of choice and meaning. Here, users utilize neoliberal ideologies to mix the religious and the modern perspectives on marital relationships. In the next section, we'll see how for some, the religious language is enough, and these users utilize the new media spaces to promote a traditional, transactional approach to relationships.

Transactional Partnership: The True Goals of Marriage

Unlike the other two perspectives I've outlined, the transactional partnership perspective suggests a more traditional approach to dating and marriage. This perspective proposes that for Jewish men and women, the ultimate goal is to "build a house in Israel"—to have children. To do so, you need two: a *man* and a *woman*. Romance has little to do with this—it's all about building a good and stable partnership, not unlike a business partnership.

This perspective can be found in many of the explicitly Jewish dating websites, such as JWed (which focuses solely on dating with the purpose of marriage), SawYouAtSinai (which has professional matchmakers assigned for each users), Yenta (which is location based), TheJMom (in which parents can do the matchmaking), and more. While many of the Jewish websites recognize that a variety of Jewish lifestyles and religious adherence exists, they focus on and promote a traditional and religiously oriented approach to dating. This approach is made clear in the different websites' focus on the goals of marriage and childbearing, their emphasis on religious identity, and in some cases, the involvement of a traditional *shadchan* or matchmaker or even one's parents.

This traditional perspective can also be seen in the profile building process, in terms of highlighting religious ideologies and identities at the onset of dating. Many of the dating websites are aware of the differences and nuances between the religious streams and help users self-identify their religious identity as part of their profile. For example, S-net (Shidduchim-net) offers six categories for religious affiliation: *Dati Leumi*, *Haredi Leumi*, *Dati* light, *Haredi*, former-*Dati*, or *Masorati* (traditional). In that way, users can self-identify, select their dates based on their religious belonging, and know the religious "level" of the website itself. Another example can be found in the popular Israeli website 7brachot, which has a warning pop-up that reads: "This website in not meant for Haredi people. For them we are currently building a different website, which will not include pictures."[48]

In addition, an emphasis on marriage and creating a family is quite explicit throughout these dating websites. For example, a site called 2become1 explains that "creating a family in the religious sector is a very important action from a social and religious perspective. The man and woman about to be wed [...] are partaking in a religious act of great importance."[49] Arguably, it is the focus on the religious aspects of matchmaking that allows users and rabbis to feel comfortable when embracing these online practices. Through these socio-technological choices that the website designers made, they are able to utilize new media tools and affordances to promote traditional perspectives and practices regarding dating and marriage.

In direct continuation to the review of possible online dating websites, it is worthwhile to explore how users assess and feel about these dating websites in these online religious forums. It seems that many of the users utilize the various religious forums to complain about online dating, and even warn others against it. For example, in a thread discussing similarities between dating and job interviews, users reject online dating and instead begin to discuss the various contexts to meet someone offline: singles Sabbath, religious dating clubs, speed dating, and so on. They reject online dating because it is not "serious enough" or because of potential deception. In a different thread, users discuss how, online, people can hide facts (like that they are married, or divorced with kids), to which one of the users explicitly says, "Just don't date online." While others do say that they met their husbands online, the general consensus in the forum is that dating should occur offline, and through offline networks, but you can use online tools to discover some basic information before dating. These users try to normalize dating behaviors that emphasize transparency and seriousness, with the goal of marriage in mind.

This type of normalization of behavior is not limited to online forums dictating online dating: it also happens from the screen to the offline dating experience. For example, a user on the Kipa forum started a thread with the title "Veganism" and in it she asks when, or if, she should tell her date that she is vegan. Most responders say that, well, best if she doesn't say at all, because "this is a big issue for men."[50] While some users argue that "when love is strong," you can handle any difference, most others insist that "you cannot deny that this is a serious burden." Some users mentioned their own experiences dating a vegan or vegetarian, and one female even mentions dating a male vegan—but the overall assumption in the discussion is very gendered and operates under the idea that "men eat meat." In these ways, the user is corrected—she should consider not how or when to reveal that she is a vegan, but rather how far she is willing to go for her future husband. Users bring up the point that "in a relationship you need mutual respect. That means you will also have to make sacrifices for him and not just expect that he will compromise for your ideals which he doesn't hold."[51] They say that she should consider if she is willing to go to a steakhouse with him, watch him eat meat, or "make him a fish/meat dinner?" In this example, we can clearly see how the user, and any person reading afterward, gets the pulse of the society regarding what is expected of this type of a relationship: a gendered, semitraditional approach that highlights compromise and sacrifice.

This attitude reflects an attempt to push against the notion of "true love" and instead focus on realistic expectations in a transactional relationship. For example, a rabbi's article on dating myths is shared and discussed on a Supertova forum. One of the rabbi's points is that there is no concept for "the one" and instead, people should be less picky and that "one has to have confidence and faith in the person with whom you wish to take the next step—but one who expects to hear a 'divine echo,' or to feel butterflies in the stomach, will keep waiting and waiting."[52] The rabbi is clearly trying to reduce the notion of a divinely appointed match, and make dating more "down-to-earth" and less romanticized. Most of the users find this helpful, and they comment that these are "words of wisdom, so rarely encounteted [sic], offering hope to those of us who are still in search of true love. Thanks for sharing!"[53] and "So very true. Many of us have an unrealistic view of romance."[54] One user does oppose the rabbi's opinion, using religious sources that show that your potential date is "the other half of your soul." But in general, this approach seems to be accepted and appreciated.

Another way in which the more traditional approach is strengthened online is in highlighting the role of religion in dating. Users constantly debate the importance of one's religiosity in the dating world. For example, in one of the more popular threads on Supertova, users debate if one must be a believing Jew or not if they are using this Jewish dating service: "Why would an Atheist be on a Jewish dating site? I'm sure Atheist singles sites exist."[55] While other users hurry to explain that Judaism is a peoplehood and not just a religious creed, the relationship between one's religiosity and who they date seems to be a critical issue. Even in the Kipa forum, in which all users are assumed to be religious, varying levels of religious observance play in important part in dating. For example, replying to a man that was complaining about a date that felt like an interview because the woman asked too many questions, one user says: "I think her questions/remarks are legitimate. A certain religious observance level is important for her. Very legitimate. It's not clear if you could build a good relationship if there are meaningful gaps on the religious level."[56] This sparks a conversation in the forum between those who think getting to know someone is a process, and those who believe that certain parameters—like religiosity—are better stated clearly in the beginning, to avoid what they understand as "incompatible" partners. Thus, we see again how these forum discussions work to explain and correct, and to negotiate and make sense of, Jewish dating. And in the case of this specific normalization, they are pushing toward a traditional understanding of marriage that is based on compatibility at the religious level. Of course, not all users accept this traditional approach, and some even explicitly express how the religious society makes them feel stressed into marriage; for example, a twenty-seven-year-old user writes in the OKclarity forum that "especially as an older guy in the frum [Orthodox] world, my prospects of marriage don't look good, for I feel like leftovers/2nd class to younger guys."[57] In other examples, users express feeling that they must date within a specific religious lifestyle[58] or that marriage is predominantly for procreation. But these reactions tend to be downplayed by the other users in the forums who embrace the traditional approach regarding dating.

This approach to dating translates to a very gendered understanding of married life, an attitude that highlights the need for understanding the difference between the genders and acting accordingly. A strong example of this are two articles written by Emuna Braverman, one titled "What Women Really Want" and the other, "What Men Really Want," and two videos staring Rabbi Tzvi Gluckin, one titled "Marriage—For Men Only" and the other, "Marriage—For Women Only." Braverman's articles have received the most comments within the Aish sample (fifty-eight and ninety-eight, respectively), and the videos, while not as popular, still received more comments than the average for Aish (twenty-five and twenty-six, respectively). Although the articles and videos are authored by different people, they seem to indicate similar conclusions—men need respect, women need love. Braverman's articles are quite explicit about this and claim further that if men do not get respect and women do not get love in a relationship, their marriage is in danger:

> *What Men Really Want*: It's not complicated. What men really want from their wives is appreciation, respect and love. "He wants to be her hero. When she is disappointed and unhappy over anything, he feels like a failure," says relationship expert John Gray. [. . .] Appreciation, respect and love. Does your husband get nagging, criticism and resentment instead? Do you welcome your husband at the end of the day, or greet him with a barrage of complaints? [. . .] It's not about who has what job; it's about attitude. "If you treat him like a king, he will treat you like a queen." (Menorat HaMaor).[59]
>
> *What Women Really Want*: Like men, women certainly want admiration and respect, but our deepest desire is to be loved. As the Chazon Ish, a prominent rabbi of the last century, wrote, "A woman's nature is to find favor in her husband's eyes." A woman's nature may also be to run big corporations—I'm not suggesting anything limiting or demeaning—only that love and accolades from our

partner is what nourishes and sustains us and our marriages. [. . .] men need to constantly express and demonstrate their love. [. . .] What do women really want? [. . .] "The way to handle a woman is to love her, simply love her, merely love her, love her, love her."[60]

The ideal marriage portrayed in these articles is one in which the husband and wife, by understanding that the other is like them but also different, give their spouse what they need—love in the case of women, respect in the case of men. To love a woman, according to Braverman, means to show gratitude, to praise her, and to not criticize her. To respect a man, according to Braverman, means to make him feel like a hero, and praise him even if he does not help at home—to stop seeing him as a nuisance and start seeing him as "a king." Rabbi Tzvi Gluckin is even more explicit in his advice to newlyweds by presenting a view of marriage as a partnership between essentially different genders. In his humorous videos, he tells women, "Women! You have married an immature, pre-adolescent, festering ball of ego! Every man thinks that he's his wife's knight in shining armor! He needs to know that you appreciate all that he does, that you depend on him to solve all your problems."[61] And, according to Gluckin, a wife can let her husband know this by doing the following: "When he comes home from a hard day's work, he's exhausted, beaten by his day, and he is not able to listen . . . you need to be dressed nicely, greet him with a smile, ask him if he needs to sit down, give him a snack, pour him a drink, rub his shoulders, let him know that you appreciate all that he does for you, and give him a few minutes to relax. Once he is comfortable, confident and firmly in charge, then you can stick it to him!"[62] The video style and text of the video is seemingly humorous, but the content is consistent with other material on the website in which gender norms are presented and understood traditionally and marriage is understood transactionally.

The users commenting on these videos wonder if Gluckin is serious or not: "Is this guy kidding."[63] While Braverman receives mostly agreement in the comment section, many of the commenters explicitly disagree with Gluckin, claiming that these videos are insulting. As one of the users writes, "[I feel] disillusioned. I'm not sure what to say: I love Aish, and this was the first thing on the site that ever rubbed me the wrong way. I'm disappointed in the cynicism present in this video, and the attitude toward relationships it presents."[64] Out of the twenty-six comments reacting to the video advising women, twelve resist his message, while five accept and find it amusing and true. One comment reads, "I'm newly married, and I enjoyed this very much. Frank, funny. Thanks."[65] Another reads, "Too true. I have seen this happen with my husband. And since I have returned to work, it has gotten worse. I needed that reminder. Thank you."⁶⁶ The advice video for men is much more accepted by the users: out of the twenty-five comments, fifteen were supportive of Gluckin's message, and only five explicitly resisted it. The greater support for the video advising men is probably because the message is deemed less insulting—while in the video to women, Gluckin suggests that women rub their husbands' backs and get them a drink, in the video to men, Gluckin advises men to listen when their wives talk:

> Men! Your wife needs to talk! [. . .] When she starts talking, she'll probably be emotional, and you are probably somehow the cause of her problems. She will launch into a tirade filled with exaggerations seemingly directed at—you! Because you are a thickheaded hyena i.e., the typical male, your giant yet fragile ego will get bruised . . . you will get defensive, your natural instinct will be to defend yourself—watch out! This is a trap! [. . .] Let her talk, smile, be concerned, empathetic, and listen to her. [. . .] When she is done, she'll feel good, she got it all out and she knows that you care.⁶⁷

This video, although it portrays both men and women in a less-than-pleasant light, is generally well accepted by the users. What is interesting about both videos, aside from the way they portray gender, is how they operate within the structures of both traditional and internet culture. While the message is similar to that mentioned in other articles, the presentation is inconsistent with the usual Aish style. There is no mention of religious content—neither Torah citations nor religious words of wisdom—and the content is not presented as a lecture or article. Instead, the editing rhythm is upbeat, with a jump cut every few seconds, extreme close ups on the rabbi's face, and a clean green screen as background. Gluckin looks more like a YouTube celebrity than a rabbi. Presented in a style that is similar to internet media logic, Gluckin's message is easier to dismiss as a joke, but many of the users take it quite literally. It is unclear if Gluckin meant for his advice to be taken seriously but judging from the resemblance of the content to the rest of the material on the website, he probably did. This could be a case of a rabbi trying to be "cool" by improperly using media logic—using hyperbole while the advice is nevertheless meant to be implemented. It seems that the "culturing" of this media logic works. The religious meaning-making trumps the dismissive tone.

In both articles and videos, traditional gender stereotypes play an important role in "saving your marriage." According to the logic presented here, men are emotionally challenged and respect-motivated, and women are fragile, talkative creatures in need of love. Not only are the stereotypes for each gender traditional, the relationships portrayed are also stereotypical and traditional—women at home, men at work. These messages also claim that for a relationship to work well, men need to be better at listening and women need to show more respect. As one user commented, "Get this word out and marriages would be restored all over the world, along with womens [sic] confidence."[68] While both authors and the users who support them seem to understand that this way of thinking is not so popular in contemporary Western secular society, they present this traditional "Jewish" type of gender relationship as safer, more meaningful, and better for both men and women. One user defends this patriarchal concept thus: "What's wrong with this way of thinking? Men & women are different, and react differently. [. . .] When we realize that we're completely different species and how the other reacts, and use that knowledge—we communicate better. [. . .] When this was the way of thinking—pre feminist era, what was the divorce rate? Compare that to today's society."[69] In other words, this comment and others in the Aish website call for a "return" to traditional gender roles in order to save marriages and lower divorce rates. Here, feminism (and modernism) is mentioned as the source of problems in marriages, and the solution is to understand the inherent differences between men and women and to build heterosexual relationships that are based on that understanding. This digital discourse suggests the following marital logic: "I need to understand the other person so that I can save my marriage. The other person is of another gender, and it is her/his gender that makes them what they are. Therefore, staying within my gender requirements and understanding their gender role will help the important task of keeping the peace and the love in our home." In other words, it is through traditional approach to gender that we understand the other person in marriage. And through this understanding we keep the peace in the Jewish home. Divorce—although Halachically legal—is less than ideal, and more than a few articles in Aish, Kipa, and Chabad discourage it.[70] The traditional, patriarchal, perspective is alive and well in these online new media spaces, and digital media tools and logics (such as multimedia, participation, etc.) are utilized to promote this approach to dating and marriage.

Summary

This chapter highlights how marriage is (re)intensified as an important part of Jewish life by giving marriage spiritual and social importance through specific

Jewish online dating websites; online communities and forums discussing dating; and popular Jewish websites, articles, and videos. The chapter shows how marriage is central to the discussion of gender roles, and how gender roles—especially traditional ones—are defined and maintained through discussing dating and marriage behaviors. Three perspectives were explored: a modern(ish) one, which emphasizes love and connection; a traditional one, which emphasizes patriarchal gender roles in a transactional relationship; and a mixed, neoliberal one, which highlights spirituality and self-empowerment as results of adherence to traditional dating and marriage mindset.

Online communities especially play a central role in helping religious users make sense of dating and marriage, and in the process of these debates, the normalizing of gender roles happens. That is, through niche dating websites that take advantage of technological affordances, such as specification, online community, and website comments, a negotiation of what is means to be married takes place. The dating websites mold the characteristics that one should care about (religious denomination and level, for example), the online forum communities discuss how one should choose their mate, and the online articles and comments negotiate the meaning of "wife" and "husband." Together, these work as a discourse, and because this discourse is online, anonymous, and belongs to all, it can be viewed as representing "what everybody is thinking" and, thus, work as a strong normalizing force.

The online discourse regarding marriage created in these websites further suggests understanding the female gender—women—as giving and internal and therefore as people who will flourish from marriage and motherhood, in which they get to give. The discourse not only explains women through their roles as wives but also frames marriage through gender roles. Thus, maintaining traditional gender roles is presented as crucial for maintaining marriages and as a way for women (and men) to be empowered in their "true self." The next chapter explores one of the potential difficulties couples encounter once married: the bedroom.

INTERLUDE 1

Window Installation
Technological Affordances

Like many middle-class '80s kids, I grew up getting familiar with computers (not the internet) with a deeply rooted notion about their materiality. My father worked at a cybersecurity company, and while he dealt with math and concepts, I would sit with his colleagues and watch them take apart a motherboard or weld some chips. My first summer job was at this company, and I was what you'd call a "rack girl"—I'd collect computer parts and deliver them between departments, monitor the servers, and do whatever other little jobs that were needed. In those big, cool rooms, between racks of servers with no screens, my first realization about computers was born: they are things.

This tension between the material aspects and the social elements that inform its creation and uses is at the heart of many discussions about digital media. The idiom "the media is the message"[1] has been well established, analyzed, and deconstructed. Scholars have shown that while the materiality of communication technologies matter, we should not ignore the historical, cultural, and social environments in which technologies are made and used. Instead, an approach that I find more useful and nuanced is to consider specific medium's "technological affordances" and their uses.

Technological affordances are defined in various ways in scholarship, but the definition that I found most helpful is Jenny Davis's, which explains that these are the ways in which technologies "push, pull, enable, and constrain" social interactions.[2] Davis and others examine how technological affordances ask that we look at what the technology itself allows and constrains—for example, Facebook asks the user "What's on your mind?," thus "pushing" the user to contribute content that is personal. Twitter, on the other hand, asks us to share "What's happening?," thus "pushing" us to engage in social conversation. While both platforms depend on users' content, their structure asks different questions, thus pushing toward different types of content and interaction. Of course, users might end up sharing personal thoughts on Twitter or political ideas on Facebook—the technology allows for that. But by paying attention to the technological and social "invitations," we can start to note the ways in which these platforms construct different expectations for uses.

It's important to note throughout the book how technological affordances shape the discourse that is happening. A prime example of this is in the design and functionality of dating websites. For example, the dating websites described in chapter 3 use digital media logic of narrowcasting (selling or marketing to a specific, niche group) to promote themselves; they are talking to and operated by a specific religious community. They do so through their use of specific language and their various technological choices. They also use specification, which helps religious users navigate online dating more easily. That is, by adding various dating specifications, such as religious denomination and familial aspirations, they normalize those elements as important social cues to notice when dating. These dating websites, by crafting a specific profile information grid, standardize what the important features of one's spouse are. Of course, the choices they offer are based on (offline, traditional) social and religious demands, but by listing it in these ways, the websites' creators and editors use technology to de facto regulate dating norms.

One of the unique features of the websites based in Israel is their strong emphasis on religious lifestyle. For example, the FAQ page on the 7brachot website makes it explicit that people who do not observe the Jewish religious dictum of *shomerae negiaa*, or abstinence from any physical contact with the date prior to the marriage, are not welcomed. The websites emphasize their religiosity in different ways. For example, the website Grapevines (בענבי הגפן),[3] which offers matchmaking services for the Haredi population, carries rabbinical endorsements, thus communicating its commitment to the Jewish law and possibly becoming more attractive for some of the religious population. This specific website functions with a payment system, in which couples pay to the website if they choose to marry—as is the custom with offline Haredi matchmakers.

Another example of the impact of technological affordances can be noted in the Q&A and comments sections throughout the websites. As shown in chapters 4 through 6, the fact that these websites allow for a comment section—a technological, platform choice—allows for internal community conversation and, thus, negotiation. This is especially prominent when examining religious Q&A sections, where the rabbis' answers are supported by technological affordances and negotiated using the comment section. In a study I conducted in 2020, Heidi Campbell and I examined 567 Israeli Q&A sections from the Kipa website. We noted that these online Q&A discussions create a discourse in which "responsa becomes a horizontal line of information transmission instead of a vertical one. Instead of referring to old media such as religious books, the rabbis referred to new, easily accessible sources of information."[4] That is, the rabbis use the technological affordance of hyperlinks to complement and support their answers with various links (some to other rabbis' answers, some to secular sources). They also tend to provide shorter answers then those found in religious Q&A books, thus adhering to the media logic and technological affordances that push for short content. Furthermore, the practice of online Q&A discussion, and the comment sections, allow for participation that was previously not possible. However, as seen throughout this book, this technological invitation for participation is often used for peer regulation and, as I have called it elsewhere, a "technological incitement to confess."[5] In these question and comment sections, people share personal stories and struggles under the cloak of anonymity allowed by the technological affordances of the websites. Then, "these personal confessions, when displayed publicly on the websites, are enabling a new structure for religious regulation and normalization of gender and sexual norms."[6] By noticing how the technology allows for certain behaviors online, we are better positioned to understand the discourse that is happening.

In short, technological affordances are important to consider when we examine any communication and especially when we examine the ways in which technologies limit and enable certain types of communication. Throughout this book, I note the affordances that construct the discourse: the participatory elements in forums and comment sections, the anonymity allowed in these spaces, and the invitation to engage in the push and pull of community discourse. What users do with these affordances is where things get really exciting—users deploy anonymity to ask taboo questions, and yet, they also utilize the democratic elements to support a traditional power structure.

Chapter 3

Being Intimate

Our bodies—how we look, feel, and want to be touched (and by whom)—can be a complicated topic for most people, regardless of religion, race, or age. It is especially so for those who are raised in certain religious cultures in which sexuality is a taboo, an unspoken topic. This chapter examines how new communication technology, the internet, helps Orthodox Jews explore their sexual behaviors and identities, expand, and negotiate them, and at the same time restricts and normalizes certain sexualities and bodies.

As someone who grew up in Orthodoxy, I can relate to the type of confusion and complexity expressed by users regarding the topics of sex, the body, modesty, and sexuality. I can remember as a young girl, in various settings, older male rabbis would come to speak to us about how and why we should dress and act modestly. At first, I was just embarrassed. But as my feminist sensitivities evolved, I started getting angry. One day I asked one of my female teachers—are men so out of control, that the sight of my elbow is enough to make them go crazy? She said something along the lines of, "Of course not, but why poke a sleeping bear?" I wondered then how you can become intimate with someone you were brought up to see as a threat. It can't be easy. It wasn't for me.

Back then, these notions bothered me not because of a sexual desire (which I didn't yet possess) but because I felt that these practices and worldviews were creating an Othering mentality in which men and women are alienated from each other and from each other's spheres. As someone who always had an easier time befriending men, I was confused as to why those relationship should be considered "dangerous." And, living in a modern world in which this type of gender segregation does not (explicitly) exist, I could not understand why females should be policed or restricted in any way. But when I asked these types of questions, I mostly got shut doors or unsatisfying explanations, and I felt alone in my frustration. It seems, however, that I wasn't so alone. The same concerns and inquiries are reflected in these online negotiations, and new and creative solutions—both bending the laws or restricting them—are present online today.

In the previous chapters, I have theorized how Jewish online spaces are used for the negotiating and reframing of gender norms. In the last chapter, I looked at a topic near and dear to many women's heart: finding love and getting married. While most young women in Jewish Orthodoxy are excited about the prospect of getting married, dreaming of their wedding dress and day, many of them are hesitant, if not fearful, when it comes to the wedding night. This chapter explores what happens once one gets married—that first night and sexual intimacy after. In a society in which intimacy is taboo, the introduction of the internet, where one can find information and ask questions anonymously, has allowed a growing discussion of sexuality within these communities. This has inspired scholars to examine how religious individuals who wish to explore sexuality without abandoning their religious community might use new media for such purposes.[1] Thus, this chapter theorizes and exemplifies the pivotal role the internet plays in three important ways: first, the internet allows women's voices, worries, and hopes—women's sexuality—to be heard and become a part of the Orthodox discourse (for the first time); second, the participatory affordances of digital communication allow lay men and women the chance to publicly negotiate sexual norms; and last, normalizing power of this online discourse reduces innovation and increases an repressive approach to sexuality.

Like in the previous chapters, this chapter provides examples and analysis from three mainstream Orthodox Jewish websites, Chabad, Aish, and Kipa, as well as examples from open pages on social media in which Jewish norms are discussed. And, like the previous chapter, I've highlighted three general attitudes toward this topic: a more traditional, strict, and even fundamental attitude, which calls for strict adherence to sexual "purity"; a middle position, which portrays traditional sexuality (more specifically, modesty) as a liberal, positive, and empowering choice; and a modern, even progressive position, which attempts to recognize female sexuality and reshape Jewish norms regarding sexuality.

Before delving into the online discussions, some background is necessary to understand them. The next section provides an overview to mainstream Orthodox attitudes and norms regarding sexuality and intimacy. As discussed in the introduction, it is pivotal when researching online religious communication of any kind to understand the history and worldviews of that religion. When it come to the complicated issue of sexuality, the history and worldview inform what people know and how they think about their own bodies. Therefore, understanding current attitudes, as informed from Jewish history and religious-legal texts (Halacha), allows us as readers and researchers to analyze what people say and do online in light of their religious and ideological views. It is important to note that Judaism is complex and the next section is, as stated, an overview, and thus certain nuances are lost in favor of providing general knowledge.

The Body and Intimacy in Judaism: An Overview

Judaism, by and large, regards sexuality as a positive aspect of human life rather than an inherently "dirty" or "sinful" action. However, as shown in this review, sexuality is only considered positive under certain normalizing rules, namely, a patriarchal, heterosexual system. Within this system, intimacy between a husband and a wife is very important and positive, and it is one of the duties a husband owes his wife. That is, to some extent, female sexuality is recognized. For example, there is a saying in the Talmud (collection of canonic Jewish writing, completed about 500 CE) that if the man reaches orgasm first the child will be a girl, and if the female reaches orgasm first the child will be a boy[2]—meaning the rabbis of the Talmud recognized female sexuality and even to some degree encouraged it. (Since male children were more desirable, by suggesting that female orgasm helps to conceive a boy, the rabbis of the Talmud encouraged their readers—men—to actively seek their wife's sexual pleasure.) But in general, and more prominently, sexuality and intimacy are conceptualized from a male perspective with little to no attention paid to female needs and pleasures. The above saying from the Talmud is one in an ongoing discussion on sexuality, of which one popular conclusion is that among a married couple, "whatever a man wants to do with his wife—he can."[3] This text, along with the fact that throughout Jewish history, religious texts and norms were dictated by men, showcases the male-centered approach toward sexuality found in Judaism. One of the most prominent pieces of evidence for this male-centered sexuality is that during the wedding night, the man and woman must consummate their marriage through penetration, which, as seen in the analysis below, can be traumatic for many young women who have never touched a man before that night. While there is a famous Halachic debate between the Maimonides and rabbi Yosef Karo (author of the important Halachic book *Shulchan Aruch*) concerning whether it is allowed to "kiss or touch that place [i.e., the vulva]" (Maimonides allows and Karo forbids), many Modern Orthodox rabbis and Halachic rulings minimalize intimacy to penetration in the missionary position.

In most Orthodox societies there is little interaction between the sexes: boys and girls study in separate schools and have separate after-school activities; men and women are segregated in synagogues and in some public spaces in Israel and in the United States; and general interactions between the sexes are frowned upon. This circumstance changes depending on how strict the Orthodox community is—for example, most Dati Leumi (National Religious) and Modern Orthodox communities have mixed kindergartens, and adults study in mixed universities. Ultra-Orthodox tend to be stricter about gender segregation. In either case, the large majority of Orthodox youth spend most of their time unexposed to the other sex, and (are supposed to) have no sexual interactions before marriage—including no kissing or hugging. Once engaged to be married, the young couple is slowly encouraged to spend more time with each other—not alone, and not to be intimate, but to get to know each other. Before the wedding day, women and men receive rabbinical council about marriage and intimacy. Usually, men meet with male rabbis who will explain to them about family purity, the religious approach to intimacy, and how to treat their future wives. Women will meet with a female—it could be the rabbi's wife, or the more official "bridal guide" (*Maderichat Calot*)—who will instruct the woman about how to keep family purity, the religious approach to intimacy, and what is expected from her as a wife and mother. Since in many Orthodox communities, men and women have less social interaction, the purpose of these meetings is to prepare them to live with the other sex and, specifically, to discuss intimacy and family purity.

Family purity consists of rules regarding how to behave around a woman's menstruation and labor. According to the Bible, any bleeding (or semen, for that matter) from one's reproductive body parts makes one unholy. In order to become pure again (and as a result, be allowed to touch and attend temple worship) they need to wash in a ritual bath. In biblical and Temple times (up to about 70 CE), ritual baths were used to purify people from a variety of things: touching dead bodies, spilling seed, some skin diseases, and menstrual and birth blood. All of these necessitate ritual cleaning.[4] After the Temple was destroyed, only menstrual and birth blood still necessitated ritual cleaning; in some more pious Orthodox communities, spilling seed also demands ritual cleaning. Contemporary Orthodox understandings of family purity dictates that during a wife's menstruation, and for seven "clean" days after, she and her husband cannot touch—this includes sexual activities, but also hugging or, in some extreme interpretations, passing food to one another (so that their hands do not touch). Some Jews sleep on separate beds during those weeks. Once the wife goes to the ritual bath, she is "pure" and intimacy is restored.

Sexuality and intimacy also have to do with modesty (*Tzaniut*)—that is, in the ways the female and male bodies are conceptualized. Modesty is important for both men and women, married or single. However, modesty rules concerning women are far more detailed and stricter than those for men, and married women have an additional Halachic ruling to cover their hair as well as their body. The issue of modesty concerns three aspects: dress, relationship with the opposite sex (touch), and overall behavior. For example, women are not allowed to sing in front of men. While makeup is not Halachically forbidden, putting on visible makeup is considered immodest. Men and women cannot hug, touch, or shake hands with the other sex (as discussed in the previous chapter). Overall, both men and women should not act or dress in a way that draws attention to their bodies. Specifically for women, they should wear clothes that hide their arms, legs, and cleavage; skirts and not pants; and clothes that are not see-through or tight. In other words, they need to dress in a way that abstracts their body. Young women are often told that their bodies are a distraction for men, and that it is their moral duty to cover up in order to help men "control themselves." Speaking about sexuality too is considered immodest, and most young people receive no official sexual education in Jewish religious schools.

Contemporary attitudes toward sexuality and modesty in Orthodox Judaism tend to adopt a more restrictive approach.[5] According to Yakir Englander and Avi Sagi, modern approaches to sexuality and the body "pose a new challenge" for Orthodox communities.[6] Scholars suggest that this growing anxiety about sexual "purity" is a response to the sexual "promiscuity" of the modern, Western world. This anxiety creates a reactionary attempt to control and regulate sexuality more forcefully in contemporary Jewish Orthodoxy. For example, Tamar Elor describes the current reactions to modesty and sexuality in Orthodox communities as a "tornado" that aims to constantly control more aspects of female dress and behaviors.[7] As Orthodox Jews live within secular, modern societies, they are exposed to immodest and sexual behaviors in the media and in the street. As a result, a need arises to protect one's traditions and worldviews, and this need often translates to more restrictive and extreme approaches.[8] In an attempt to explore current trends within this community, Stadler interviewed contemporary (postmillennial) Israeli ultra-Orthodox students and surveyed the handbooks and audio and visual materials the students received. She found that the rabbinical material focused on overcoming one's bodily needs, counting sexual desires as one of the most dangerous needs.[9] Stadler further describes how in Israel, the ultra-Orthodox discourse about sexual modesty has become "militant" in its presentation of sexual purity as a battle against the evil inclination.[10]

I've added topics such as family purity and modesty to this chapter on intimacy because they are both religious practices related to how the body should be conceived. These issues—sex, modesty, family purity, and touch—all showcase how gender and sexual norms are dictated through Halachic rulings. In other words, how these behaviors, which normalize religious Jewish thinking regarding body and sexuality, are prescribed by religious creed and changing Halachic rules. For example, it is the Halachic code that describes what is considered modest for women—that they should cover their hair, wear skirts of a certain length, and an array of other restrictions and rules regarding being modest. While modesty is not explicitly about sex, it is related to how one understands one's body and understands the proper relations between the two sexes. These rules and norms work to make women understand their bodies (and themselves) as something that should be hidden, secret, protected. Similarly, family purity rules dictate that married couples do not touch each other during the woman's period and thus tend to understand the female body in those times as unclean and impure. In these ways, the rules matter—not only in dictating everyday behaviors but, in a deeper manner, in constructing the ways in which one understands their own body and what it means to be touched.

When these norms are discussed online something big is at stake—not only the personal issues of a specific person or couple but a reframing and negotiation of how Orthodox Judaism conceives of bodies and sexuality. Since, as previously stated, sexuality is not openly discussed in most of these communities, the internet allows for a revolutionary discussion to take place: a public discussion of these private matters. However, when these Halachic codes are discussed online, they are already informed by the ways people understand their bodies and their sexual norms. So a kind of conceptual cycle is happening here, where users online discuss these issues based on their offline, traditional, knowledge and experiences, and by doing so, they contribute to an open, public discourse that de facto reframes these norms. As discussed earlier in this book, to understand a religious—or any type of ideological—group or discussion happening online, we need to understand the offline tradition and societal norms informing these discussions. And, once these discussions happen online, they themselves become part of the normalizing discourse for that specific topic, thus informing the offline behavior.

To recapitulate, online discussion pushes and shapes the very norms discussed in these religious websites or forums. In these online materials, people share their personal stories in either the Q&A sections or in their comments to published "official" articles. By sharing these personal stories, they expose and challenge current norms. The official articles also reveal much about the current Jewish Orthodox mindset toward sexuality and the body. The rest of this chapter explores this current negotiation as it takes place online. I begin with the topic of modesty, showing how restrictions are reframed using postfeminist language as a form of liberation. This represents the "mixed" position, which embraces traditional norms but frames them in a neoliberal language of personal empowerment. Then, I present the traditionalist perspective through an exploration of positive online representations of "kosher" sexuality. Last, I offer some examples of using online media for resistance and bending of sexual norms. The chapter concludes in short summary, highlighting the trends and ways sexuality is negotiated and represented in these online religious spaces.

Modesty as the Great Liberator: Online Religious Endorsement

Modesty—the way women dress, look, and behave—is inherently tied to the ways sexuality is thought of and experienced. But because it is not such a private topic as intimacy, as women are seen—on the street and in the media—it tends to be discussed rather openly in religious schools and texts. Not surprisingly, the issue and meaning of modesty seem to also generate a lot of discussion on all the websites examined in this book (Chabad, Aish, Kipa) as well as on social media. What seems to be constantly communicated in these online sources is that modesty is not a burden or a legal restriction but rather a "natural" and "liberating" choice. Various "modest fashion" groups and pages can be found on Facebook—all of which emphasize modernity and style with names such as "Modest and Chic" or "the Modest Vibe"—including the successful ModLi company, a modest clothing line that has more than 103,000 followers on Facebook.[11] These pages highlight style and individuality over Halachic restrictions. For example, the page "Modest fashion for Jewish women" writes in their "About" section, "This is a community for Jewish women *who choose* to dress modestly."[12] Thus, these social media sources provide the sense that modesty is a choice. But for many, if not most, Orthodox women modesty is a religious obligation—not a choice. Or, if it is a choice, it is a choice that has social and personal consequences.

Modesty has consequences because it plays an important part in how one is seen and, as a result, who she can date. Therefore, one way in which modesty is dealt with online is in association with dating and dating difficulties. Two online articles exemplify this: an article from Aish titled "Dating with Dignity," commented on by twelve users and shared 418 times on Facebook, and an article from Kipa titled "Research: Religious Girls Dressed in Secular Style Will Have Difficulty Finding a Husband," commented on by seventeen users and liked 347 times, the most liked of the Kipa articles in this study's sample. These two articles have very different styles, but they both offer a "modern" explanation and meaning for modesty rather than a religious-legal one. The Aish article is written in a similar style to a Buzzfeed article or an advice column, with five "pointers" for a successful date. Most importantly, the article stresses, is that love takes time to develop, but respect "begins at day one."[13] While the actual tips suggest listening and being curious and present, the tone of the article is that humbled and respectful behavior is the key for a successful date and relationship between the sexes. In that way, the article suggests (albeit, implicitly) a traditional approach to women's behavior as quiet, nonaggressive, polite, and modest. The Kipa article is written in journalistic style, commenting on the "discoveries" of some research without passing Halachic or religious judgment on modest dress codes or behaviors. The Kipa article begins by describing the phenomenon of "later singlehood" in the National Religious community in Israel. It asks:

> What is the reason for later singlehood? [. . .] Doctor Yaarit Bokek attempted at answering this question by interviewing various young people [. . .] one of the [findings is that] [. . .] *young religious women that dress like secular girls, with jeans and tight or sleeveless shirts have a hard time meeting their destined groom*, because they do not look religious in the eyes of men that would have dated them if they only knew the women are actually religious. [. . .] Dr. Bokek concludes for those who want to have a relationship: "A person needs to know themselves and be consistent in behavior. [. . .] Those who have an unclear religious identity might consider seeking therapy to establish a consistent and coherent religious and social identity."[14]

While the article takes a neutral position regarding modesty by not explicitly describing how one should dress, it does "reveal" that dressing immodestly might delay one in attaining the important goal of finding their soulmate. The article instead places advice and judgment in the voice of the academic authority, Dr. Bokek, who clearly states that a "consistent and coherent religious identity" is needed in order to date. In other words, to date religious men, women need to dress in a way that will please them and communicate religiosity: they need to dress modestly. Unlike the article author, the users commenting on this article are less than impartial. Many of the comments state clearly and explicitly that women who do not dress modestly are simply not religious. One comment reads, "The reason is simple—they [the women] are not religious. A woman that doesn't give two cents about *Halacha* is not religious. Even if she says she is."[15] Another states that "a girl that does not follow *Halacha* is not religious. Why make it more complicated?"[16] These commenters argue that dressing modestly is Halachically prescribed, and if a woman does not dress modestly, she is not adhering to Halacha and as a result should not be considered an Orthodox Jew. We see in these comments how the participatory elements of the internet—the option to comment—are employed by users who have a traditional, if not fundamental, approach to modesty. They promote a binary and dichotic thinking in which modest dress is the only allowed interpretation of the Halachic texts, and women who do not follow those specific rules are simply not religious. Furthermore, they present this attitude, policing women's dress, as the mainstream and a reasonable attitude, using phrases like "Why make it complicated?" and, "It's simple." Only two users question and negotiate the definition of modesty and its relation to religiosity. The first states, "Look at how you talk? The road to rabbi Shienberg [an extreme ultra-Orthodox leader] is very short! [You] immediately blame—'Not modest . . . ' 'Not religious . . . ' 'Not like us . . . ' You have become a disgusting, sick herd, hypnotized by your 'purity.' I have news for all you 'pure' people. You are disgusting."[17] The second commenter writes, "Why are you saying that wearing pants is immodest? What's the relation? You are right, it's better to have a skirt that sweeps the road. Insane. Help! There are ultra-Orthodox here."[18] Both comments mention ultra-Orthodoxy as an extremity that they believe the Religious National Orthodoxy in Israel has not yet arrived at. In fact, they use that extremity to define what they are not—their understanding of this community is as one that is not extremely modest or obsessed with modesty and "purity." These users are upset to discover that most users commenting are prejudiced against women wearing pants. What is negotiated here is not only the definition of modesty—rather, through female modesty, the entire community is measured and the female herself will be judged as "religious" or "not religious enough." Here, we see a deliberation on the boundaries and norms within this religious community regarding female dress codes. Two related layers of normalizing discourses can be highlighted here: one concerning the female body and the other regarding the boundaries of community. The first is the attempt to police the female body through three strategies: first, through suggesting, as the journalist does, that immodest dress will result in loneliness; second, through suggesting, as the psychologist, Dr. Bokek, does, that people need to maintain a coherent religious identity; and last, claiming, as the majority of the comment section does, a religious, Halachic dictation of the female dress code. Both the secular approach (journalistic and scientific) and the religious approach focus on the individual woman's body and dress. On the other hand, the second layer focuses on the community as a whole and can be found explicitly in the comment section. Here, it is through the female body that the community is saved or damned—the community and its boundaries are defined through the attitudes people express toward modesty. In both layers, the internet plays an important role both as the playground and as that which sets the rules of the game; it is the space in which these negotiations can happen, and through its participatory culture and technological affordances—sharing and commenting—it sets the rules for who can speak and how. So, while the article enacts "old" media logic of journalistic discovery and expert opinion, the "new" media logic of commenting plays a significant role in this discourse. It is through the comments that the "mainstream" opinion is revealed and maintained and in the comments sections where resisting voices (while few) can be heard. The internet, thus, plays a significant role in formulating the concepts that then shape the community.

For most online authors in these Jewish religious websites, the issue of modesty is framed around the individual, not the community (at least, not explicitly). As was observed in the social media examples, modesty is tied with concepts such as dignity and respect. For example, in the Chabad website's explanation of modesty, it is considered a "staple of Jewish life" and it is explained that "the basic idea—for both men and women—is to wear self-respecting clothing."[19] The reason to be modest, according to the article, is that "when we refrain from calling undue attention to our external selves, our human core, the Gdly spirit within each one of us, can shine through."[20] Similarly, in the Aish article "Dating with Dignity," the author assures her readers that "a real, lasting relationship [is] built on the foundation of respect."[21] In these articles, and in others, modesty is a way in which people show respect to their bodies and let their internal, "holy" aspects represent them. "Our external selves," our bodies or sexuality, are dismissed and negated. This coding of modesty and sexuality into concepts such as "respect" and "dignity" is echoed by the readers, who tend to be more explicit about the connection between sexuality and modesty. For example, one response to the mentioned Aish article reads, "Why don't you mention that respect also means NO touching."[22] Another user gives additional dating advice, such as, "Maintain appropriate boundaries if you are a man."[23] In the reactions to the Chabad article on modesty, users quickly connect "respect" with "sexuality" as in this comment: "So ladies, please help me and other men not to lust, by not putting temptation in [our] path. Let us admire and be attracted to 'you' and not your bodies."[24] While this comment is written by a male, some of the females commenting also see immodest dress as a way to sexualize them: "I have never worn shorts or short skirts. It makes me feel very exposed. I don't like the way some men think of women as objects."[25] Most of the users commenting on this Chabad article are interested in sharing practical advice, such as which garment is considered modest, how to cover one's hair, and how to deal with dressing modestly in hot weather. The practical tone of the article, which gives specific restrictions and instructions for modest wear, is reflected in the comment section. Thus, this specific understanding of modesty is reaffirmed in the comment section. Participatory technological affordances are used to normalize Orthodox, traditional views. However, a few users do object to these ideas of modesty and point to the inherent sexualization and regulation of women underscored in this concept of modesty. One user writes, "And for men? I'm confused as to why this article suggests that modesty is fitting 'for both men and women' then gives three practical suggestions that focus only on women."[26] Another writes, "Modest dress? Horrid . . . too much time spent by men on regulating and watching women."[27] These comments and articles touch on one of the sensitive topics concerning modesty: what is the meaning of modesty? Is it about regulation of female bodies and sexuality, a spiritual practice, or a communal practice of identity? These users seem to understand modesty as the regulation of women in spite of the text's discussion of respect and self-respect.

The negotiation of the meaning of modesty is found even more explicitly in other articles, such as the Chabad article "Do Women Have Something to Hide?" This article is structured as a Q&A, beginning with the questions "Why does Judaism tell women to keep their bodies covered? Is there something shameful or evil about a woman's body?"[28] The answer is an attempt to promote modesty by framing it as an act self-respect and spiritual growth:

You are assuming that the only reason for modest dress is to avoid temptation. While this may be the case in other religions, for Judaism this is not true. *The Jewish way of modest dress is not merely about how other people view women, but more about how women view themselves.* [...] The body is the holy creation of Gd. [...] The way we maintain our respect for the body is by keeping it covered. *Not because it is shameful, but because it is so beautiful and precious.* [...] This is true for men's bodies too, and laws of modest dress apply to them as well. But it is even more so for women. The feminine body has a beauty and a power that far surpasses the masculine. *The Kabbalists teach that a woman's body has a deeper beauty because her soul comes from a higher place. For this reason, her body must be kept discreetly covered.*[29]

The author, Aron Moss, explains that modesty has *nothing* to do with sexuality but is tied to spirituality. The holier something is, the more we should keep it sacred by hiding and covering it. The logic is that women, being more spiritually inclined than men, are holier, and thus need to be more modest. Here, traditional sexual norms of limiting and controlling females' bodies is imbued with spiritual meaning. The rationale argues: one does not dress and act modestly because men said so (adhering to the patriarchy), but, in fact, dressing modestly is important for one's own spiritual growth. That is, modesty receives a new meaning in these articles—as a path for spiritual development. This discursive strategy frames traditional communal roles and regulations as acts that are individualistic and spiritually fulfilling. This meaning is not solely found in online material. Lea Taragin-Zeller, in her ethnographic study of ultra-Orthodox teenage girls in Israel, has noted a similar trend—that these girls conceptualize strict modesty rule as part of their path toward "spiritual advancement."[30] The practices might be old, but the spiritual meaning is relatively new, and it is negotiated online in these articles and in the comment sections. While many users embrace and promote this spiritual meaning, others reject it for either feminist reasons (such as in the comments discussed) or for religious reasons, such as viewing adherence to Halacha and tradition as more important than spiritual or personal reasons.

The mentioned article presents women as inherently spiritual and sacred, as souls that "come from a higher place," and modesty as a way to show respect and self-respect and to protect females' holiness. This attitude can be seen in other articles. In the article "Restrictions That Free," author Dina Bacharach explains modesty as a way for her to grow as a person and to feel liberated. She writes, "Let's take wearing long sleeves, high collars and skirts for example. *It seems so restricting. But I feel so free.* I can walk down the streets and not have to be concerned that guys might have inappropriate thoughts about me. I am protecting myself so that *I can be my deepest, truest self.*"[31] While Bacharach does tie modesty to sexuality and sees it as a form of protection ("guys might have inappropriate thoughts"), she writes that she experiences modest dress and religious sexual norms as liberating, helping her be her "truest self." Here again, the concept of modesty is tied to spirituality and to empowering women to "be themselves." We see online a new twist on these traditional norms: a rationalization that ties modesty and sexual restrictions to individual growth. Her readers seem to, by and large, accept this attitude. Users write back leaving comments like "Tzniut [modesty] empowers us"[32] and saying that the article is "inspiring." In fact, the words free or freedom are the most common words used, being repeated twenty-one times in the article and comments. That is to say, in these online texts, traditional sex and gender norms are reframed and renegotiated to enhance spiritual freedom as well as the meaning of liberation and empowerment; modern, neoliberal concepts are being used to maintain traditional perspectives.

In the discussion of modesty online, then, more often than not, modesty is framed as a positive thing. This happens both in user-generated content, like social media or comments, and in editorial content, like the articles in Aish, Chabad, or Kipa. Modesty (and sexual restriction) in these online discussions is freeing, a sign of self-respect, and important when dating in maintaining your dignity. In these online texts, modesty is separated from the Halachic and from its communal and social meanings and is given a new meaning as a tool for personal, individual self-improvement. By detaching modesty from communal and traditional norms and claiming it is a matter of personal empowerment and personal choice, this online discourse removed the responsibility from the rabbis and the society, and (mis)places it in the hand of individuals. But Judaism is not an individualized religion, as discussed in the first chapters of this book. It is a communal religion, one that is based on rabbinical texts and rules. Therefore, this online discourse distorts the understanding of modesty to fit modern norms, but in doing so, it supports traditional understandings of women's bodies and of sexuality as a male-centered practice. A similar attempt is taken with sexual acts. That is, "kosher sexuality" is framed as beneficial to the individual and the couple, and, furthermore, sexuality is explicitly tied with modesty in many of the online texts discussing intimacy. For example, the online promotion of one rabbi's book on intimacy reads, "Judaism's age-old secret to building strong relationships and lasting intimacy: modesty."[33] These ideas about kosher sex are further explored in the following section, which also represents a more traditional attitude toward sexuality.

Kosher Sexuality

While modesty is glorified in these online articles, the issues of sexual norms—of how to be intimate—have a more complicated presentation online. Some online sources do promote and praise traditional Orthodox rules about sexuality, but other voices more explicitly resist and interrogate the current rules. In the section that follows this one, we'll explore the more challenging voices. But first, this section examines online sources that support traditional sexual norms, or, what it sometimes referred to as "kosher sex."

As expressed in the introduction to this chapter, sexuality is by and large a taboo topic in Orthodox Judaism. However, in online mainstream religious websites, this taboo seems to be broken. These mainstream websites and various social media outlets are populated with Jewish men and women talking about sexuality—with a varying degree of explicitness. Some sources are general and speak in a broad and vague way about intimacy. Some are more specific, targeted at men and women separately, and might even demand a short "interview" or disclaimer before a user can read or engage with the site. For example, the Facebook groups "Jewish Women Talk about Anything" and "Honest Intimacy" both have a short interview (three to four written questions) one must answer to be considered entry to the group. Even once you are admitted, regulations and guidelines of posts and users are constantly ongoing. As a result, these groups are "safe spaces" for discussing sensitive issues, but also have limited reverberation in the public online discourse on Jewish sexuality. These spaces do not act as spaces for leading change or negotiating norms explicitly but rather act as support groups or places for individual struggles. While the personal is the political, as the feminist mantra goes, these groups are not trying to be political or strive for change in the cultural-social level. In the last section of this chapter, we see an example for a public attempt at leading a discussion that bends and negotiates existing norms.

Aside from these closed social media groups, mainstream Jewish websites openly discuss some issues of sexuality. In fact, on the Chabad website the word "sexuality" alone brings up seventy-one results, including different articles, videos, podcasts, excerpts from books, and Q&A discussions. Searching the Chabad website for the word "intimacy" returns in 447 different results, but some of these results include discussing intimacy with the divine or other similar topics. Aish too offers a variety of content dealing with sexuality, and the same is true for Kipa in Israel. Throughout all these websites, sexuality is openly discussed but is clearly framed through a religious world view, which, as this section explores, allows for very specific (strict) understanding of sexuality.

Many of these sources tend to compare and contrast Judaism with modernity and modern attitudes toward sexuality. In these comparisons, modernity tends to be the source of sexual issues (like sexual harassment) and Judaism tends to be a solution for a healthy sexuality. In some cases, this is done by clearly defining "the Jewish view on sexuality" and in other cases by reflecting on current "general" events or news. This latter tactic uses events that are of common knowledge to teach Jewish values. For example, in 2012, after former CIA director David Petreaus's public affair with his biographer, which led to his early retirement, one article on Aish stated, "Another scandal involving a powerful man brought down and destroyed because of an affair with a woman he had spent an inordinate amount of time with. [. . .] It's no wonder Judaism forbids a man from being alone with a woman who is not his wife. [. . .] It's not hard to understand the underlying rationale of these laws. Judaism recognizes the power of sexual attraction."[34] The Aish author utilizes a current event to rationalize and promote Jewish laws regarding sexuality—in this case, the law of *Yichud*, which forbids men and women to be alone together if they are not married. Similarly, a different article uses a report on campus sexual harassment to argue for gender segregation. And, both on Chabad and on Aish authors discuss the #MeToo movement and earlier accusations of sexual abuse to praise "kosher sexuality" in light of these societal crises.

Aside from reflecting on general current events, other articles more explicitly offer "the Jewish view on intimacy." For example, a podcast by Rabbi Mendel Kaplan discusses "the Jewish Perspective on Love and Intimacy." He begins by stating that "the Jewish way means 'as per prescription of the Torah.'"[35] In that way, Kaplan already positions his perspective as grounded in the most sacred Jewish text, thus implicitly arguing for authority and tradition. He then moves on to discuss what Jewish intimacy is. According to Kaplan, general modern attitude toward sex is self-centered and focused on one's own desires. In contrasts, "The Torah tells us that intimacy is a gift God gave men and women so that they could be married, *so that they could create a family*, and intimacy is the glue that holds a marriage together."[36] He goes on to claim that Jewish sexuality is all about selflessness and giving yourself to the other. It is also, he claims, not for the sake of procreation (although his above definition seems to give procreation an important role) and both partners need to want it. He even goes so far as to say that according to Jewish law, there must be foreplay. More than anything, Kaplan stresses that in Judaism, sex is what makes marriage more than a business partnership and it is vital for a good relationship. He also mentions that there are certain obligations each gender has toward the other in marriage, as we saw in the previous chapter on marriage. However, there are some restrictions on Jewish sexuality—for example, adultery and rape are prohibited. The rabbi also mentions that bestiality and homosexuality (in the same breath) are wrong, and he prohibits premarital sex. The rabbi spends the most time explaining the rationale around Family Purity laws and concludes by saying, "God willing, someday in a good and healthy marriage you should all be pregnant, all of you girls here, and you should all be bringing Jewish children into the world."[37] In that way, even with his inclusion of sexual pleasure, the rabbi maintains a traditional view toward sexuality—one that positions it in direct relationship with procreation.

Other articles take a less explicit and more spiritual approach toward "kosher sex." The structure for this type of argument goes something like this: First, a declaration that sexuality is thought of outside of Judaism as natural or merely biological. For example, "Sex is the most powerful, all-pervasive force in human experience,"[38] or "Conventional wisdom says that sexuality is a natural instinct."[39] Then, the unveiling: sexuality is not the most material aspect of human life, but rather the holiest, most spiritual aspect. For example, "Sexuality belongs to the arena of the sacred."[40] However, we have to work to keep sex in the arena of the sacred, and we do so by restricting it: "Paradoxically, sex—the most chaotic, powerful, and untutored drive—can only be fully experienced when it includes an element of discipline and precision."[41] This part of the argument stresses that sexuality is something we should not speak of or become familiar with, because then we will destroy the holy aspects of it. According to one Chabad author, Mannis Friedman,

> If you become familiar, too familiar, with the intimacy of another person's life, whether physical, emotional or mental, then you've compromised the sanctity. [. . .] For our grandparents and our great-grandparents, intimate relations was a sacred thing not to be talked about. [. . .] That's why our grandparents could not talk about their relationship. They weren't keeping secrets—they were keeping something sacred.

> Today, human sexuality is something you're supposed to become familiar with. [. . .] We've removed the sanctity, all because we thought our uptight parents were keeping a secret from us. [. . .] Try as we might, we cannot ignore what our bubbes and zaides knew: the marriage bed is a sacred thing and the only way it works is when you treat it with sanctity.[42]

In other words, in the past, sexual relationships were kept "behind closed doors" and that is what kept the magic and maintained the sanctity of marriage. Today, because sexuality is discussed, it becomes not sacred, and the results are not good for the couple or for society. Indeed, a different article outlines seven axioms of sexuality, among which are "Sexuality Needs to Be Sanctified" and "Sexuality Has Value Only in a Permanent Relationship."[43] These articles highlight the need for sex to be heterosexual, marital, keeping with family purity, and taboo. This, these authors claim, will bring one happiness in marriage, prevent divorce, and bring one closer to the real meaning of sex. As Friedman concludes, "Look at those same bubbes and zaides a little closer. Those two people, who have been married fifty, sixty, seventy years, are still a little bashful with each other. They still excite each other. That is human sexuality. That is sanctity."[44] The comments reacting to these articles seem to support this mindset: "I agree 100 percent. Society has been fed this garbage from the media," and "Great, very nice read and a lot of information."[45] Reacting to Friedman's article, users write: "This is so affirming,"[46] and "I found answers to my deep question in this passage."[47] However, some resistance can be noted in the comment section. For example, one user writes, "I do understand that intimacy is sacred. However, if one remains silent on it, how do new people know how to be intimate?"[48] This notion is also echoed in other comments, such as one that reads, "Closed doors should open a wee bit. . . . We need to have a little more information out there. If it doesn't come from Jewish sources, then it will come from non-Jewish ones. When sex is 'not to be talked about,' then ignorance abounds."[49] Another, along the same lines, says, "I disagree with this article in many ways. First of all—the best way to understand how to feel sexual joy and happiness is to have a good look at nature and the plant and animal kingdom. They do not feel ashamed of their sexual nature and they do not carry around the idea that what they are doing has to be considered so extremely 'SACRED,' otherwise how on earth would they be able to be so completely in touch with their natural primal instincts combined with the pleasurable act of sex?"[50] As seen in later chapters, these acts of resistance are mostly "corrected" by other users instead of by the rabbis or the websites editors. That is, the author usually does not react, and the website editors allow these comments, and thus, to some degree, support the negotiation. It is other lay people, other users who take it upon themselves to correct those resisting. In the example of this article, one user reacts to the need for openness by suggesting that one becomes "totally comfortable with [one] self" and suppling a list of religious sources to read regarding kosher sexuality. Other users mostly take offense with the last comment, regarding a nonshameful approach to sexuality inspired by the animal world. Two users in particular stress that the author of the comment is mistaken in thinking highly of the animal world (since it is not stated in the Torah), and that "the animals do not know the difference between sacred and the mundane." Many of the users seem to accept Friedman's approach about the sacredness of sexuality, and the users who challenge the need for "sacredness" or "closeness" are corrected or coerced by the other users.

It seems that, by and large, most users assume and promote this spiritualized version of restricted sexuality. In fact, many of the authors and the users frame it as liberating and empowering for their relationships. They write and comment about how Jewish rules uplift a material need into a spiritual experience. For example, an anonymous author compared the standards in dating secularly to dating religiously, where touch between people of the opposite sex is prohibited (*Shomer negiah*), and comes to the following conclusion: "It's like an awakening that as restricting as not touching sounds, it's pretty restricting to have standards put on us as well. *Shomer negiah*, despite its restrictions, is in fact empowering to now have new options in making our own decisions."[51] Thus, the restrictions regarding sexuality are elevated in these online texts to be freeing, empowering, spiritual. As a different Chabad author puts it, "Intimate relations is a gift from Above to be guarded and cherished."[52] Online, this approach is strengthened again and again by users' commenting, sharing, and liking. In this way, users are taking part in the maintenance of traditional positions that are sometimes "dressed" in modern neoliberal language of self-empowerment. These authors and users rarely bring up the hardship and distance caused by these religious practices. As seen in the section below, some men and women do use the new affordances of the internet to try and deal with the more touchy parts of Jewish sexuality.

Let's Play: Online Religious Resistance

Not all online Orthodox discussion included in this study presents traditional Jewish gender and sexual norms in a positive light, like the sources in the previous sections. In some areas of this online discourse, certain voices begin to resist and negotiate these norms so that they include the perspectives of women and sexual minority. Usually, this happens in online "spaces" that I consider the periphery—closed forums or rogue Facebook groups. For example, Simon Theobald studied various fringe spaces, such as closed blogs for gay ultra-Orthodox men, coded Craig's lists where Orthodox Jews searched for casual sexual encounters, and secret forums in which Orthodox women discussed (anonymously) family and intimacy concerns.[53] More recently, users of the Facebook group "Jewish Women *Actually* Talk About Anything" occasionally ask about polyamorous relationships, or other "taboo" issues, less anonymously. But, in the center—in the mainstream websites that claim to be the source of Orthodox Judaism online, such voices are rarely heard. One case of an attempt to resist and negotiate sexual norms is so groundbreaking, that it deserves in-depth attention.

In August 2016, in a taboo-breaking act, the Kipa website, in association with the Yahel Center, created an online video series speaking explicitly about intimacy and challenging existing sexual norms in the Orthodox community. The Yahel Center is a unique organization seeking to address issues of sexuality in the Orthodox Jewish community. Established in 2012, the organization has worked over the last decade to spread awareness and become a source of knowledge about religious sexuality and about sexuality for religious people. They offer lectures, courses, personal counseling, and seminars. According to their website, "Yahel Center was established in order to address intimacy and sexuality openly within the orthodox community. We believe that a positive relationship between a married couple strengthens each partner and holds the foundation for a healthy family. [. . .] Our goal is to educate and provide couples and professionals with information and insight to a life of healthy intimacy with a Torah perspective."[54] In the summer of 2016, the Yahel Center sought to draw in audiences via the most popular website for National Religious Jews in Israel, Kipa. To that end, they created a series of videos publicly addressing issues of intimacy. It is unclear how many videos they hoped to create and publish, but in the end, only five videos were posted. The audience reactions were mixed. Even before the actual videos were posted, users seemed to generally resist this series and to take a stand against it. An article announcing the launch of the series was posted on August 25, 2016. This article is, in many ways, a promotional article for the Yahel Center and the video series:

> Yahel Center receives every week tens of applications by couples in need of guidance. Most of these couples do not have a sexual problem. They do not need therapy. They need directing, some information, a bit of mediation and they are good to go! [. . .] There is no magic here, just words, listening and a lot of knowledge collected from hundreds of couples that already told their personal story. A story that has already became public, but in our community it continues to remain private, sealed between the couple. [. . .] The need is clear. [. . .] We need to fix the wrongdoing that had led to a gap between us and our bodies. Us and our partners. Us and a healthy and realistic Jewish approach to intimacy. [. . .] On the one hand, we want to leave intimacy in its natural and healthy place—between the couple. On the other hand, we have a sacred duty to speak, to create an open channel that will give room and legitimacy. [. . .] For this reason, we are happy to present this video series project made in collaboration with Kipa and with a lot of love. We need to talk, but modestly, in a Godly manner, in a clear but clean and kind language, in love.[55]

This introduction presents the rationale for the video series: the Orthodox society needs to be able to discuss intimacy in a "clean" way. Unlike the previous section, in which authors suggested that sexuality should remain "sacred" by being secret, here, the authors are actively working to open things up. As mentioned before and highlighted by Theobald, Orthodox society, in general, shies away from the issues of intimacy and considers talking about it a taboo, even between friends.[56] The article mentions the results of making sexuality a taboo issue—the proliferation of sexual assault and the lack of "healthy" (heterosexual) intimacy between married couples. The way to help people arrive at these positive sexual norms, according to the Yahel Center, is through sexual education and couples' mediation—both of which can be done "in the spirit of the Torah." This promotional article has seventeen comments, which is a relatively high response rate for the Kipa articles sampled (the highest received is twenty comments). Out of these seventeen comments, fourteen were resisting this video series. Users immediately voice their concerns about this open attitude to sexuality—on the first day this article was published, it received seven negative comments. For many of the users vocalizing their resistance, the main problem is that youth (boys) will be exposed to this content. For example, "Modesty means not to speak or publish videos in public . . . there are kids and boys in this website. . . . I'm shocked [that you published it]."[57] Or, "Sex sex sex sex and only sex. Are you not tired of speaking about sex? And in public? There are kids who read here too!!!"[58] And, "Not everything should be in a website open to all. I'm surprised that *Internet Rimon* [a religious internet filter] allows this content to appear."[59] As also seen in the reactions to the actual videos, users feel disappointed that a religious website publishes such content and that these taboo issues are allowed and filtered through the religious internet filtering service. Focusing on the publicity of the website and that a child might see this article and the videos is one way in which the socio-technological affordance of the website—the open nature of the internet—works against the intended use here. The website editors and series creators want this content to be public and shared; the users feel that this offends their religiosity and the very nature of the website. Another way to voice this concern is by comparing Kipa to secular Israeli online news outlets, such as Ynet: "Did you become YNET? What's up with the Kipa website? Some things are better left taboo! Are you a website for this sector [Orthodox society] or do you want to destroy the little piece of modest content that's left? What would you not do for money? For publicity? Too bad!!! Shelve this idea!!! And keep it classy!!!"[60] We see here how even online, certain religious users want some things to be "left taboo," and that the act of sharing this content threatens the character of the website, and its ascribed audience. While the majority of the users do object to this content, the users who support Yahel Center's effort are quick to answer the other users' concerns. One user writes, "Bless you [to the author]. Better late than never . . . the issue is important and necessary; this content is available throughout the web and its best that the children are exposed to it in a clean language in with modesty in mind. Well done [ייש״ר כוח, *Yasher koach*]."[61] Another user comments, "Bless you. Can help the users of this website that probably for 99% of them the content is appropriate. Which kid surfs in Kipa? (without insulting J) and if there is a kid that visits this website then it is better they are exposed to a pure approach to intimacy and not fed only through the rest of the content online L."[62] These comments suggest that this is helpful content, a necessary project that should be public, and that if children are exposed to it, that is not so bad since the content is "clean." That is, the supporting comments raise two issues: the importance of being able to discuss intimacy and the public nature of discussing this topic online in a religious website. Most of the users objecting are more explicitly concerned with the public aspect but seem to be implicitly opposing any discussion of sexuality ("better left taboo"). In this negotiation of sexual norms, the tool—the medium of online communication—plays an important part. Yahel Center, as mentioned before, also offers offline services, but they see it as their "sacred duty" to make the topic of "healthy," "kosher" sexuality publicly discussed. For Yahel Center and the readers that support them, it is *exactly* the public exposure via digital tools that is important and blessed. For the users who oppose them, the media plays a significant part *exactly* for the reason that this content should not be accessible to all. One user exemplifies this perfectly in her response:

> I don't usually comment here . . . but in this case I could not stand silence. As a woman, I think that the discourse about intimate issues is blessed, important, emancipating. . . . I am totally for it! But there are appropriate and inappropriate platforms. . . . It's important for me to say that I'm shocked to see such open talk without any control on who has access to it. Young boys, teenagers . . . Not at all appropriate! This is a blessed video series for the appropriate audience! But please! Do not publish such a series openly and publicly on your website.[63]

For this reader, it is not the *discourse* she is concerned with, but the *online* aspects of it—the fact that it is being talked about online, and as a result anyone (young boys) can have access to this content. Here, the question of how the online is used comes into play. Perhaps, if this was a closed forum or restricted section of the website, more readers would feel comfortable with it. After all, the online content of the videos is meant to be religiously inclined—to use "clean" language and speak of Halachic sexual norms. In this way, the technology of online videos is cultured for religious needs. However, many of the users feel that this is an improper use of the cultured technology.

Yahel Center and Kipa uploaded all the videos within the same month the mentioned article appeared, during August 2016. Each video is two to six minutes long, presented by a different woman, and each one deals with a different aspect of Jewish sexuality. The reaction to the initial announcement article is higher than the reaction for each individual video (seventeen comments on the article versus an average of five comments for each video). While the reactions dwindle in volume, the strategies and narratives presented in the comments to the announcement article are reflected in the videos' comments. Users reacting write comments along the lines of "there are kids here"[64] or "disgusting."[65] However, overall, the responses to the videos are more positive than those posted to the announcement article. For the announcement article, four out of seventeen comments were positive, in which users wrote that they see this discourse as an important one, while thirteen commenters strongly resisted. Out of the twenty-six total comments on the five videos, twelve were positive and fourteen resisting—46 percent positive reactions. The videos were also liked via Facebook, which can be read as a sign of support—while the average number of likes on articles from the Kipa sample was forty-three likes, these videos received on average a little over forty-six likes. This trend means that, in comments and via liking on social media, users are actually supportive of this video series, unlike the initial response to the series' announcement, which was negative.

The higher support for the actual videos compared to the announcement article can be explained in various ways. First, it is possible that the announcement article might have received more exposure than the actual videos. The videos are all posted under the "Women" section of the Kipa website but the article announcing a "new series" on Kipa might have been pushed by the website editors to promote the series itself. Another possibility is that the announcement article triggered more reactions because it was not examining one specific topic but rather dealing with the meta question of "Should we discuss sexuality in public?" That kind of general debate, one that frames the future of this website and, therefore, this online community, might have resonated with more people. It is also possible that once the videos were posted, users saw they were not as bad as they expected, or maybe they even agreed with some of the content. Regardless of the higher positive reactions to the video versus the announcement, the majority of the reactions were negative. That is, 61 percent of the total comments on all the videos objected to this series and were negative, and by the end of August 2016, no more videos were posted.

The videos are groundbreaking in regard to Orthodox online discussion of sexuality in several ways. First and foremost, this type of open discussion of sexuality does not exist in any other format within the Jewish online discourse. The videos do not only hint at sexuality, like previous articles discussed, but use clean language to actually describe practices and give advice. In other words, they speak relatively openly about an unspoken, taboo issue in these communities. Second, the videos feature women talking about sexuality and Halacha—not only having their voices and perspectives heard but de facto acting as teachers and religious authorities. For some Orthodox communities, this is unthinkable—women should not speak in front of men, teach Torah, or generally teach in public. Even in those sections of the Orthodox communities in which women do teach, they usually teach "modestly" and only to other women—not publicly to all members of society on a taboo topic. Having a woman explain, teach, and even speak "in public" (online) about her and others' sexuality is radical and, to some extent, revolutionary. That being said, the gendered use of this technology is still evident, both in the women's need to assert authority and in the users' comments, which question that authority.

While the videos' content is revolutionary in some ways, the women presenting are clear and careful to position their teaching within the Torah's spirit. Yehudit Yeser-Weinstein, in her video *It's OK To Laugh*, begins by reading from the Bible the story of Isaac and Rebecca in which Isaac is "playing" with Rebecca.[66] She uses the authority of the Bible to frame her stance toward sexuality. Yeser-Weinstein goes on to explain this "play" between them as a biblical way to discuss intimacy, similar to the biblical use of the word "knowing." But "play," Yeser-Weinstein offers, is less serious than "knowing." In this way, the Torah teaches us to take intimacy humorously and playfully. Furthermore, Isaac, according to Yeser-Weinstein, was a biblical patriarch that is known for his love for his wife. Therefore, we learn that playful relations are the normal way of "Jewish loving." Yeser-Weinstein invites both females and males to take sexuality more lightheartedly and to experiment with it—to play with it. She also frames this attitude as what the norm should be.

This negotiation of relational norms is evident throughout the videos. Some are trying to create new norms—such as playful intercourse[67] and speaking about sex after and during intercourse with your partner.[68] Others are trying to navigate and bend existing norms—even if it means examining and challenging Halachic ruling. Two videos deal directly with Halachic issues: *Niddah* (family purity) and the wedding night. Ella Ben-Shitrit's video concerning *Niddah* does not challenge any religious ruling, but it does encourage women to think of themselves first.[69] The day of the ritual washing after the period of separation between husband and wife following the rules regarding menstruation should be dedicated to rest and relaxation, to prepare the wife for her wash and the intercourse that will follow. More importantly, Ben-Shitrit urges women to be in touch with their bodies and urges couples to create an environment in which this night will become a refamiliarization with each other's bodies, rather than a stressful night in which intimacy (e.g., penetration) must be achieved. For those women (and men) who experience the night of return to intimacy after two weeks of being separated (during the female's menstruation and seven clean days) as stressful, Ben-Shitrit offers alternatives such as hugging, going on a date, or simply being together and removing the expectation of intimacy for that night.[70]

When it comes to the wedding night, the situation is more complicated. According to Halacha, the couple should try to have intercourse on their first evening—mostly to prevent the groom from masturbation or "spilling his seed." In one of the most daring videos, Hanna Ma-Tov asks newlyweds to not force themselves to arrive at penetration on the wedding night.[71] Most religious youth have little to no sexual experience before getting married, due to the custom of *Shmirat Negiaa*. As a result, the wedding night becomes a night of "from nothing to everything" and for some of the women (and probably some of the men too), this can be traumatic. Furthermore, because of the rules of family purity, after any bleeding the couple needs to be separate again for at least seven days. This, according to Ma-Tov, can be very difficult emotionally. Ma-Tov approaches this situation with authority and says: "You do not have to 'do it' that night. *I strongly recommend not to*."[72] She goes on to advocate a different approach:

> Sit together ... hug, and kiss and get to know each other's body ... with no commitment to that moment ... you can delay it [penetration] for a few more days ... so you will have a meaningful, healthy and loving experience and not a trauma. ... That it should be *from her will*, from her love to arrive at it, for you [male] and for her ... I really stress this and strongly recommend *not to do it that [first] night* ... enjoy, a day or two or three ... be together and enjoy this game ... get to know her body and she will get to know your body and you will arrive at it with pleasure and joy.[73]

This text is not only explicit by the standards of Kipa website, it is also seemingly against Halachic ruling, which dictates penetration the first night of marriage in order to consummate the marriage. The users are quick to point this out: "This is against *Halacha* what you are saying,"[74] "This is the opposite of what the *Halacha* says,"[75] and simply, "Reforms."[76] A learned Halachic discussion then takes place between the users, with one user trying to defend Ma-Tov and this perspective using Halachic and religious sources. Other users who endorse this video simply note that it is brave and beautiful advice. One user even goes so far as to dismiss the Halacha in face of this woman's teaching: "Very beautiful. Above and beyond any *Halacha*. Common sense that can save a marriage for years to come."[77]

What arises from this video and some of the responses to it is that the issue of penetration and intimacy on the wedding night has been so far dictated by (male-centered) religious ruling, and it is through the work of women like Ma-Tov that this issue is beginning to receive a female perspective. Furthermore, it seems that the Halachic approach has caused pain and distance between married partners (see the last comment implies), a pain that is crystallized and addressed in the last video of the series and, more generally, in the work of the Yahel Center.

The video titled *Not to be Afraid to Touch*, presented by Moria Tassan-Michaeli, is the most liked among all the videos (seventy-six Facebook likes).[78] In the video, Tassan-Michaeli describes married women who are afraid of intimacy with their husbands and try to avoid it, even avoid hinting at it. She tells a story of a woman who does not call her husband in any endearing names such as "dear" or "sweetheart" because, in their relationship, using an endearment means being available for intercourse. These women in fact feel relaxed and more comfortable in the two weeks in which they are "forbidden" to their husbands (during menstruation) because there are no reasons for "stress" or "expectations." According to Tassan-Michaeli, this is a result of the first intimate encounters these religious couples had and the existing religious norms regarding intimacy.[79]

Tassan-Michaeli argues that the extreme move from no touch to sexual touch and penetration can create a dissonance and result in distance and defamiliarization with one's own body as well as with a partner's body. Tassan-Michaeli therefore suggests that couples need to differentiate between "loving" touch and "sexual" touch—which can get mixed up because of this "all or nothing" approach. In cases like these, any touch from one's husband—hugging, stroking, caressing, even a brush of the hand—will be immediately translated to pressure to arrive at penetration. While recognizing that this is a problem that is created through social norms and cultural enforcement, that is, a sociological macro phenomenon, Tassan-Michaeli offers couples a solution that is privatized and personalized: change your communication patterns, go to therapy, and so on, thus offering a solution at the level of the individual, a psychological resolution instead of a sociological one. Tassan-Michaeli bravely opens for discussion a topic that is taboo and unspoken for most married couples: their broken intimacy. She suggests changing deeply rooted social norms and encourages people (who usually barely talk about their bodies with anyone) to talk openly about intimacy with their spouse. Surprisingly, this "scandalous" video receives only one response—and it is positive: "Thank you!! An important issue! From a married woman."[80] As mentioned above, this is the second most liked article on Facebook from the entire Kipa sample, indicating that users have found this content acceptable and perhaps even relatable. The fact that Tassan-Michaeli does not challenge Halacha, but instead offers solutions at the level of individual therapy, could possibly contribute to the acceptance of this video.

In summary, the Yahel center and Kipa website offer here an open "kosher" discussion of sexual norms. Digital media—videos posted on websites and their comments—allow for a negotiation of these norms and for women to voice their concerns and needs. This is revolutionary beyond doubt. But, as the section before highlighted, not all online Orthodox media is used to break taboos. In fact, most of it is used to maintain traditional norms. When it comes to the sensitive topic of sexuality, mainstream Orthodox websites generally seem to say less rather than more, and that by itself says a lot.

Summary

In this chapter, issues of negotiating sexuality online were considered. Examples of debates on modesty, on kosher sex, and on playful Jewish sexuality were provided. The online platforms allow, in many cases for the first time in Jewish history, systematic acceptance of female perspectives into the Jewish corpus. Online, women's voices became part of the discussion on Jewish rules regarding sexuality. While the participatory nature of the internet allows both men and women, rabbis and lay people, to openly discuss sexuality, in most cases, this negotiation tends to be dominated by traditional and patriarchal notions. Jewish sexuality in these online spaces is largely restricted, confines the female body, and adheres to male-centered ideas of sexuality.

This chapter highlights three general directions concerning the online discourse on the meaning of sexuality as presented in the above videos and articles. The first is a spiritualization of modesty and sexuality using neoliberal terms and concepts to maintain traditional norms. The second perspective highlights traditional norms toward sexuality, mainly arguing that the Jewish approach to sexuality is better than the modern approach and that sexuality should remain a taboo issue. The third perspective is a negotiation of sexual norms and "Jewish intimacy" publicly and openly, via digital tools, in an innovative and groundbreaking format. The media of the internet and these websites, which allow for user reactions, further complicate things as users react and reject—negotiate—both the traditional views and the innovative (modern) ones.

The major takeaway of this chapter is that two seemingly opposing trends are happening online: on the one hand, the internet allows for an open discussion of sexuality within Orthodox Jewish communities. On the other hand, the open discussion tends to encourage a restricted and highly regulated sexuality. The next chapter deals with what happens after sex, when intimacy is achieved, procreation established, and babies follow. How do Jewish women use these online platforms to makes sense of their roles as mothers? The negotiation of Jewish motherhood is explored in the next chapter.

INTERLUDE 2

Looking Through Windows
The Power of Everybody

Since its early inception, and even more so after "the Arab Spring," the internet has been theorized as a democratic force,[1] a public sphere in which every citizen can voice their concerns, can directly interact with powerful entities, a "space" where everybody is on the same playing field. Of course, scholars have noted again and again that the internet is not so equal—that internet companies have more power than their users,[2] that governments still control a lot of the online communications; in other words, that traditional sources of authority still have more power than citizens, even online.

This debate about power online is also present when it comes to digital religion. Scholars have been researching new modes of religious authority as they shift and change online. More concretely, Pauline Cheong suggests three ways to understand religious authority online: through the logic of disjuncture and displacement, in which we see the ways digital media has decreased the power of traditional religious authority; through the logic of continuity and complementarity, in which digital media strengthens religious authority; and through the logic of dialectic and paradox, which accounts for the complexities of religious communication online.[3] But one area that requires our attention, I argue, is not the power of official authority, but a (new) form of power: the power of "everybody."

Humans are social creatures and, as such, have always sought to conform to what others around them do. We see this with small children, who copy behaviors from others around them. But you can also see it in yourself; in a new environment, you might examine how others talk and interact to assess how you should behave. We all want to be considered "normal" within the community that we wish to belong to. One way in which we learn what acceptable behaviors are today is through digital communication.

In other words, digital media becomes our window to the street, a way for us to examine what is right and wrong in the eyes of others. Of course, this gets more complicated, because (1) there are millions of online spaces from which to learn, and (2) those whose voices get heard online are not actually everybody. Regarding the first point, this is easier once you select your community—in the case of the Jewish Orthodox discourse, there are limited online spaces in which these conversations happen. I have tried my best to select online sources in this book that represent "mainstream" Orthodoxy, so we can assume that users in these websites belong to and are searching for information regarding mainstream Jewish thoughts and behaviors.

The second issue is more difficult to unpack. If, on a question regarding premarital sexuality, the rabbi says "no way" and fourteen users also say "no way," one might be tempted to conclude that *everybody* (or most people) in Orthodox Judaism are against premarital sexuality. Maybe that isn't actually true, but the sense we get from these websites is for a majority position. This impacts how we would judge our own ideas and behaviors.

For example, the forums discussed in chapter 2, as can be seen from the multiple examples, are digital spaces were people try to make sense of the dating experience in a communal space. They use the community attributes and feelings to share personal stories of success and failure, of their hopes and fears, and of their real experiences. Through religious and emotional support, the users help each other process and progress with the clear goal in mind: to find their destined mate. The online community's help also works to solidify what is the ideal and correct gendered dating behavior. The digital, because it produces a discourse, as explained in chapter 1, because it reflects the "street" or your average community member, is a prime tool for normalization. In other words, in these digital religious spaces, the reader is exposed to what "everybody is thinking" and thus learns how they too should behave.

This normalization happens through repetition and peer regulation. The online discourse operates as a space for peer regulation, which works toward the enforcement of social norms. That is, whenever tension or resistance is present, for example, in the comment section, users are active in regulating those voices to fit with the opinion of the authority. In that way, traditional (or even fundamental) views are upheld not by the authority but by "everybody."

We can say that the online discourse operates like a public sphere, where various voices are heard. The openness and accessibility of the internet makes it "public"—all the sources discussed in this book are open sources, which any person can read, comment, and share. While most of the authors are leaders and rabbis representing traditional views, the interactive elements allow for users to react to "official" stances. And, unlike in previous public spheres in history, here, women utilize these digital media affordances to voice their disagreements, concerns, and experiences. Of course, users' input is always already tinted by the offline ideologies and experiences they are exposed to; for example, while users might resist how motherhood should be presented, they do not fully resist the importance of motherhood for the Jewish religious community.

It's important to note that offline and online sense-making go hand in hand. But the online provides a sphere where anonymity and multiplicity of sources can allow a user to be more experimental or "rude." One can try and stretch the norm so it can be renegotiated. Online, users can stretch and expand what they know, but at the same time, digital media can be a safe space to express what one feels because of features like anonymity. Trying to (re)own Jewish womanhood, some women use digital media to lend their voices to the discourse and shatter the ideal image of the fully devoted, never-tired, will-die-for-her-children Jewish mother. But who gets the final say in this public discourse? That is a question that is difficult to answer, but for now, it is safe to say that the longer Orthodox women use these digital media, the louder their voices will become. In that way, a new "everybody" can be found online—an everybody that includes previously silenced voices.

Chapter 4

Becoming a Mother

When my friends got married, I felt that I would lose them to motherhood—that's how I thought back then. Getting married has an immediate result, and that result was, as discussed in the previous chapter, procreation. As I'm writing this book, I'm pregnant with my first child, at the age of thirty-six. Like many women in the late twentieth and early twenty-first century, I was able and chose to "delay" motherhood. But for many religious women, regardless of religion or location, that is not a socially acceptable choice. Most of my liberal and modern religious friends had children (plural) before the age of thirty, and for many of them that was a source of joy and meaning and, at the same time, constraint and hard work.

The general Jewish religious social expectations are for women to become mothers. This can be seen in many ways: statistically, Pew research shows that Orthodox Jews have on average 4.1 children—compared with US Jews in general, who have 1.9 children on average.[1] My mother, for example, gave birth to her fifth kid in a hospital in Jerusalem where each week a woman gives birth to her fifteenth child. Sixteen percent of Jewish women in Israel give birth to their first child before the age of twenty-four.[2] Socially, religious Jewish communities in Israel and the United States also have communal resources to help with and encourage childbearing, such as free or price-reduced childcare and secondhand stores for maternity clothes, strollers, and so on. It is also not uncommon to see older children (say, eleven or twelve years old) taking care of younger siblings in these big families. In other words, socially and culturally, motherhood is encouraged and supported.

Like many women in the modern world, women in the religious sector try to "have it all"—family and career. To do so, women often select career paths that would allow them to focus on the house, like teaching or social work. In my religious upper school program, for example, many of the girls choose to be a teacher-soldier as a preparation for a path into a career in education. We also had regular discussions on how to balance career and family (even though none of the students had her own family or career) and learned how to deal with this and other "feminist" dilemmas. There are also religious women who are doctors or lawyers or who work in technology, higher education, or one of many other higher paying jobs. But from a young age, females are encouraged to put their future family in focus, to concentrate on getting married and becoming a mother. I remember in the religious high school that I attended, we did not have career days but spiritual growth programs that focused on the self and the women's role in society and in the Jewish family. The emphasis on motherhood began in high school, if not earlier.

In public lectures and programs, and in the general cultural "feeling," motherhood is depicted as the goal and the path to Jewish womanhood. This is also true online, where an array of online material by religious leaders—articles, videos, advice columns, podcasts, and recorded lectures—highlight the importance of parenthood. For example, each of the popular Jewish websites, Chabad, Aish, and Kipa, have sections dedicated to parenthood. However, the gap between the promise of motherhood and the reality of motherhood is voiced throughout the online discourse. On social media and in comment sections, users—especially women—push back. They share their struggles with parenting, ask for help, and debate the meaning of their sacrifices. This chapter explores how motherhood is framed and then reframed through the digital discourse.

Furthermore, this tension between the "official" narrative and the narratives found in the comment sections and on social media is used in this chapter to theorize the networked digital sphere as a public sphere. But it is not necessarily a rational discussion, where opinions are formed through expertise, but rather a more emotive discussion, where affective reasoning and personal experience frame the social norms. As discussed in previous chapters, neoliberal discursive strategies that focus on "choice," "empowerment," and "self" seem to be strongly present in this online Jewish discourse.[3] For example, in the previous chapter, many of the online sources focused on individual difficulties with sexuality rather than a systematic issue with rabbinical law concerning sexuality. In these previous chapters, we saw how the "participatory" elements of the online discourse—like the comment section—were used by people who accepted this type of self-regulation. In this chapter, however, we see how the digital public sphere allows for the public to raise questions, to raise their voice. This chapter presents a tension between the edited, official articles and videos that present a more ideal version of motherhood and the users, in forums, social media, or in the comment section, that question this ideal based on their real-life experiences. Like in the previous chapters, I offer three general perspectives: a more traditional perspective, which presents motherhood as a divine power; a more modern perspective, which tries to argue for a Jewish womanhood that is not defined through motherhood; and a middle ground, which sees motherhood as a sacrifice, but one worth having in order to achieve your spiritual goals.

Through these three perspectives, the digital discourse serves as a "public sphere" in that it is "a domain of social life where public opinion can be formed."[4] However, as discussed in the first chapters of this book, I argue that these online discussions go even further than forming public opinion—they serve as a mirror and a window: a way to understand ourselves, and to view the world. Thus, this push and pull between the "official" and "unofficial" descriptions of motherhood also informs individuals on what it means to be a Jewish mother.

The title of "Jewish mother" is burdened with history, culture, and complex contexts that span outside the realm of only the digital discourse. Therefore, the chapter begins with a brief survey of the cultural and religious attitudes toward motherhood. Then, we explore how those ideals are presented online, in three distinct perspectives: one that idealizes motherhood, one that discusses the hardships of motherhood but maintains its importance, and one that calls for a space for Jewish womanhood that is not focused on motherhood.

Jewish Attitudes Toward Motherhood

As stated earlier, building a *Jewish house*—starting a family—is a very important concept in Judaism in general and, specifically, motherhood is an important part of a Jewish woman's life. In this section, I provide a general overview of traditional Jewish attitudes toward parenting, but more specifically, toward motherhood. As early as Mishanic and Talmudic times (the second century CE), mothers were revered and held a special place in Jewish life and literature.[5] The Bible itself mentions that one must respect both parents—father and mother—and offers a few heroine mothers. The importance of these biblical and early canonical texts should not be overlooked—they serve as motivation for the Jewish communities to this day.[6] In their seminal edited book, *Mothers in the Jewish Cultural Imagination*, Marjorie Lehman, Jane Kanarek, and Simon Bronner dedicate various chapters to examine the importance these earlier texts play in the role of Jewish motherhood today and showcase that "images of the mother have been a hallmark of Jewish culture."[7]

Today, most Orthodox women become mothers at a relatively young age and have large families.[8] This is both a result of the general prohibition against the use of contraception (although today some rabbis in some cases do allow birth control pills) and of the ongoing communal and social drive toward motherhood, the constant expectation in Jewish and Israeli society to bear children.[9] As mentioned in the introduction, Judaism is a matrilineal religion/ethnicity, and as such, mothers play an important part in the Jewish family and peoplehood. After the Holocaust and especially in Israel, motherhood became a national mission, and many Jewish Orthodox women see it as their goal to help the nation of Israel grow.[10] For example, Jewish religious women are open to and active in various medical fertilization, for example, egg freezing, which is "now becoming naturalized as acceptable and desirable precisely because it cryopreserves Jewish motherhood, keeping reproductive options open for Jewish women."[11]

As such, motherhood takes on a prominent role in women's lives, even though from a purely Halachic perspective they are not obliged to have children. It is men who are obliged Halachically to have children through marriage (and not illegitimately) and to take care of their children—to feed them, find marriage partners for them, and take care of their futures. For example, fathers are charged to take special care of their male children—a father must circumcise his son, teach him Torah, and help train him in an occupation. However, throughout Jewish history, and in some contemporary Orthodox communities, as men spent most of the time out of the house (either working or learning Torah), the job of educating young children fell de facto on the mothers.[12] Furthermore, mothers are entrusted with educating their daughters with keeping a kosher household and preparing for a married life.[13] Jewish motherhood, therefore, includes all the expectations of modern motherhood (managing a household, cleaning, cooking, doing laundry, educating, helping with homework, nursing, and providing emotional support) and also includes specific religious Jewish elements (making sure the house is kosher, preparing for holidays, keeping Halacha, keeping family purity, and, usually, having many children). Institutional support and religious leaders' encouragement for big families further increase women's motivations toward motherhood.[14]

Like in other patriarchal traditions, the "Jewish Mother" was, and still is, very much an idealized symbol of self-sacrifice.[15] From biblical icons like Rachel Imeinu ("Our Mother Rachel"), who died while giving birth, to modern depictions of mothers during the Holocaust[16] and the trying times in the beginning of Israel,[17] Jewish mothers are asked to give sons to the nation, even at the cost of their own life. Even in the extreme conditions of the Holocaust, Jewish mothers did their best to be present for their children and protect them to the best of their ability.[18] And, as many scholars of early Zionism point to, mothers played a significant role in the construction of the State of Israel and many young women were called to become mothers for the future of the Jewish nation.[19] This demographic battle for the survival of Israel is present even in today's Israeli and Jewish culture.[20]

A Jewish woman's children (in some cases, especially the sons) are her pride, and, to a degree, the lens through which her own status is measured.[21] In contemporary United States and Israel, where most modern religious Jewish women both work and raise children, many times the child's well-being and success will trump the mother's professional and personal needs. A study from 1986 showed that "other things [being] the same, including other family income, Jewish woman have a lower labor supply than other women if there are young children in the house."[22] This, Barry Chiswick argues, supports the hypothesis that Jewish mothers invest more time in their children, even at the cost of their own careers.

Jewish mothers also carry, especially in the twentieth and twenty-first century USA, certain cultural concepts and stigmas. Jewish mothers are "nagging," they care too much for the well-being of their child, they guilt their children into submission, and they "love their children—to death!"[23] This image of the strong and always-present Jewish mother has made its way into becoming a well-known figure in various pop culture artifacts throughout American entertainment history.[24] The Jewish mother is hailed and criticized for being very involved in her children's education, career, and love life. In some ways, according to Joyce Antler, some of the behaviors of Jewish motherhood have become common among general contemporary parenthood, in which parents are more actively concerned about their children's success. Thus, Antler suggests, in many ways "we are all Jewish Mothers" today.[25] That being said, Jewish mothers, and especially religious Jewish mothers, face a specific set of expectations and attitudes. These expectations are communicated implicitly and explicitly in discussions within families, educational institutions, and in traditional texts. They are also presented and prescribed in various ways online. It is these online expectations—and the reactions to these expectations—that this chapter reviews and analyzes.

In this chapter, three types of sources are analyzed: social media and forums, online materials for "family" or "parenting," and online material that is more generally for women but which discusses motherhood. Social media and forums include some discussions from a popular Facebook group for Jewish women; a forum called Imamother for *frum* (religious) Jewish women; and a Kipa forum dedicated to parenthood. The second type of sources includes online material specific for parenting like Jewish parenting blogs and material from Chabad, Aish, and Kipa specifically dedicated to parenting. The last source, online material, like in the previous chapters, includes both official, edited articles and videos and the comment sections. In these comment sections and on social media, the negotiation of the tension between idealized motherhood and "real" motherhood is crystallized. For the first time in Jewish history, mothers' struggles are heard, shared and archived, and they become part of the religious discourse. Women use digital technology's affordances of anonymity and accessibility to congregate and create their own story of what it means to be a Jewish mother. And, when these experiences clash with the idealized mother prominent in Jewish discourse, a new, negotiated Jewish Mother is born—one that demands rights and appreciation. However, as we saw with dating and intimacy, even as the official, traditional narrative is negotiated via digital media, certain elements of it are reestablished, sometimes even with more zest and zeal. In the case of motherhood, it is clear both from the unofficial material (forums and social media) and the mainstream websites that the importance of motherhood as the main aspect of Jewish womanhood is upheld and even reproduced. With digital communication, as seen in the next section, motherhood is further normalized so that every action a mother makes is assessed through the online religious discourse.

Motherhood: The Underlining Ideal of Jewish Womanhood

Parenthood seems to be always present in religious online material targeted to women. Even when motherhood is not the explicit subject of discussion, it seems to be woven like a thread throughout many of the articles for women on the popular websites of Chabad, Aish, and Kipa. Within these websites, articles' titles and topics tend to be centered on womanhood and marriage, with headlines such as: "Don't Get Divorced," "The Role of Women in Judaism," "A Woman's Place in Torah," "Men, Women and Forgiveness," and "Lousy Body Image"—but these articles almost always implicitly discuss motherhood. The traditional perspective on motherhood, highlighted in this section, positions motherhood as the goal and natural path of womanhood, and, as such, it is always already present in discourse about gender and sex. It is the underlining assumption around all official discussions of dating, marriage, and intercourse. As discussed in the introduction of the book, Judaism is a matrilineal ethnicity, that is, only Jewish women can give birth to Jewish kids. While there are no Halachic rules concerning how to be a mother, and women are not even commanded to have children, motherhood is seen as very important in a woman's life in traditional Jewish culture.[26] All three websites—Chabad, Kipa, and Aish—as well as the other digital sources examined, seem to encourage and support motherhood and parenting as important Jewish values and, as seen from the analysis, seem to understand motherhood as a fulfillment of womanhood.

Motherhood is generally described in the online discourse that is traditional in a positive light. For example, reacting to the article "Men's Rights,"[27] one user comments, "Jewish men ARE sensitive and loving because the wonderful mothers that have taught them and raised them."[28] The importance of the mother as the center of the house and the one in charge of education has inspired some to even craft specific "journeys" for Jewish mothers—either metaphorically, through written material, or literal journeys, in the example of the organization MOMentum.[29] MOMentum is an organization that seeks to empower Jewish mothers by giving them the opportunity to engage with Jewish values through an eight-day journey to Israel. The organization's founding director, Lori Palatnik, who was dubbed "the mother of mothers in the Jewish Diaspora,"[30] was recently recognized by the State of Israel and given the high honor of lighting one of the six traditional beacons lit every Israeli Independence Day.[31] When interviewed about her work, she clearly explained that "this is an investment in the Jewish Mom. Why? Because she is the main influencer at home. If you invest in the mother, if you inspire her, she will awake the family, and they will awake the community."[32] For Palatnik, to invest in the mother does not mean a financial or structural investment, but rather, investing in her self-empowerment by teaching her the Jewish values of courage, peace and wholeness in the home, faithfulness and trust, and so on. Everywhere on the website, women are directed back to their families. For example, under the "taking action" tab, the description reads, "By setting personal goals, becoming role models to our children, and growing as leaders, we can make a difference for ourselves, our families, our communities, and the world."[33] Thus, through one's motherhood, one is invited to change the world.

Jewish mothers, while at times criticized for being too controlling,[34] are generally lauded as the spiritual hero and savior.[35] This attitude can also be seen in the websites of Chabad, Kipa, and Aish. According to most of the websites' authors, and some of the commenters, motherhood is the highest form of being one can aspire to. For example, the author of the Chabad article "No, I Am Not Satisfied with Women's Status in Judaism" reminds her reader that "by exempting women from time-bound mitzvot, Torah reminds us that essential to our relationship with God is the understanding *that building a Jewish family life is a priority* that can never be sidestepped."[36] The author goes on to explain that this is an important role that has a high value in Jewish life, a role that is uniquely reserved for women: "What I love about Torah Judaism is the central position given to children, who are our future. As a family-based religion, the ideal of raising children is considered most significant. It is a responsibility that is shared by both parents, but Torah realizes the unique talents, techniques, and intuition that women bring to the fore."[37] According to the author, Chana Weisberg, Judaism recognizes and cherishes childbearing and child raising. In Judaism, the family is given a place of respect—it is significant, and mothers are honored for their work. Furthermore, it seems that women are uniquely gifted to be mothers, as they have "talents, techniques, and intuition"—hinting at motherhood as a natural, essential element for women.

Motherhood is also the desire of many Jewish women, or so the articles on these websites suggest. For example, on Aish one can find articles about the internal call to freeze one's eggs if they haven't had kids before the age of thirty-seven "because the Jewish women knew, even in their darkest hour, a day would come when they would sing"[38]—meaning, she is still preparing to be a mother. There are many other articles discussing the joy of motherhood or how motherhood makes you a more successful woman (see, for example, an article on how being an Orthodox Jewish mother made the author a better CEO[39]). On Kipa, on the other hand, women write about choosing to be a "present mom" over a "working mom."[40] While the choices might be different in these articles, the underlying assumption is the same: for a religious Jewish woman, being a mother is a must.

This idea is emphasized so much so that, in a different Chabad article, it is argued that childbearing is what makes females into women: "Women [were] born with a womb and the ability to carry and bear a child, and men were not."[41] This highlights the ability to bear children as the essence of womanhood, as is crystallized in one of the supportive comments to this article: "G-d breathed into us that role of nurturer not only for our children but our husbands too—this is why a man leaves his family and cleaves to his wife. G-d is reminding his daughters to return to our husbands and take no worry in what the world would see as a move in the opposite direction for feminism; the world is calling us to the workplace but our G-d is calling us home!"⁴² According to this user and the general spirit of these articles, motherhood is given to women by God in order for them to accomplish and live out their inherent nature as nurturing and giving individuals. By sanctifying motherhood and making it holy, God-sent, this discourse gives meaning to motherhood that is beyond the communal and practical. It gives motherhood a spiritual meaning. This spiritual meaning is found not only in the official discourse written by community leaders and rabbis but also in some of the forums and social media content. One forum user in the Imamother forum even created a poll to examine if Jewish women believed that taking care of children is a spiritual activity, and the results are telling: 81 percent answered "definitely."

And what is it that makes caring for children spiritual? The forum users argue that the job itself is compared to other *mitzvoth* (commandments) and spiritual qualities. For example, changing diapers is teaching the baby to be clean; by dressing children, one is "emulating Hashem [God] who clothes the naked."⁴³ More generally, the work of motherhood is the action of *Chessed*, or mercy, compassion. As one woman puts it "We are doing *Chessed* all the time, and *Chessed* inside the home is on a *greater* level than outside the home."⁴⁴ Furthermore, according to some of the users on the thread, motherhood is their *tafkid*—their role in life, and fulling one's role, one's designation, is a high spiritual role in Jewish theology.

Other examples highlighting the spiritual meaning can be found in the popular blog and Facebook page JewishMOM, which collects a variety of sources and posts about Jewish motherhood. "Mothers are like the Sun,"⁴⁵ one post claims. On a Facebook post, one user shares that moms are "the ground upon which children grow."⁴⁶ In another post, a description of Jewish mothers as spiritual heroes reads, "Ongoing coping with difficulties and overcoming them, this is eternal heroism . . . [this is the quality of] JewishMOMs. When we remember all the things we JewishMOMs do on a daily basis that we (just between us) would rather not do. But we do them anyway. For our kids and for our husbands and, of course, for Hashem."⁴⁷ Here, some indication of the work of motherhood that women might rather not do is expressed. However, that work quickly becomes sacred work, actions done by Jewish women for the sake of not only their children and husbands but also God, *Hashem*. In this way, mothers' conditions or issues are overlooked and their sacrifice become a religious act. And, similar to comments in the official websites, here too users react positively to these types of messages, thanking the author and claiming that this is "very empowering, thank you."⁴⁸

But what happens when this spiritual, natural role includes hard labor, exhaustion, and disappointment? Using the participatory elements of digital media, women online voice the paradox of motherhood, how it is meaningful and not respected, wonderful and painful, fun and tedious. The next section examines how women negotiate this ideal image of Jewish motherhood by mixing religious ideology with modern perspectives and their real-life, personal experiences.

Motherhood: The Works

From a young age, children are taught to respect their parents in Jewish religious education. I remember how much it was pressed onto us as kids, the importance of being a respectful child. But I also recall that respect translated differently in relation to mother and father. For the father, we would respect him, by, for example, being quiet and speaking politely to him. I distinctly recall at elementary school, we were told that a way to respect our fathers was to never ever sit in their seat. Well, my father didn't have a traditional seat at the head of the table, so this was a problem for me. I wanted to prove (to my teachers, parents, myself) that I was a good and obedient daughter, and so I introduced my father to his new seat, and then religiously guarded (pun intended) it from my siblings, who thought this was a great new game. But when it came to respecting mothers, the tone was a bit different: we were told that we respect them by helping them around the house, helping them set the table or prepare the Sabbath meal. Respecting mothers meant landing a hand in the housework. While fathers deserved inherent respect, motherhood was all about the work.

My own mother, a mother of five and a successful filmmaker, used to tell me how much the work of motherhood is underappreciated. She would say something like "I love being a mother to my children, but I hate the work of motherhood." While her position totally made sense to me, even before I became a mother myself, it was a voice I rarely heard in Orthodox society. Most mothers looked tired, sure, but the mantra was "joy is children."

Online today, however, the narrative is a bit more complex. While the importance of motherhood is not easily decreased in online sources, women do use these digital tools to negotiate certain elements of motherhood and to raise their voices about the struggles related to motherhood. That is, not all users view motherhood as wonderful or spiritually meaningful. Quite a few of the users write—in their comments on the popular websites, in blogs, forums, social media or other online spaces—about the physical and mental work associated with motherhood. They wonder if that work is indeed spiritual and if it is really appreciated and respected as a Jewish religious "job," like being a cantor or having similar leadership or educational positions in the religious society.

Reacting to the mentioned poll about seeing childcaring as spiritual, one women comments, "My impression is that most women do not think that diapering, bathing, feeding and shopping for their children are spiritual activities."[49] She continues to ask, "What about this—I have read and heard that it is very important to get household help. So tell me, if you clean the house, it's spiritual. What about if the Polish or Mexican lady cleans your house. Is that spiritual for them? If you're too busy or distracted to think about your home being a miniature *mikdash* [Temple] and your work in the home as the *avoda of the kohanim* [priestly work], is what you do spiritual regardless? Or only if you have that intent?"[50] Other users active in this debate react to her questions by claiming that, yes, it is indeed only spiritual for Jews, or more accurately, for people who are dedicating this work for the well-being of other Jews, their Jewish education, and their ability to worship God (versus making money, for example). However, some of the users claim that you do not need intent—even if you are not experiencing your housework as spiritual, it is inherently so because it is *Chessed*, compassion. The original user reacts to this idea by writing that "washing the woodwork is not inherently a *mitzva*. It's a *mitzva* if you make it into one with your intent."[51] This user claims that, unlike acts like praying or eating *matza* in Passover, women are not commanded to do housework, but they *can* make it into a spiritual activity if they infuse it with religious meaning. Which, it seems, a few of these online texts try to convince women to do. Infusing housework with spiritual meaning is a way to negotiate and make sense of the work of motherhood; it deals with the realities of motherhood, often ignored by traditional texts, by adding a spiritual (neoliberal) layer, which is apparent in a several examples from the blogs and the websites. An author on Aish argues that staying home to care for children, cook, and clean is more important than going to the synagogue: "Women have not been 'assigned' the lesser work. Society has presumed that work to be lesser simply because it has traditionally been performed by women."[52] The author goes on to argue that the job of motherhood is the holier work; many of the women commenting on the article agree with her and thank her for sharing this "Truth." A few users do push back, asking questions like, "Shabbos [Shabbath] may be a day HE [the husband] can go off to shul and daven quietly without one child in need of attention ... so since mom is home doing exactly what she has been doing the other six days [taking care of children] . . . how is it a day of *menucha* [rest] for her???"⁵³ While these online discussion allow women to voice their frustrations about the work of motherhood, none of the users, or the author, seem to question this division of labor. Instead, many are happy to attribute a type of holiness to the labor associated with motherhood.

Another prime example can be found in the JewishMOM blog, when the blog author discusses in several articles the work of preparing for Passover, specifically the importance of cleaning for the holiday. According to Jewish law, in Passover, houses should be completely free of bread (or *Chametz*, leavened bread, to be exact), and this commandment becomes a rationale for a deep spring cleaning, one that usually takes two to three weeks, and includes not only the kitchen but the entire house—all the closets, bags, beds, and various rooms must be checked for *Chametz*. Women have nervous breakdowns and houses go into panic mode around that time because of the need to make sure that the house is "really" clean. This includes a lot of tedious housecleaning activities, like cleaning the cabinets, washing backpacks, cleaning and organizing the basement, and so on. Some women, like the blogger JewishMOM, try to elevate these activities in articles like "Why I Think Pesach Cleaning is Spiritual." In the article, the blogger writes:

> Cleaning for Passover is a *mitzvah*, which means that every moment you and I spend scraping grime out of our stoves or searching behind our children's bunk beds for well-hidden chocolate-covered wafers, we are performing *Hashem*'s [God's] exact will at that moment. [. . .] I also do other things to prepare spiritually for Passover—like listening to lots of classes (while I clean) about the deeper meaning of the holiday. But I still believe that my most meaningful spiritual preparation for the holiday is actually physically preparing for it—cleaning and organizing my home, shopping, cooking. Because sometimes the holiest act possible doesn't feel holy at all!⁵⁴

In short, in this blog post and in others, JewishMOM argues that the physical is the spiritual, and that by cleaning, women are preforming God's will. This argument does not address the lack of housework obligations for men (if it's so holy, should they not also take part?) nor does this argument examine the realities and histories of housecleaning. But this discourse, which spiritualizes housework, seems to hit home with users on her blog and elsewhere. Users comment by thanking her and by writing that they are encouraged by this type of thinking. Thus, it seems that this type of discourse, which spiritualizes the work of motherhood, is popular in online Jewish spaces and makes sense for many of those who take part in this online discourse.

But do others in the Jewish community see housework or motherhood as an act of religious importance? Do men, children, rabbis, and religious leaders really understand this work as *avodt chohanim* (priestly work) that should be respected and cherished? According to the online female users, especially those commenting and in social media, not always. For example, reacting to an article on the topic of the respect that should be given by wives to their husbands, one user resists by making the following argument: "Let me tell you. Men need to respect us women more. We are out working too. Its [sic] not just a man's world. I am a VERY DEDICATED mother to my kids. I drive from sport to sport, watching their games, taking them to their friends [sic] houses, etc. I do it all. I work, too."[55] Motherhood in this article is mostly presented in an ideal fashion, but the nitty-gritty aspects of it (such as housework, driving kids, etc.) are discussed in the comment section. The material and psychological aspects—the *work*—associated with motherhood are commented on by several women, but with different attitudes. Some, like the user above, see it as a reality and a sign of dedication, but one that deserves more respect and appreciation from men. The need for further respect is in comparison to the esteem other practices—like praying in the synagogue—receive in Judaism. In a different article, which mocks women's "constant complaining" about their rights, the author suggests that if women were obliged to go to the synagogue, they would complain about that too.[56] A discussion then takes place in the comment section about women's commitment to prayer—private or in the synagogue (or in a *minyan*, a prayer group). One of the users then asks, "Yes, times have changed since then, but women still do the lion share of household chores and child-rearing. Even if women were allowed to participate in a *minyan*, how many would actually do so? Most of us struggle to get our kids to school on time, go to work, cook dinner, and do a myriad of other things until bedtime. So where does this really leave women? Still somewhat underappreciated, because it's not about having the time to pray, but about counting as much as a man."[57] This user suggests that women still do most of the work associated with parenting. Indeed, the Jewish religious web sources seem to support her claims: most sources on parenting are written by women, for women. Even as they use words like "parenting," these website sections usually refer to "mothering," since women—mothers—are the ones burdened with most of the actions related to parenting. For example, educating the children is clearly a task that is in the mother's court, but does not belong solely to her—the father, rabbi, and school systems matter too. On the Kipa website there is a section for "parenting" and an insistence on parenthood being equal. So much so that one author encourages partners to "switch between the jobs and roles at home [...] the children will see the flexibility and the fact that no job belongs only to one gender."[58] Another example is from the Chabad webpage, which has a section for parenting that is separate from the "Jewish Woman" section. But some subsections, like "birth and parenting," appear both under the parenting tab and the Jewish Women tab. Examining the digital media—the website's organizational scheme—reveals underlined norms and attitudes toward motherhood. In the parenting section, for instance, most of the articles are written by male rabbis, but most of the comments and questions sent in are written by women, mothers. In one representative article from the parenting section, the commenters were fourteen females, seven males, and fifteen uncertain.[59] Another telling example is from the advice column in "parenting" where one user says, "Dear Tzippora, I want my husband to help me more with the kids."[60] Through the expert's answer, we learn that this comment "reflects a classic family struggle. Mom spends much more time with the kids, and begins to feel like she's the expert."[61] So while the fact that there is a parenting section on this website seems to hint toward an attitude of shared responsivity for child raising, the main focus is still on mothers.

The Aish website is also a perfect example. Under the section of "Family" the website suggests a few tabs, such as marriage, parenting, mom with a view, kosher recipes, and so on. There seems to be a distinction between "mom with a view," a section dedicated to mothers—therefore, women—and parenting, a section for both mothers and fathers. But a quick scroll in the articles in the parenting section reveals that they are, too, mostly written by women for women. Furthermore, the few articles written by men tend to deal with disciplinary issues (like "When Your Child is the Wicked Son" or "5 Ways to Stop Your Kids Getting Spoiled this Chanukah"). Similarly, in the Kipa forums for parents, most of the active users are females, mothers. Thus, as the suggested by the user above, in terms of online discourse too, "women still do the lion share of household chores and child-rearing."

The user also brings up another point in her comment—that mothers' work denies them religious leadership and participation, and that it is underappreciated. According to the user, in Orthodox Judaism women "do not count as much as men." The underappreciation of motherhood these users describe tells a different story than the "official" narrative offered by the authors of the articles in this online discourse. There seems to be a contradiction between the articles, in which motherhood receives many praises, and their comments, which describe the burden of motherhood (driving children, housework, etc.) and the underappreciating of motherhood. It is more than likely, however, that while the articles might represent some ideal position, in reality, many Jewish mothers are probably not well respected by their husbands, children, or community. They might receive praise at the dinner table but not monetary compensation or "real" respect. Compare the duty of a father praying at the synagogue and the reality of a mother clothing the children. No one would say, "Don't bother her now, she is doing the important act of keeping her children clean and well dressed." That is, the position of motherhood many times becomes "natural," "hidden," or simply taken for granted. At the same time, religious obligations such as studying Torah and going to the synagogue—traditionally done by men and not women—are seen as holy commitments, actions for which one receives honor from both the community and God. For example, in a parenting forum on Kipa, users share their High Holidays experiences.[62] Almost all the women stayed home and could not participate in prayer. Some of the women lament this and say they feel like they are missing out. Others try to offer advice and reinforcement about the importance of staying home with young children, for example: "What helped me in these years [of having young children] was to sing the *Niggunim* [liturgical songs] of the High Holidays at home. It got me and the mood, and taught the kids indirectly. This year my son in in third grade and he sat next to his father and sang a lot of the parts, and I think that's partially because of the preparation I did when he was young."[63] Similarly, many of the other women in the forum see their absence from the synagogue as an important opportunity to educate their young children. But they also share the frustration that comes with that, the feeling of missing out on spiritual or religious obligations—the feeling of being left out. As one woman clearly writes, "It's not like being partners in prayer. [. . .] The important thing is prayer itself."[64] Another users shares, "First year without going to any of the prayers . . . so somehow I feel like it wasn't really *Rosh Hashanah* and there is the feeling of missing the prayer, but it's OK, every stage in life has its beauty."[65] As can be seen in these forums, mothers use these online sources to makes sense of what the work of motherhood means—religiously, spiritually, and materially.

Using online sources, mothers begin to ask for this respect, or at least for a narrative that shows the complexities of their realities. They mix the traditional approach to motherhood by still positioning it as holy, but negotiate it by voicing their frustrations, mostly anonymously. They reiterate my own mother's position, which recognized the hardship of motherhood. But they do not question it or explicitly work discursively to challenge this system. In the next section, we'll see a more explicit attack on the position of motherhood as the goal of Jewish womanhood. Specifically, the next section examines nonmothers, who use the online discourse to wonder about the place of childless women in Judaism. While mothers might not be as respected as they should, the fate of nonmothers, discussed in the following section, is even grimmer, as they exist in the liminal space between Jewish womanhood and motherhood.

Nonmothers and the Goal of Jewish Womanhood

My sister, now thirty-six, does not want to have children (at least right now). While she is no longer Orthodox, she grew up in this environment and still lives in Israel, where most women are mothers at that age. She constantly feels the pressure to become a mother from the society around her and, at times, even feels inadequate or unvalidated in her choice. She is not alone. The online discourse, anonymous and easily accessible, allows users to ask about the value of women who are not mothers—either by choice or not by choice. This conversation is present throughout the online sources: in the religious websites, on social media, and in the blogs. These discussions tend to highlight the importance of being a mother—and what is lost when that does not happen.

A clear communicator for the need to become a mother is that on two of the mainstream websites—Chabad and Kipa—there are subsections dedicated solely to fertility. Aish also has a lot of content related to fertility; a search on their website for the word "fertility" brings back 324 results. Some religious traditions—for example, some branches of Evangelicals or Catholics—are suspicious of fertility treatments because they "intervene in God's plans" or are in some other way considered immoral.[66] But for Judaism, and Orthodox Judaism too, fertility treatments are a way to uphold the first commandment given to Adam and Eve: "Be fruitful and multiply."[67] There are some concerns for Orthodox Jews—a preference not to use donor sperm, for example. But even with these concerns in mind, it seems that (religious and secular) Jewish women by and large do not avoid fertility treatments, with Israel being one of the leading country in the world for IVF (in vitro fertilization) births and various fertility treatment centers creating and caring about their Orthodox Jewish clientele.[68] More importantly for the purposes of this book, fertility seems to be a central issue when women's health and parenthood are discussed online. In Kipa's online articles and forums, which are mostly populated by women sharing their pains, concerns, and hopes, motherhood is clearly the goal. One heartbreaking example is from a personal article written about the hardships of infertility, in which the author writes, "I try to act like a good Jew. I try to connect to God, and I try to help others connect to God. I feel like a good Jew. But I don't feel like a good woman. I have not done what women do: bear children."[69] As can be seen from this example, in these online spaces, the pain of those who want to be mothers is expressed. And this pain is related not only to their personal disappointment but also to their relationship to God, religion, the community, and the self. Like this author, they feel that they are failing in doing what makes them a Jewish woman: becoming a mother. Even the blog JewishMOM—an online blog space clearly dedicated to motherhood—features stories of childless women, but always with the assumption that these women want to become mothers. These include stories of women who prayed for children (like the Miracle-Working Washerwoman[70]) and heartbreaking stories of women who lost their children or who cannot have children. One striking example really showcases the strong association between having children and being a woman. Here is an excerpt from an anonymous letter sent to the webmaster of JewishMOM, by a woman who is mourning the fact that she will not have children: "I am writing anonymously because I am someone whom it is difficult to look at, somebody bad. A woman who has not fulfilled her mission in life. A childless single woman who is Israeli, and furthermore, religious is *muktseh*, set apart out of disgust. I am someone who has something wrong with her."[71] She continues to write that as a forty-one-year-old unmarried women, her chances of having children are null. And that even though she dated for twenty years, she couldn't find her soulmate. So now, she is mourning the loss of her unborn children, and, as the text reads, her failure to fulfill her mission as a woman. In the comment section, other women reflect on her pain and the part society might play in how she feels about herself. Many of them ask what they can do to alleviate her pain. They suggest praying, being kinder, more actively engaging in matchmaking so that no woman is left unmarried, and "maybe be more sensitive about what we say in the presence of other people."[72] In all the various responses, compassion to nonmothers is clearly expressed, and these responses, along with the letter, crystallize the underlying assumption that being a Jewish woman means becoming a mother.

In light of this assumption, what is the fate of Jewish women who are not mothers? In an article titled "A Feminist Quest for a Place in Jewish Life," the author Donna Halper remembers her correspondence with the Chabad Rabbi Menachem Mendel Schneerson. She reached out to him many years ago. Even though she was not Orthodox she sought his advice about the place for a feminist, childless woman in Judaism. He sent her a letter back, and now, years after, she recalls this correspondence: "He understood that I was seeking some guidance as to what *mitzvah* a childless woman is supposed to perform, and I thought that his response was both beautifully expressed and very, very compassionate: There is a role for every woman, whether a mother or not, in Judaism."[73] While the Rebbe's answer does seem to indicate acceptance of childless women, he does not, in his letter, specify any *mitzvah*, roles, or practices they should perform.[74] This is noted by some of the users. One comment asks, "So what were the *Mitzvahs* that childless women could do? Teach? Influence? So they have no family, children, or grandchildren. Then again they are to teach others children and influence them? Seems barren to me. Shabbot without a family, isn't Shabbot. No family to be with or get ready by sundown? So to me life within Orthodoxy for the childless is still very hard."[75] Another comment reads, "Oy vey!! In this article, the author's attitude and the Rebbe's letter, as well as in the comments, there is completely missing ANY understanding of the deep, devastating pain the infertile woman feels!! I was not moved by this article as I have nothing in common with this author—she was untouched by being childless. My experience has been that the Orthodox community simply has no familiarity with or understanding of infertility. So disappointing. You are leaving a whole group of women (and men) without any spiritual comfort or guidance."[76] Both these users, along with other commenters, feel that for them, it is very hard to be a woman who is not a mother—for whatever reason—in the Orthodox community. It is not only a question of your religious belonging (which *mitzvah* they should perform) but more of a concern for the daily life that, in Jewish communities, centers on the family. What is a childless woman (or man) to do in the weekly Shabbat or the multiple holidays each year, all of which are meant to be celebrated with one's family? For an infertile woman who wants to have children, like the second user cited above, this can be a devastating experience as your personal pain is overlooked and made worse by a child-focused society. As the user highlights, "The Orthodox community simply has no familiarity with or understanding of infertility." And, regardless of your ability to have children or not, it is life without family in a family-oriented world, as the first user points out, so no matter how many other children you teach, as a woman (and probably as a man too), to have no children of your own, no family, makes life in the Orthodox community very difficult.

These experiences of the Orthodox community not being a welcoming place for childless women are echoed in other articles in Chabad, Aish, and Kipa. For example, Kipa published an article on a few religious couples who, like my sister and her husband, choose not to have children.[77] This was presented as shocking and abnormal. Many of the users reacting to the article question the prevalence, stating things like, "You've taken two bizarre girls . . . and made it into a phenomenon."[78] Other users vocally disregard them, saying, "Every Jewish person has a duty to have children,"[79] and "This is unhealthy behavior."[80] While four users' comments do seem to accept this position of not having children, the other twenty-three comments strongly resist, meaning 86 percent of these user participating in the online discourse resist the phenomenon of childless couples.

Reflection on the choice to not have children is mostly focused on women. These women are seen as opposing their predetermined role of motherhood, and thus losing the meaning of their womanhood. This strong association between woman and mother is challenging for childless women but also for women who see themselves as more than mothers. For example, this user reacts to the article "The Role of Women in Judaism," saying:

> Subject: No Meaning
> I was interested to see that it is not *halachically* required for a woman to marry or have children. *This article has nothing to say to such women, since it defines womanhood strictly in relation to marriage and children.* Furthermore, for those women who do choose to marry and have children, childbearing, child-rearing and menstruation take up less than half of a woman's life. *The article identifies no religious meaning for the other 40 years?*[81]

This question about meaning outside of motherhood is brought up in other users' comments. One such comment reads, "I think it is time for the Chassidic world to recognize that women are in this world not just to have babies and raise families."[82] Furthermore, these women are actively asking and seeking meaning that is outside motherhood: "Maybe all who read this post will disagree! But, there are some jewish [sic] women who may not feel like they are mentally, emotionally, or physically capable of having children. What about the passion to learn *torah* [sic], that these women have, why can't this chassid [sic] community foster that? It hurts to want to be more observant and find that the only way I can join a jewish [sic] community is not by studying *torah* [sic], but by having babies."[83] The roles of women outside of motherhood are further described in other users' comments. While some feel ostracized by being childless, others do try to argue for a space for women without children in Judaism. One user, for example, brings up the need to express for women merit not via marriage or childbearing; she suggests an answer for these unmarried, childless, women: "My sister is unmarried and we are very close. She leads a very fulfilling life [. . .] and she's very loving and giving to everyone, so her contribution is great. There are many ways to be in this world. The union of communion is also what we find in the unity of being part of community, married, or not. [. . .] Many women are mentors to others and do shine, as one single candle lights the night."[84] According to this user, there are other ways to be a woman aside from marriage and motherhood—through mentorship, loving, and giving. While not contradicting the essence of the article she is commenting on, which argues that women's nature is internal and is focused on giving, this user suggests other ways of giving outside of having your own family. She does not suggest leadership, but she does allow for mentorship. Some users are even more explicit in rejecting this ideal traditional Jewish woman who is a dedicated mother. Their resistance is voiced in various ways; one user writes, "While I enjoyed reading this article one question remains unanswered. I am an unmarried woman without children and living alone (not by choice!), were does this leave me? Living in a large international, intercultural, and interreligious country (Holland) I feel I need something visual to remind myself of my Jewish identity, and I very much wish for something like *tzitzit* or a veil. Anybody know what I mean??"[85] Another user comments, "Wow well i'm [*sic*] so glad that my existence in this world is to make sure that my husband is doing everything. Great. As if I don't have enough to worry about just with myself. thank you Chabad for another wonderfully sexist article where i [*sic*] am once again relegated to the kitchen and to motherhood. g-d forbid a woman should want more than that."[86] The first comment represents users who might agree with the message in principle, but their personal experience contradicts these ideals. In the case of this user, she is unmarried and does not have children, and is thus unable to be a wife or mother. As a result, she is seeking other ways to *be* a Jewish woman—she suggests a ritual dress. The second commenter is much more aggressive in their resistance. They see the article as "sexist" and are angered by the fact that it renders women only as wives and mothers: "I am once again relegated to the kitchen and to motherhood."[87] The use of the expression "g-d" instead of God or god in the comment suggests that the writer is a religious person (since religious Jews avoid writing the name of God). That is to say, this is likely not a case of an internet troll or a person external to the community but rather is a person who is within the community and takes part of the communal online discourse—as can also be seen from their religious language and from the language of familiarity "thank you Chabad for another wonderfully sexist article." The insider capable of criticism is important to the making of an online discourse—the negotiation that takes place on these websites is not only with (or against) the modern, secular world but also within the various religious interpretations and practices.

In these examples, Jewish women voice their pain: how they feel they have no space in the Orthodox Jewish community without raising a family. They use digital media to express this loneliness and what they feel as a lack of belonging. They push against the traditional narratives and seek new meanings that relate to them as people, not mothers. This third perspective takes on modern concepts of individualism and feminism to argue for the worth of a human life outside of their communal role as mothers. They seek a modern way to be a Jewish woman, one that has to do with religious leadership or ritual and not with home-bound duties. Thus, there seems to be a gap between what these users describe as their experiences—both as mothers and as nonmothers—and the picture portrayed in the "official" articles. Article authors suggest that motherhood is holy and has a spiritual meaning and that, at the same time, Jewish women who are not mothers also have a role to play in the shaping of the community. However, the users tell a different story: they feel that motherhood is underappreciated and that nonmothers have no "home" nor role to play in these communities.

Summary

In this online discourse, it seems that motherhood plays a pivotal role in defining Jewish womanhood. The role of motherhood goes hand in hand with the understanding of a woman as internal and giving, a nurturing creature in her essence. Motherhood is not only expected of women but is redefined in this online discourse as spiritually meaningful—a "'call from G-d' to 'return home,'" as one user comments. The importance placed on motherhood is present throughout the various online texts: in articles, videos, blogs, forums, and social media. Mothers in this idealized discourse are the "sun" and the "ground" from which Jewish children nourish. Mothers are not only the ones who bare children, and thus continue the existence of the Jewish nation, but they also educate, protect, and raise children—making them the heroes and saviors of Judaism. Mothers' work—the mundane aspects of cleaning, cooking, bathing, and so on—is elevated and compared to the work of priests in

God's Temple. And those who cannot become mothers mourn not only their unborn children but also the loss of their own identity as a Jewish woman. Numerous articles highlight how Judaism honors mothers, and one article even lists five specific ways: in stories about heroic mothers, by singing "Woman of Valor," through the commandment to "respect Thy Mother," honoring parents after their death, and by seeing them as partners with God.[88] As the author writes, "In Jewish thought, motherhood isn't only raising a child; it's being partners with the Divine." But one must wonder if similar articles about the ways Judaism respects rabbis exist; in other words, does the fact we need to write it mean it is not a common practice?

Indeed, examining the "other part" of this discourse—the users' comments and reactions to various posts and stories—showcases that respect is not always the Jewish mother's experience. Users bring up stories of frustration, exhaustion, feelings of emptiness and lack of recognition from their general environment. For example, reacting to idealized stories of motherhood, women call out that "men need to respect us!" and simply that they feel overwhelmed by the amount of work motherhood entails. Using online forums, women survey themselves about the spiritual value of motherhood, and debate how the work of motherhood—the cleaning, feeding, driving—fits with their spiritual goals. Childless women use these online platforms to raise their voice and ask, "What about us? What is our role as a Jewish woman?" The interactive aspect of the digital plays a part in the negotiation of motherhood, as women throughout these texts challenge both the way mothers are treated and the association between motherhood and womanhood. As one of the users points out, "Being a mother is not all that I was, I am more than a mother, more than my career, more than my hobbies, I am a collection of all those things, including daughter and friend."[89]

This is the power of online discourse—to bring together various voices within the same community or with a shared goal in order to make sense of a social norm or phenomenon. When online discourse becomes a digital public sphere, it, ideally, allows for a dialectic tension that should bring about understanding and shared meaning. Through the tension between the ideal and the lived experiences, users can have a more open discussion about motherhood. In that sense, the internet serves as a platform for online discourse that can then reshape the attitudes and norms surrounding Jewish motherhood. In the next chapter, we will see how similar digital tools and discursive strategies are used to negotiate feminism and the meaning of being a Jewish woman in modernity.

INTERLUDE 3

Breaking Mirrors
Using the Internet for Resistance

Much of this book highlights the ways in which traditional power structures operate in online discussion—as becomes clear in the conclusion. But, as you probably already noticed, there is a lot of space for resistance, for the voicing of divergent opinions, throughout the content explored in the book. This section examines the ways in which internet technologies allow, and even encourage, the breaking of hierarchies.

Previous research on resistance online has highlighted the power digital media afford to the public in resisting existing systems of power.[1] The most renown example of the power of social media in mobilizing movement is the "Arab Spring"—in which, it is argued, social media played a pivotal role in combating dictatorships. Inspired by the Arab Spring, the Occupy movement also utilized social media to be "everywhere."[2] These movements used what Innocent Chiluwa describes as "sociolinguistic issues such as virtual community, identity, language variations and social interaction."[3]

In other words, digital media, and especially social media, allowed voices of resistance to connect with each other, plan in safety, help each other, and create impactful media artifacts. Through using social media, people were able to create communities and identities around activist issues, thus strengthening these movements and enabling them to have a stronger presence off- and online. Social media's focus on spreadability[4] and connectivity[5] is exactly how these movements of resistance—like the Arab Spring, #BlackLivesMatter, or #MeToo—were able to exist and thrive. Furthermore, these movements of resistance rely heavily on the "logic of networks"[6] in which both communication and aggregation play important roles. According to Jeffery Juris, the logic of networks "entailed a set of embodied social and cultural dispositions shaped by informational capitalism that oriented actors toward

(1) building horizontal ties and connections among diverse, autonomous elements (e.g., movements, organizations, groups, etc.); (2) the free and open circulation of information; (3) collaboration via decentralized coordination and directly democratic decision-making; and (4) self-directed networking." The logic of networks thus builds on individuals who have various weak ties, who then make self-directed decisions to join a network based on diverse and open circulation of information within that network, which allows for collaboration. Digital media can be easily used—and has been used—for such purposes, through comments, listservs, direct messages, forums, and more. This type of use of digital media for resistance has also been employed by feminists, who generally use digital media through postfeminist lenses that build on networking, individualism, choice, and agency.[7]

Interestingly, when it comes to studying various forms of online *religious* resistance, there is less research to be found. Some studies have highlighted how online spaces can be used to challenge traditional religious authority—what Pauline Cheong has referred to as "the logic of disjuncture and displacement."[8] For example, when religious individuals turn to the internet to learn about theological issues instead of going to their local religious leader, they avoid these religious "gatekeepers" and thus, at least implicitly, resist their authority. Religious digital creatives, forum moderators, or website editors become, at times, de facto religious leaders—even if their official status is that of lay people. In other words, previous studies have shown that digital media technologies have, to an extent, dismantled traditional religious hierarchy and allow for a flatter structure of religious power.

Perhaps unsurprisingly, much of the interest in online religious resistance is tied to issues of gender and sexuality.[9] Kristin Peterson, in her book on the digital activism of religious feminists, has pointed out that "one of the primary ways in which digital media has been essential for feminist activism within religious traditions has been in providing creative spaces."[10] Online creative spaces and satire[11] have been used by women and queer individuals, traditionally marginalized voices in religions, to resist and bend norms. But more often than not, these tactics are used in marginal spaces—in the periphery of the religious internet. In this book, we examine the mainstream online spaces of a religious community—so what does resistance look like there? What digital tools and tactics are used?

You can find various examples throughout this book for resistance, but here, since we are focusing on tools, I want to highlight three aspects of digital religious resistance: *anonymity, communal negotiations,* and *(inadvertent) religious innovation*. Anonymity allows for explicit opposition to traditional norms—we saw this in the case of the users voicing disagreement in the comment sections of mainstream articles. In the chapter on motherhood, for example, users explicitly resisted prescribed role of women as mother by posting statements like "This article has nothing to say to such women [unmarried or without children], since it defines womanhood strictly in relation to marriage and children."[12] This kind of anonymous comment explicitly rejects the article's claims and resists gendered norms in Judaism.

Communal negotiations, on the other hand, are more complex. They tend to happen in forums where users form relationships and even friendships with each other. While these forums still allow for anonymity because users return and have continuous interactions, they work together to make sense of norms. For example, in chapter 2, we saw how users of Lo Kala Derchenu were trying to make sense of gender norms in dating. Last, some resistance seems to happen through various innovation, which might be happening inadvertently. The best example for this is the video series on "kosher sex" created by the Yahel Center and posted on the Kipa website (discussed in chapter 3). These videos were innovative in several ways: the format (video content); the content (open discussion of sexuality); and the authority (women as speakers). However, the resistance—at least from the website editors' perspectives—might have been inadvertent. They might have thought they were putting out some "juicy" content—but were they ready to take part in and support new norms in regard to Jewish sexuality? Because digital media encourage interaction, web editors might be more inclined to post material that will drive user participation and thus publish content that is innovative, that pushes the boundaries of norms. In this way, religious resistance online can happen through innovative content.

We see through the examples in this book that resistance within mainstream religious online communication is a bit different from other forms of online resistance. It is done not through creating creative spaces or building networked communities of like-minded activists. It is done from *within* the community by utilizing online affordances like anonymity, communal negotiations, and innovative content. It is done, in other words, by participating in the online discourse of the community, by partaking in the "push and pull," the internal negotiation of gender and sexual norms.

Chapter 5

Dealing with Feminism

From a young age I knew I was a feminist. My first encounter with gender constructs (that I can recall) was in kindergarten, were I was mocked by the other kids because I was coloring with "boys' colors." My mother was a painter at the time, and I was quite educated about warm versus cold colors, and I knew there are no gender-specific colors, but no matter what reason I used, the kids were convinced that yellow was a masculine color and I could not use it. This is where I started to suspect that there is something terribly wrong with the distinctions made between boys and girls. I was about four years old.

My next (feminist) trauma was when entering the first grade. All my friends up to that point were boys, but in the religious school I was sent to, like most religious schools in Jewish Orthodox society, classes were segregated based on gender. In a split second, I was separated from my friends, and left alone in a classroom full of kids (girls) I felt I had nothing in common with. My family moved a lot, so the next few schools I went to were not gender-segregated, and I quickly made new friends—most of whom were boys. However, in the religious educational system, middle and high schools are always segregated, so by the time I was eleven I was back to being surrounded by girls. Of course, as I grew older, I made friends with girls—usually the nerds, weirdos, and outsiders like me. My friends in middle school loved and mocked my feminist sensitivities, and even wrote a song about how you should not say certain words around me or I would go into a tantrum about feminism. I was a good student and generally didn't cause a lot of trouble, except for constantly pushing back against gendered ideas in the classroom or in any special lecture on these topics.

I learned feminism at home, from both my parents, and I brought it with me to school. In the Orthodox religious system in Israel, gender plays into education in various ways: not only are the schools segregated but the material is different: boys learn Talmud and Halachic text, they learn how to think and argue like a rabbi; girls learn some Torah stories, basic *Mishna*, maybe Jewish philosophy, and home economics. They receive additional religious education in the form of inspirational speakers giving lectures on topics like modesty, relationships, devotion to God, and what it means to be a Jewish woman. In these classes and lectures, the message is given both implicitly and explicitly: your role as a religious woman is to serve, not lead—internal, at home, mother, and wife. The difference between what educational content boys and girls receive, however, is limited mostly to the religious sphere. Other areas of study, like math, English, and biology, are more equally present in both schooling systems. (This is true for Orthodox schools. In ultra-Orthodox schools, there may only be religious content taught.) There are still some discrepancies; for example, most female religious high schools do not offer topics like engineering or computer science, maybe because excelling in these areas might lead girls to be recruited to the Israel Defense Forces (IDF), which is something most religious families in Israel want to avoid. While members of the ultra-Orthodox communities in Israel avoid the IDF altogether, for the National Religious stream, only girls are discouraged from joining the IDF. There are many reasons for that, but we'll get to that later.

So, back to school. You can imagine that this young, homegrown feminist was not very happy with the educational messages listed above. But mostly, I had a passion for studying, and I saw—as many Jewish men and women do—studying religious texts as my religious obligation. And so, while I was a good student in most classes, I was a very rebellious student in *religious* classes. I was sent to the teacher, the head teacher, and the principal more than once for speaking up on these topics. I was told that it's very nice I have this passion, but it should be redirected toward my obligations as a woman. It didn't always end that way, though. One brave principal took me up on my offer and said that if I could find ten more girls interested in studying Talmud after school hours, he (the principals of these institutions are usually males) would personally teach us. Maybe he didn't believe that I would find others, or maybe he didn't think we would be willing to stay in school after hours to study more. But sure enough, we did, and he kept his side of the deal, and we started a small Talmud class in that school, that mostly focused on stories, not legal elements, from the Talmud.

My experiences up to that point in my life was a strong dichotomy between religious institutions and feminism. In school and at the synagogue, women were told to take the back seat, sometimes quite literally. I believed that this could change and from a young age worked—together with my father, who was teaching me Talmud at the time—to create spaces for women to study and lead. When we moved to Jerusalem, I found that the communities there were much more open to these ideas. I was able to give sermons in our local synagogue and was now graduating from a liberal religious (non-Orthodox) high school, where young men and women studied Talmud together. But the most powerful experience was when I was able to join Midreshet Bruriah, a religious one-year upper school for girls that offers full, "male-like" Talmudic studies, and encourages and helps girls join the IDF.

Midreshet Bruriah (also known as Lindenbaum Seminary), named after the Talmudic sage Bruriah (the only female to participate in the legal discussions in the Talmud), was a unique place in the National Religious Orthodox society. It offers a one-year after-graduation education, including room, food, and a full program. This school does two things that are outside the norm in the Orthodox communities: allow girls to study Talmud and encourage them to go to the IDF. For Orthodox feminists, this was *the* place. But even girls who did not consider themselves feminists joined Bruriah, seeking to deepen their understanding of Judaism and to serve their country in a meaningful way. Many of the girls who went to Bruriah didn't want to become leaders—they wanted to become teachers and people who support their community. And Bruriah helped them become soldier-teachers, which would assist in their future professions. However, as one of the main donors said in her speech to us, "Here, feminism is the norm." For the first time in my religious upbringing, I felt I had a home, and that my aspirations for a world where Orthodoxy and feminism are combined were indeed achievable. But I found out as the year progressed that there are still boundaries. While I was a feminist growing up, there were a lot of things even I didn't consider, like leading prayer, reading from the Torah during service, or putting on *Tefillin* (Phylacteries). But a few other girls, a small group of us who quickly became friends, were interested in these activities. One morning a friend of mine was "caught" putting on *Tefillin* in a public space—the study hall. She was called in for a talk, asked to keep these types of activities private, and all of us had a special session on the history, legality, and social norms surrounding *Tefillin*. We were told, I specifically remember, that the Orthodox community is not prepared for women wearing *Tefillin*, not prepared for female rabbis. And if you want to create change you have to work from *inside* the community, not the outside. So even here—in the nexus of religious feminism, I was friends with the weirdos and outsiders.

It became clear to me that the tension between feminism and religion is not easily solved, and these experiences helped me become the woman I am today. They constructed my understanding of feminism and my understanding of myself. I was not able to do this journey with the aid of the internet, but for many religious women today, the internet plays a pivotal role in navigating these complexities. This chapter thus explores how digital media is used in the process of the construction of the self as a religious woman in the twenty-first century. For me growing up in the '80s and '90s, my family, friends, and educational systems were the places in which I learned who I was and constantly reconstructed that. Today however, much of my identity is explored, learned, constructed, and framed through digital media, from my profile picture on social media to sources of information on how to write academic books or breastfeed. Similarly, the texts analyzed in this chapter showcase how Jewish women use these online sources to explore and express their identity. Through articles, comments, information from organizations, and social media, Jewish women use screens as a mirror to see—what does it mean to be a Jewish woman?

We see in this chapter how feminism, as the social movement, the call for gender equality, or even just a signifier of modernism and secularism, plays a major role in the online discussion of gender norms and identity. The analysis in this chapter examines the ways in which feminism is understood and used by online authors and users. Like in previous chapters, feminism in this discourse is discussed in three ways: it is either negated (traditional), redefined (mixed/neoliberal), or negotiated (modern). In some of the articles, it is framed as a destructive and dangerous force; in some, it is an ideology that Judaism needs to conform to; and in others, authors and users promote their own specific kind of feminism, a religious Jewish feminism.

In this chapter, data is analyzed from the same three websites examined throughout the book (Chabad, Aish, and Kipa), along with related organizations' websites and some social media sources. I mostly use sources that explicitly deal with feminism, but even in those articles that discuss modesty, dating, or motherhood, feminism is mentioned in the comment section. Some of these comments were analyzed in this chapter as well. In short, texts that either explicitly or implicitly deal with feminism were brought into consideration here. After a brief review of the history of feminism and Judaism, the chapter is divided into three sections, each discussing an approach to feminism found online: negating, redefining, and negotiating.

In each section, we also see how digital media's focus on identity plays a significant role.

Judaism and Feminism: A Complicated History

In some ways, it can be argued that Judaism has always had a space for women. From the early days of the Torah, the Matriarchs were featured alongside the Patriarchs. In the *Mishna*, women had specific commandments special to them. However, as becomes clear in this section, the space crafted for women was usually internal—inside the home, as a mother and wife. As mentioned in the introduction to this book, Jewish religious discourse concerning gender and sexuality is mostly concerned with separating the domestic (female) and the public (male). This discourse takes place and derives its power through the Halachic (legal) discourse. As a result, the main issue concerning Jewish feminism is how to combine Orthodox Jewish life, which is based on Halacha, with feminist ideas. This can also be seen in the feminist impact on legal or Halachic aspects in Israel and in the United States.[1] As made clear by the prominent feminist Jewish scholar Rachel Adler: "Whether gender justice is possible within *Halacha* and whether a feminist Judaism requires a *Halacha* at all are foundational questions for feminist Jewish theology that have no parallel in Christian feminist theology. [...] Appropriating the terms and method of *Halacha* itself, many feminists concluded, drew them into a game they could not win [...] *Halacha* became the feminists' elephant in the living room."[2] To deal with this elephant, some Jewish feminists outright reject Halacha. Furthermore, several important leaders in the feminist movement—especially in second wave feminism—are secular Jewish women, from Betty Friedman to Ruth Bader Ginsburg. But from an Orthodox perspective, it is not possible to separate Halacha from Jewish life. Therefore, Orthodoxy has to negotiate both feminism and Halacha.

While early reports of women who could be considered Jewish feminist can be found (the biblical figures of Tamar, Esther, or Devora; the Talmudic figure of Bruriah; Rashi's daughters; and more), Jewish feminism as a movement is usually tracked back to the 1970s with roots in the United States. There were, to varying degrees, religious Jewish feminists writing and working before and in other areas of the world; but as a movement, it is convenient to point to that time and place.[3] Early Jewish religious feminists were mostly concerned with the incorporation of women in prayer spaces; religious leadership; and Halacha by and large.[4] In the early 1970s, Rachel Adler published what would become a canonic article for Jewish feminism, aptly titled "The

Jew Who Wasn't There: Halacha and the Jewish Woman."[5] Other women were concerned with feminizing God, finding religious female role models, or even exploring possibilities of gender-bending with Jewish texts.[6] Others yet were concerned not necessarily with religious leadership roles for women, but with ensuring that Halachic rules protected women's rights (for example, sexual safety and the possibility to divorce).

These second wave influences on Jewish feminism later gave birth to a few movements and reactions within the Jewish Orthodox world. On the one hand, organizations like the Jewish Orthodox Feminist Alliance (JOFA), Women of the Wall, and Kolech (in Israel), to name a few, were established throughout the 1990s and early 2000s to promote and protect women's rights within Orthodoxy. On the other hand, many leading Orthodox and ultra-Orthodox rabbis and lay people explicitly called for feminism to be rejected, seeing it as an external threat to Judaism.[7] It should be mentioned that by and large, feminism was adopted in religious Jewish streams outside of Orthodoxy, like Conservative, Reform, and Reconstructionist. These denominations have today female leaders in prayer, service, and legal positions. But for Orthodoxy, feminism is either negated or negotiated. The tension is mostly rooted in attitudes toward females in religious leadership positions and as legal judges (learning and applying Halacha) and, more generally, in what should be the gender roles in and outside the house. Because Orthodox Judaism has praxis as its heart, these debates tend to be boiled down to the degree to which Halacha can accommodate feminist ideas.

According to Ronit Irshai, combing Halacha and feminism is not an obstacle but rather a necessity. Irshai considers Halachic discourse as a discourse in the Foucauldian sense, meaning as a site of struggle, one that has the potential to change and shift. That is, she suggested that all people participating in Halachic discourse have the option to resist, construct, and take part in the discourse. She did not think that this is a game in which feminists "could not win," but rather, one they have to play wisely: "I suggested at the outset that, in the manner suggested by Foucault and Fish, the halakhic community functions as a player in the game and already has the power to influence the shaping of the hegemonic halakhic narrative. But that is not the full picture; for one who is empowered must know as well how to deploy that power wisely. Only in that way will it be possible to achieve any sort of consensus."[8] Irshai is optimistic that because of the changing nature of Halacha, it is bound to eventually incorporate modern feminist ideas, because those who participate in the discourse—religious men and women—already practice these ideas in other areas of their lives. As we see from the online material, this is true for some women. But other women feel that the feminist ideas presented in the general society go against their nature or against their religion, and as such, they reject them and support the hegemonic Halachic narrative.

As mentioned in the introduction, Rachel Biale, in her epilogue to the book *Women and Jewish Law*, suggests that there are a few ways in which Jewish feminists can deal with Halacha—approaches that range from rejection, to adaptation, and to a reframed acceptance of these roles. Her focus tends to be on sociopolitical options for feminist Jews.[9] In this chapter, however, we see that the digital discourse creates another avenue for the negotiation of feminism and Orthodoxy. In this avenue, the discussion seems to move from the broader social implications to the personal ones.

Online, in many of the discussions, comments, and resources, the debate about feminism is explicitly or implicitly tied to one's identity. Users share about how feminism (or the rejection of it) shapes their *own* identity as a woman. Some talk about how the rejection of feminism helps them connect to their true self, their divine feminine. Some redefine feminism to fit into their identity as a religious woman—seeing, for example, the exclusion from prayer spaces as an empowerment of their intimate connection with God. And others, maybe not unlike the donor from Midreshet Bruriah mentioned in the introduction to this chapter, see their ongoing work on religious feminism as their identity marker—they are not just a religious woman, but a feminist-religious woman.

To an extent, feminism was always an ideology that is tied into people's personal identity (hence the feminist idiom "the personal *is* political"). This is also historically the case with religious Jewish women.[10] As can be seen in the mythical story of Yentl, wanting to fight existing oppressive systems (that prevent you from studying, for example) is often kindled from a personal, inner fire. The internet contributes to this tendency of tying feminism to personal narratives. It even emphasizes it. This is because internet "media logic" suggests that one should use the internet for self-expression— you have your personal email, personal website, personal profile, and so on. You can personalize almost any app or website. And, while there are some anonymous, nonpersonal, communal online expressions (Wikipedia is probably the most notable example), many online interactions are about creating and maintaining the self.[11] While this is true for all the data presented in this book, special attention is paid in this chapter to highlighting how online discourse on feminism is part of Jewish women's digital identity.

In short, Orthodox Judaism does not inherently oppose feminism, but neither does it embrace the concept. Rather, Orthodox Judaism as a denomination offers a variety of reactions to feminism.[12] Religious individuals with feminist sensitivities might choose a passive form of resistance, like covering their hair in public but learning Talmud at home, or an active form of resistance, such as creating egalitarian Orthodox synagogues in Jerusalem.[13] Feminists might choose to leave Judaism altogether or at least abandon Halacha and, as a result, Orthodox Judaism. Few try to create a combination of Orthodox Feminism.[14] By and large, however, most consider combining the terms Orthodox Judaism and feminism to be an oxymoron,[15] and while some Orthodox communities might accept a certain number of equal rights "outside" (e.g., allowing women access to education), most Orthodox communities reject feminism in the synagogue and at home. This is true especially when feminism seems to endanger traditional norms or Halachic rules, as it often does. With the embrace of digital media, these varying perspectives are displayed and discussed, and they play a vital role in Jewish women's understanding of themselves. The rest of the chapter explores each of these perspectives: negating, redefining, or negotiating Jewish feminism.

Negating Feminism Online: "The Way of the Torah"

As mentioned above, there are several ways in which the Orthodox community reacted to feminism. One such way is by negating it, seeing it as a threat to the Jewish lifestyle and trying to maintain a "traditional" understanding of gender relations. However, when this negating attitude is examined, it is usually the voices of the male leaders that are spotlighted—for example, journalistic or scholarly articles about Rabbi so-and-so's rejection of feminism. Exploring the digital discourse allows us to see how laypeople, and especially women, may also hold the attitude that feminism endangers traditional Jewish norms.

This approach toward feminism is somewhat hostile. It considers feminism as a "male-bashing agenda,"[16] dangerous to marital relationship and to self-actualization. Some online authors and commenters see feminism as a movement that has harmed both men and women. For example, the article "Mom with a View: Men's Rights" by Emuna Braverman starts with the assertion, "After years of taking a beating by women and the feminist movement, it seems like men are finally starting to stand up for themselves again."[17] In a different article, the same author writes about a study that confirms that feminists are less happy in their marriages because, as Braverman explains, "not only were women created to play a specific role in the marriage, we want to play [a] defined part."[18] Feminism denies women the self-actualization of fulfilling their role, and as a result, makes them unhappy. A different author, reviewing Betty Friedman, gives her article the subtitle "Breaking Free of Feminism's Constraints."[19] As can be seen from these examples, this attitude is quite explicit for writers on the Aish website but can be found in other online spaces as well. For example, an article on Kipa covering an all-day seminar against recruiting girls to the IDF, highlights a female leader and speaker who explained that "the modern world thinks all kinds of things, but forgets the fundamentals"[20] and that "we are not contaminated by the disease of feminism." This language explicitly rejects feminism as a dangerous "disease." Reactions to this article in the comment section are full of praise and appreciation, with comments like "so nice to read the truth." On the same website, an opinion piece from a leading rabbi proclaims: "It is not the culture of others and the values of western feminism that should lead us, but the way of *Torah*, which is wholesome and lacks nothing. We should not ask 'what can a woman do' but 'what does the *Torah* tells women to do.'"[21] As can be seen from this material, online sources are not shy about their rejection of feminism in favor of what they consider "the way of the *Torah*," meaning, their interpretation of ideal, traditional gender roles.

Some online material, conversely, is not as explicitly negative toward feminism as the articles mentioned above. This material tends to negate feminism by attacking the principles of feminism, such as the idea of gender equality. An excellent example of this is Tziporah Heller's Aish article "Jewish Views on Gender Differences," in which she explains her perspective about men and women:

> To get a clear picture of the Jewish view of womanhood, we must go back to the beginning—the *Torah*. [. . .] But why, then, didn't God create two identical beings? The answer is that in order to maximize giving, the recipient must be different from the giver. [. . .] But what are these differences? [. . . The] feminine manifestation and strength is more internal, while the masculine focus and expression is more external. [. . .] This emphasis on the internal has many practical implications. [. . .] For example, women, who are more internal—and in a sense private—will usually find their direct connection to God most efficiently through private prayer. Therefore Judaism encourages them to express this through regular daily private prayer, although of course they can pray in a synagogue if they

prefer. [...] Gender is a pivotal quality in each person's identity. Men and women are fully equal but different—and that difference is good. [...]

King Solomon's beautiful poem *Eishes Chayil*, "A Woman of Valor," describes all the different roles a woman can play, including teacher, businesswoman, mother, wife—but all of them as a woman. By giving her the tools to grow morally and spiritually while maximizing her unique strengths, the Torah frees a woman to be herself with self-esteem and joy—and no apologies.[22]

Although feminism is not mentioned explicitly in this article, I suggest it may be read as part of the online Jewish discursive negation of feminism, since it does deal with the issues at the heart of any form of feminism—gender relations, differences, and meanings. According to Heller, the Jewish view on gender is that there are gender differences, but both genders should be appreciated and valued. They are "equal but different." This attitude claims a binary opposition between internal (female) and external (male). It then uses this binary to explain the division of labor in Jewish religious patriarchal systems: women stay at home because they are good in managing internal affairs; women cannot lead in the synagogue because that activity is defined as external, and leadership in the synagogue is in conflict with their essential nature—they will achieve more spiritual benefits from private prayer.

The discursive strategies should be highlighted here. First, at no point does Heller mention what women cannot do according to Halacha. For example, she does not write that they cannot lead service in the synagogue because of Halachic reasons, only that because of women's internal abilities, "Judaism encourages them to express this through regular daily private prayer, although of course they can pray in a synagogue if they prefer." The language is very soft and seemingly nonregulatory—"encourages," "express [yourself]," "although of course they can," and "they prefer." This does two things: it makes the traditional patriarchal structure a matter of choice and of joy, and it portrays traditional female roles as spiritually meaningful. The last sentence of Heller's piece concludes this perfectly: "By giving her the tools to *grow* morally and spiritually while *maximizing* her unique strengths, the *Torah frees a woman* to *be herself* with *self-esteem* and *joy*—and no apologies."[23] The spin is quite clear—traditional patriarchal gender roles are not a matter of oppression and denial but of growth and empowerment for women.

The last phrase, "and no apologies," is a hint at the feminist movement, which robbed women of their essential selves and made them have to be apologetic about wanting to be internal, a mother and a wife—"themselves." In this way, the subject is governed by itself through concepts such as choice and personal responsibility. Heller calls for a type of religious "self-improvement" that encourages the readers to maintain traditional gender roles as an act of personal responsibility. Furthermore, one's identity is at stake here—her "inner self" and the expression of that self. Thus, a form of religious governmentality is enacted through the discursive strategies of self-regulation and self-improvement. Readers are steered into not resisting traditional gender division of labor by framing domestic duties as a joyful choice, an inherent part of one's identity.

The contradiction between the prescribed "true" empowered self and the realities of gender segregation and oppression in these societies should, supposedly, result in some form of resistance.[24] However, it seems that this discursive strategy is by and large accepted and even lauded by users of the website. The article was shared 244 times on Facebook, which is, for a website like Aish, a relatively high number. Furthermore, the comments in general seem to agree, accept, and praise this approach to gender. Out of the twenty-one comments to this article, twelve in some way or another reinforce the article's perspective. For example, "I loved this article on the differences. . . . Finally something that says it's o.k. to be what you are created to be."[25] Or "Excellent! Many questions are answered in this article with both *Torah* erudition and a splash of secular, worldly awareness. Very useful in what is a very modern debate."[26] Conversely, not all the users commenting agree with Heller, and those who disagree make their case quite clear. For example, an anonymous comment reads, "You stress the differences—what about the similarities?"[27] A comment made by the user Mara reads:

> Subject: Disagree
> I am a heterosexual female. All of my life I have been "man-like." Why I enjoy relationships, I find emotional involvment [sic] taxing, it is the comraderie [sic] that I crave. I am very facts and figures, very masculine right down to the intimate aspects of my life. I do not possess even a single "feminine" trait. And yet I am comfortable with myself and do not feel like a "freak." We are not robots or dolls to fit a certain image. We are all individuals.[28]

Using her personal experience, Mara rejects the article on the basis that some people (herself, in this case) do not fit the mold, so to speak. Here too, identity plays a big role—Mara is not inherently disagreeing with Heller, but rather, she wonders what this means for her and her identity as a Jewish woman. As a response to Mara's objection, one of the users comments, "As the article mentions, everyone is an individual. What you are is what you are, and like every possible set it has its advantages and disadvantages. Understanding male/female polarity, and the different desires/needs that are in play, is still helpful to anyone."

The importance of highlighting feminism as related to identity (and not a social condition or movement), and that this identity might be in conflict with Judaism, is stated not only in web articles but also in forums. On the Kipa website, there are multiple forums discussing topics from parenthood to cars. A search for explicit mentions of "feminism" shows that it is often referred to in a negative way. For example, in a debate on which doctor to see in relation to pregnancy—male or female—one user writes, "I will not sacrifice myself on the altar of feminism,"[29] and she explains that because men have more time to dedicate to their profession, she prefers to do the serious exams and treatment with an expert (a man). Other women say that they just feel more comfortable with a female doctor, and that feminism has nothing to do with it. In either case, the users refer to these as "preferences" and "choices" that has to do with their own personality and not societal structures. Similarly, in a completely different forum discussion on dating, one male user complains about how "women lie"[30] because they say they want sensitive men, but they are really looking for a strong man that shows no emotions. This opens up a debate on what it means to behave in masculine or feminine ways. One user says, "This is nature, why go against it? Yes, what women find attractive are masculine qualities. A woman wants a man to lead . . . similarly, a woman needs to be feminine. Look good, be soft and pleasant (that doesn't mean she can't be smart and excel in any other area)."[31] In these comments, users constantly essentialize masculinity and femininity and call for women to behave in feminine ways. While some users accept this statement, a few resist, writing that this perspective is chauvinistic in essence. One user writes, "I don't have a problem with your personal taste [. . .] the issue is the generalization, as if there is only one proper way to express 'masculine' sensitivity."[32] Another female user even offers warning, stating that thinking in this stereotypical way could endanger one's relationship. And repeated are the notions that are summarized by one user's post: "It has nothing to do with feminism, and everything to do with your personality."[33] Again, feminism, inherent gender difference, and identity are weaved together in these online sources.

The stress in these articles and in the comments is on gender differences and how important it is to "be who you are"—to relate to your identity properly. What is less explicit are the rights and responsibilities given to each gender, and the (theological, Halachic, social) inability to move between those rights. That is, if a woman, like Mara, wants to be more "external," from a Halachic perspective that will be problematic. This is explained away by redirecting these as "abnormal" desires to the "natural" "male/female polarity" that is stated in these sources. In sum, in these mainstream Orthodox web spaces, online authors and users tend to react to feminism by implicitly rejecting it and explicitly creating meaningful gender differences—or rather, by reinstating traditional gender differences but embedding them with personal meaning and empowerment.

Redefining Jewish Feminism: "Woman Is Beautiful"

The second approach found in these online sources regarding feminism is to redefine it, usually by combining neoliberal postfeminism with Jewish theology. The examples in this section provide a peek into a worldview that basically says that being an internal, nurturing, receptive Jewish woman *is* my feminism, because it is a form of respect to the feminine. This approach is, to a degree, a redefining of feminism, because it tends to ignore structural oppression of women; or to redefine this oppression as liberation. For example, if women are prohibited from leading prayer, this approach will redefine it as women empowered to do their individual prayer—and so on. This approach is not solely unique to Judaism—in fact, it is very much in line with other postfeminist thinking, for example, positioning industrial beauty standards (like lipstick) as a feminism choice.[34] There is, of course, a danger in redefining, which has been brought up in feminist circles; how far can the redefinition go? And who are the gatekeepers of the definition, in this case, of feminism? For some, redefinition can even be considered a logical fallacy (for example, if we redefine "bats" as "flying animals" then all birds are bats).[35] But the purpose of this section is not to evaluate the truthfulness of this approach. Instead, we examine how online discourse allows women to negotiate and redefine Judaism, feminism, and what it means to be a Jewish woman—their own identity—using their own experiences and voice.

Digital sources that exemplify this approach appear in all three websites and other online Jewish spaces as well. For example, on Aish, one author, Yaakov Rosenblatt, defines himself as "the Feminist Rabbi."[36] He begins by stating that his definition of feminism might be "at odds" with others', thus showing some acknowledgment for how this redirecting of the use of the word "feminist" is not in line with the general conception of feminism. He goes on to provide his definition: "A feminist is one who validates, encourages, and celebrates the feminine tendency. A feminist—male or female—is one who recognizes the prominence of femininity in the family unit, social and commercial relationships, and the development of a modern, moral society." As can be noted from this definition, the emphasis here is on the *feminine*. He continues to explain that according to Jewish thought, both men and women have masculine and feminine sides. The difference between his and "modern feminists'" approach is that he believes that "healthy" men are mostly masculine and "healthy" women are mostly feminine. And, while he agrees that *some* men and women do excel in the other's territory, this is an "an individual's achievement"—not a feminist one. Furthermore, by pushing women into masculine tendencies and fields, modern feminists are causing pain to women. He writes that because of modern feminism "millions of women are unattached, disconnected and discontented." *Traditional* or, Jewish, feminism, on the other hand, provides women with safety, because it "encourage[s] women to marry young but to choose inspired men who appreciate providing and protecting, whose relationship with God and position in their community doesn't allow them to be dishonorable." In other words, traditional feminism encourages women to be feminine—mothers and wives—but to find men who will not leave them, who will support them and play their role in the couple's goal to establish a family. For, as Rosenblatt writes: "the Judeo-Christian ethos is that co-dependent marriage and co-dependent child-rearing is the secret to a wealth of human satisfaction." Here, women and men share the same goal, and "traditional feminism" helps women achieve that goal with greater satisfaction than "modern feminism."[37]

On the Chabad website, a similar attitude toward gender relation is taken by the authors. For example, in the article "The Role of Women in Judaism," the author describes her experience in a gender studies class, and how the feminist approach made no sense to her.[38] She therefore set out to find the Jewish meaning of being a woman. She writes that according to Judaism, there are distinct masculine and feminine qualities—and both men and women have a combination of them, on a spiritual level. However, "in actuality, or on the most physical of realms, a woman cannot produce seed, and a man cannot house or give birth to a baby"—only by bringing the distinct qualities into union can babies be created: "This child is the culmination of the *chochmah* [a Kabalistic quality of masculinity] of the man and the *binah* [a Kabalistic quality of femininity] of the woman. It is the best of both worlds." Therefore, and because "the true way that we define ourselves, and come to understand and reveal our potential, is through the focus on the other," both men and women are only complete in relationship with the other. In her conclusion, this author writes, "And when we acknowledge that we are able to both give and receive, and that both are very active roles, then we can rejoice in the qualities and attributes that are uniquely ours as women, and start celebrating who we are, while bonding and building, rather than competing, with who we are not."[39] She does two things here, and throughout the article: first, she shows that according to Jewish thought, both men and women have masculine and feminine sides; and second, she subtly argues that women should accept their femininity and use it to create with "the other"—the men. This argues against her feminist teacher (who represents external-to-Judaism feminist thought) because it suggests that women shouldn't fight men to take their place, but rather work with men—each gender in their place. Gender roles remain distinct, and women are encouraged to be "internal"—feminist ideals of equality are replaced with respecting and treasuring the feminine qualities.

This article seems to strike a chord with many, as it has received eighty-three comments. Forty-four of them are overwhelmingly positive, with statements like "Just wonderful. You touched our heart, our soul and reveal our role as we feel it is: woman is beautiful."[40] Some users do resist the attitude described here, making comments like, "You clearly should have taken better notes in the gender studies class. There is a difference between 'gender' and 'sex'"[41] and "The rabbis throughout history have placed women as something to control and manipulate."[42] But these comments are in a distinct minority (about six users voice their objections) and most users support this approach and laud the article.

Other authors on the Chabad website take this approach a step further and more clearly call for a unique kind of "Jewish feminism" or, more specifically, *Chassidic* or *Chabad-nic* Feminism. In her article *Chassidic Feminism*, Rivka Slonim describes the following:

> I would describe myself as a *Chassidic feminist*. The two terms are not mutually exclusive, though their combination is not without tension. [...] I was born into a Chabad-Lubavitch family that never questioned the intellect or ability of a woman. I grew up surrounded by female role-models of strength, character and intelligence.
>
> As I was growing up, there *was nothing I felt was beyond my reach, except perhaps synagogue life as enjoyed by the men.* This often seemed

unfair, but there was an understanding that this was just the way it was. As I grew older, *I realized that I enjoyed being female*. My femininity was more than just the way I was; it was a unique part of who I wanted to be and how I wanted to express myself. [. . .]

I feel grateful to the feminist movement for the positive changes it has brought for women. It has brought opportunity, equitable pay and respect to the female half of society. My perception is that the feminist movement has helped society catch up to the Chassidic world. *Today, we see a feminism more grounded in the female self. We see a new generation recognizing the joy and fulfillment in motherhood*. There is a dawning that we women *are* different, biologically, psychologically, intellectually, spiritually and in every other way.[43]

This type of feminism can be understood as a form of religious postfeminism, which essentializes womanhood as unique and inherently different from manhood, not just biologically but also "psychologically, intellectually, spiritually and in every other way." This attitude does not challenge the traditional gender relations or division of labor, but instead views motherhood and femininity as the main form in which women should be celebrated. This type of feminism sees women as *essentially* more spiritual and more internal, therefore women have no need for public work or leadership positions (for example, not participating in the synagogue, as mentioned in the above article).

The article portrays a type of joy and empowerment in the domestic position, by describing women as "role-models of strength, character and intelligence" and their domestic chores (such as being in charge of the kitchen) as a "joining with the Divine." Here, this writer is aware of the political or social meanings of traditional gender roles, stating that "nothing I felt was beyond my reach, except perhaps synagogue life as enjoyed by the men." And although "this often seemed unfair," she rationalizes this disparity by concluding that "this was just the way it was." Hence, the logic underplayed in this article is that while gender differences on a personal level are a discovery of "who you really are," gender differences on the sociopolitical level are "just the way it is." The author is not against feminism—she even goes as far as thanking the feminist movement. But she continues to remark that the "feminist movement has helped society catch up to the *Chassidic* world"—implying that the *Chassidic* world was already feminist, and does not need the external, secular feminism, or any further progress.

The reactions to the article are interesting. On the one hand, the article was not shared widely (only eight shares on Facebook, way below the average sharing in the Chabad website, which is about 129 per article). This could indicate disagreement, or a wish to not be associated with feminism (as the title of the article is "*Chassidic* Feminism"). On the other hand, out of the thirty-one comments to the article, twenty-one agree with it and praise Slonim's writing. They say things like "What a wonderful article! Thank you so much for this beautiful expression!" and "From this great article I am learning that it is OK to be a traditional Jewish woman and that there are things that we do and there are things that the men do."[44] Some commenters more explicitly state the theological relation between femininity and the coming of the Messiah, which is the core belief for Chabad followers. One reads, "Embracing the conciousness [sic] of Feminism and Chassidius [sic] is *to rejoice in G-d making us a woman*!! There exists an allure of this world but it is so false and pales when we truly understand and *accept our roles as women, wives, and mothers with all the joy* and glory G-d has intended for us!! *We are now in the Messianic era*, and must be humble and loving as we channel our G-d given spiritually intuitive light. This is truly a gift from G-d to the women."[45] In this comment, and throughout the Chabad website, the role and status of women is tied to the theological understanding of this current historical moment as the coming of the Messiah. As mentioned in the introductory chapters of the book, Chabad is a movement that follows "the Rebbe" (Menachem Mendel Schneerson) who passed away in 1994. The Chabad movement, to a degree, sees the Rebbe as a Messiah figure, and works religiously to bring the days of the Messiah closer. Some even believe we are already in the end of days or a messianic era.[46] This association with the messianic era gives feminism a whole new meaning, a religious one. That is, some Chabad writers believe that equal rights or the feminist movement are signs of the messianic moment in which we are currently. However, the type of feminism that is to be embraced is a religious-traditional take on feminism, an "equal but different" approach in which women are to be adored for their internal roles as mothers and wives. A woman is a goddess, but a goddess restrained by her femininity to her home.

There are other ways in which feminism is incorporated into Judaism without being explicitly feminist, or through redefining feminism. One such important avenue that is hinted to in the above example, is the journey to empower the *self*—to become a "strong" woman. Digital media offers the religious woman avenues to explore this without necessarily defining oneself as a feminist. One example of this is the Israeli website LeOran.[47] The Israeli website LeOran (Hebrew for "in their light") launched in 2016 by the organization LeOran, is dedicated to inspiring young religious Jewish girls by offering a range of female models from various walks of life. The website has various categories, such as sports, science, art, agriculture, politics, and education, and under each category, users can find names of outstanding Jewish women who excelled in this area. Most of the women are contemporary and religious, for example, Tamar Ariel, the first religious female to become a military pilot (under "security"), but some examples also include Zipporah Zion, an Ethiopian empress from the fifteenth century (under "politics"). The website also showcases how to use this information in educational settings (such as school bulletin boards).

The purpose of the website is to help young religious women in Israel craft their future by following the examples of these outstanding women. While not explicitly feminist in any of their descriptions of the website, the organization, or the women, the website implicitly offers a feminist alternative to the life roles and paths offered to girls in Israeli religious education. In general, Israeli religious education, while providing girls with access to STEM and other professions, most of the time educates girls that their main future role is as a nurturer, as a mother and a wife. As a result, most Israeli religious women end up in professions like schoolteacher or social worker, where they can be home in the afternoons and move into their "second shift" as housemakers. This is not surprising, considering the context and history of gender roles in Judaism. LeOran offers them a different path: the path of inspiring women who became trailblazers in various avenues of life, while maintaining their religious duties and feminine responsibilities.

What is interesting about LeOran is that the website is not explicitly religious or feminist. This allows it to play the feminist-religious game wisely. The content is feminist-religious, but that is never clearly stated. Only when checking the specific women, will one find that the website mostly highlights religious women. They also put forth articles and press coverage of these women that tend to highlight how they are loyal to their religious path while maintaining their professional career (for example, Tamar Ariel as holding a weapon and a religious book). They also use, especially in their Facebook communication, religious phrases and terms, such as "The righteous shall flourish like the palm tree."[48] In these ways, they make the implicit argument that religiosity and female self-achievement (feminism) can happen simultaneously—but no one needs to know you're a feminist. Furthermore, in some of the examples, the website links directly to news articles that highlight how these women achieved what they did—without breaking a single Halachic law, while staying completely devoted to Orthodoxy. Here again, one can achieve self-actualization without changing anything in the current religious systems.

If a nonreligious Israeli was to stumble into this website, it would not be easily recognizable as *religious* or *feminist*. I suggest that the reason for this is that LeOran wants to shape a discourse in which religion and gender become a nonissue, where they place no boundaries on one's path to success. Here, too, like in the Chabad or Aish examples, the self is at the center of the feminist debate: her path as an individual. This is not unlike other neoliberal feminist media content,[49] which ignores structural issues and places the burden of success on the individual.

As a project, this is a unique and important website that offers feminist content for the religious society in Israel. And, unlike similar websites—like, for example, Kolech, which is discussed in the following section—LeOran does not declare itself as a feminist project. In so doing, this website also redefines feminism by "being feminist" without being feminist. LeOran, Chabad, the Feminist Rabbi—these online sources give voice to a larger movement within Orthodox Judaism that seeks to, in part, reconcile Judaism and feminism, but on traditional Jewish terms. To that end, feminism is redefined to either be outside of the religious realm (in the case of LeOran); a form of respecting the feminine (the Feminist Rabbi); or a celebration of feminine divinity (Chabad)—all of which maintain traditional gender roles at least at the level of religious commitments. And, as seen in the section about negating feminism—the self, one's identity, is at the center of the online discussion, as is often the case in digital discourse. The next section shows how even when religious systems are challenged by religious feminism, the self, the digital representation of identity, still plays a major role.

Negotiating Feminism, Staying Orthodoxly Jewish: "I'm a Feminist!"

So far, we have explored Orthodox Jews using online media to take as either a negating or redefining approach to feminism. But not all users in the Jewish digital sphere discard the feminist movement in these ways. In general, authors and users taking what I call "the negotiating approach" tend to write and think about feminism not as a religious praising of women (redefining) or a destructive unnecessary movement for Jewish life (negating) but rather as a movement that Judaism needs to struggle with or conform to.

Some Jews use online sources to take a feminist stance clearly and proudly and support the feminist movement. For example, in her article "And You Shall Tell Your Daughter" (paraphrasing the biblical "and you shall tell your son" [Exodus 13:8]) Mariam Adler "tells" her daughter that she is a feminist:

—Mom, are you a feminist?
—Yes.
—What is a feminist, mom?
—A feminist is a woman (or a man—yes, there are feminist men) that believes that men and women (and all people) were born equal.[50]

Adler unapologetically describes herself as a feminist and tries to combine her feminist identity with her religious Jewish one. Adler clearly writes in response to the question "Why are you a feminist?" that "everyone should get equal opportunities in this world, and equal rights. Equal pay at work, for example. Equal authority in legislation, for example. Yes, even when it comes to "our" rules—Halacha, decrees, customs. Everyone should have a place in the synagogue."[51] Here, religious feminism is not a way to explain women's internal nature but a desire for equal rights in both secular and religious spaces. In the previous attitudes (negating and redefining), even users who agreed with some feminist principles, kept those principles "outside" the religious realm. Here, Adler explicitly calls for feminist ideas of equality to be inserted into the religious world. Interesting to note that even as Adler points to social structures (such as Halacha or the synagogue), her argument begins from her *identity*. She doesn't write about what is feminis*m*, but rather, what it means to be a feminis*t*, she frames this ideology through her own self, her personality.

The reactions to this article are rather harsh. Out of the fourteen comments to the article, only two are supportive, and the others resist in various ways. Some highlight the truthfulness of rabbinical Halacha as higher than social movements such as feminism—"Rabbis decide for men and women, for tall people and short people,"[52] and "The god of Israel is true, Moses is true and his Torah is true."[53] Others remind her of the inherent differences between men and women and how they are not equal: "God chooses different people for different tasks [. . .] people of Israel were chosen [. . .] the tribe of Levi and sons of Aaron (and not daughters!) were chosen."[54] Still others dismiss her writing as Conservative or Reform,[55] thus othering her perspective, placing it outside of what they understand as traditional Orthodox Judaism. Overall, the reactions are negative and strengthen traditional patriarchal Jewish understanding of gender. At the same time, the webmasters of Kipa have Adler as one of their regular writers (she has written a total of sixty-eight articles in Kipa since 2013) and thus keep this conversation about religious feminism going.

This article from Kipa is obviously not the only source online to promote this type of religious feminism. However, since this attitude is less popular in Orthodox circles, one would be hard pressed to find many sources like this in the mainstream religious websites of Chabad, Aish, Kipa. But if one searches for "Jewish feminism" or "Orthodox feminism" online, they are bound to come across one of the well-established Jewish Orthodox feminist organizations: JOFA or Jewish Women's Archives (JWA) in the United States or Kolech in Israel. These organization are all active offline in creating events, offering support, and facilitating community meetings. Online, these organizations seek to provide information and promote their offline activities, fostering a sense of community for religious feminists. For example, on the homepage of JOFA the first button is for "details about upcoming events." The idea of identity and belonging is also communicated in JOFA's logo, which clearly marks this sense of identity and community with the motto "where you belong," and the tabs on the homepage include "events" and "community"—using the online to establish and enable this community. Under the tab for community, one will find sources like JOFA's blog, podcast, and webinar series' archives. There is also a "prayer finder" for finding gender inclusive prayer services and resources for specific holidays. The website offers a research library and an array of religious content written by feminists. A user of the website will find enough sources to practice as an Orthodox feminist, but not a lot of ways to participate actively *online*. That is, this website seems to support *offline* feminist communities and to provide sources for feminist-religious thinking online.

The content on the website focuses on the intersections of being Orthodox religious and a feminist. Web articles include topics from workplace interactions like "Adventures of an Orthodox Feminist in Academia"[56] to biblical interpretations like "The Journeys of Ruth and Naomi."[57] Throughout the various stories, blogs, webinars, and podcasts, what stands out is the exploration of the unique identity of an Orthodox feminist Jew. For example, one author, Carolyn Hochstadter Dicker, writes about the exceptional strengthens that Orthodox women can bring to a workplace. She writes, "While at work, I came to personalize an innate set of positive values that are now integral to my religious life." As an Orthodox woman and a lawyer, she brought to her law firm values like "family pride"—a sense of pride and unity at the work place—and care for people's whole self, as workers and as individuals. This was based on her Orthodox focus on family and care. At the same time, she "consistently and confidently advocated for a level playing field for women and girls as a basic premise." Thus, she highlights how she was able to bring to work both her values as an Orthodox Jew and her values as a feminist. This is based on her personal journey, her identity. She begins her article by retelling her educational and personal story, which she summarizes with the statement "My identity as an Orthodox Jewish feminist was thereby solidified."[58] Her identity seems to play a major role in how she acts both religiously and professionally. The stress on identity is clear here, and in other articles, and is exemplified in JOFA's 2019 Shabbaton (conference), titled "Finding the *I* in Identity."[59]

Similarly, JWA and Kolech's websites are focused on offering online material that can support offline communities and individuals. JWA specifically is an archive, and their main goal is to "document Jewish women's stories, elevate their voices, and inspire them to be agents of change."[60] As such, they cater more broadly to Jewish women, not only to religious women. Kolech, on the other hand, is an Israeli organization that, like JOFA, is focused on the unique needs and identity of the Jewish Orthodox feminist. They are very explicit about how their feminism includes the religious sphere as well: "Kolech is an Orthodox Feminist organization, first of its kind in Israel, that aspires to create a social and conceptual change to promote women's status, rights, and gender equality—in *Halacha*, religious leadership, and religious institutions."[61] Like JOFA and JWA, Kolech's website offers an array of sources (in Hebrew) to support and inspire this type of Orthodox feminism, including Biblical interpretations written by feminists; resources for equal marriage, divorce, birth, and death ceremonies; archives; educational programs; and events. There are no options for interactions on the websites (no comment section, for example), but the website is linked to the organization's social media outlets, where their online community takes place.

Social media has been widely used by Jewish Orthodox feminist to share sources, build community, and spread their message, and not just by the established organizations mentioned above. For example, the Facebook public group Hagbah, which describes itself as a space "Where observant progressive feminist Jews discuss egalitarian practice, ritual and text and Jewish life."[62] Or private groups like "Seat at the Table—a Forum for Orthodox Feminism"[63] or "Teenage Orthodox Feminists."[64] In Israel, a group like "I'm a religious feminist and I too lack a sense of humor"[65] has more than sixteen thousand users. Recently, there is also the emergence of social media religious feminist influencers, like Adina Sash, known as "FlathbushGirl"; Sarah Segal-Katz, an influential Halachic teacher in Israel; and Abby Stein, a transgender activist and former rabbi. And of course, JOFA, JWA, and Kolech also have their social media presence. On social media, users come together as a community to discuss current events, personal dilemmas, share related events, and share some (feminist) jokes. For example, Adina Sash shared on her page a fake rabbinical decree, calling men to hide their faces on social media in order to help combat the COVID-19 pandemic.[66] This is a satire on real rabbinical decrees in public ultra-Orthodox spaces, which encourage women to practice modesty (usually associated with stopping some crisis, something like: "wear longer skirts for the well-being of Jewish soldiers in Israel"). Through the sharing of feminist content, events, and jokes, users can solidify their identity as an Orthodox feminist—first, because participating in these groups using their (real) Facebook profiles connects these values to their online persona and online identity, and second, because they share this content on their Facebook walls, thus clearly signaling an association of "who they are" with this perspective. Finally, online sources help Orthodox feminist users solidify their identity because they can connect with others who identify as an Orthodox feminist, and through partaking in this community, their own identity is linked with that of the group.

Summary

Throughout this chapter, we examined how online, feminism is used as either a negative term (for those negating it), a relative term (for those redefining it), or a necessary development (for those negotiating it). As a negative phenomenon, the feminist movement is described as destructive and dangerous. According to those holding this perspective, the meaning for being a man or woman is traditionally and religiously set, and the feminist movement has distorted it. Religious authority and tradition, and not secular trends, are how one should make sense of the world, of gender and sexual norms, and of their identity. In opposition to this view, those who advocate for feminism as a necessary development for religious Judaism see feminism as a movement that should steadily help women elevate their status in the house, the synagogue, and outside. Those who hold this view consider the political and social conditions and see as a problem the inequalities between men and women. In between these views, is a religiously redefined form of feminism, which seems to be the most acceptable to online readers based on sharing practices and positive comments. This view offers a unique kind of "Jewish feminism"—one that acknowledges the differences between men and women and highlights joy and empowerment in traditional roles. Some of those who hold this view also believe that females are essentially more spiritual than men (and as a result do not need leadership positions) and that female empowerment is a sign of the coming of the Messiah (Chabad). Through these discursive practices, feminism plays a major role in positioning and making sense of gender relations' meaning and norms—and of one's own identity.

Online, religious women use mainstream Jewish web spaces, like Chabad, Aish, and Kipa's websites, but also forums, Facebook, and other forms of digital media to make sense of *what it means to be a woman*—what are their roles and rights as women, and what does this mean for their innermost identity? Feminism has challenged many of the traditionally prescribed markers for womanhood, and thus, those who live in traditional worlds but are exposed to feminism need to figure out how to settle the differences between the two. Digital media allows that process to happen from the bottom up, allows for women to express their understandings of feminism and of womanhood. They can use these tools to resist male-centered interpretations of feminism or of womanhood. However, as we've seen in this chapter and throughout the book, often, women use these digital tools to strengthen traditional (chauvinistic) perspectives. Not surprisingly, when resistance does happen, it tends to be on the fringes of the religious internet. What is striking and important to note is how online, the issues of feminism are inherently tied to issues of identity, of making sense of the self. To a degree, this can be attributed to the media logic of the internet, which focuses on self-expression and presentation. The discourse found online is laden with neoliberal and self-focused language, which makes the social dilemmas of feminism into matters of personal choice or empowerment. Through this digital identity-focused language, women embrace or resist traditional gendered norms, and while the semantics are individually focused, connections and communities are also enabled through this digital discourse.

Conclusions

This book project started officially years ago, when I embarked on my dissertation project. But more deeply, it started many years ago, maybe in that sleepless night before my bat mitzvah, as I was trying to grasp what it means to be a Jewish woman. In some ways, writing this book has helped ease my own anxieties and questions; in other ways, it raised completely new ones. I hope that, to a degree, this book has offered the same to you too—some answers, some data, and some new questions. In this last chapter, I try to tie the different elements of online discourse together so we can see where this journey has taken us. I do so with some hesitation because reality is constantly changing and developing—both for digital media and for the Jewish lived experience. Still, some conclusions can be drawn out when bringing all this information and analysis together, and that information can serve as the base for new questions.

This book explores the ways in which gender and sexuality are constructed and negotiated in online Jewish Orthodox discourse. Throughout this book I highlight the ways in which religious gender and sexual behaviors are normalized and problematized through online tools. Seeking to expose the ways in which gender and sexual norms are created and maintained is a difficult task, as these behaviors are constantly and subtly corrected and reinforced. However, through emerging media, digital communication creates a new and participatory space in which, it is claimed, users can playfully experiment with gender and sexual identities, and religious and traditional hierarchies can shift.[1] In this book project I examined the ways these new digital tools are used by Orthodox Jews, who tend to have traditional understandings of gender and sexuality but are currently negotiating modern notions of sexual liberation and the feminist revolution. From this exploration, I am able to offer insight into the usage of digital tools by religious individuals for the negotiation of gender and sex as well as demonstrate more broadly the ways in which gender and sexual behaviors are normalized online.

In order to examine Orthodox Jewish negotiation online, three popular websites were chosen to represent a digital Jewish Orthodox discourse: Chabad, Aish, and Kipa. In addition to these websites, certain forums, social media accounts and content, and organizations' websites were explored. The goal was to examine "common" spaces—online spaces in which this community communicates. My investigation of this material reveals how digital communication functions as a Foucauldian discourse, a "site of struggle," in which both power and resistance take place (see chapter 1 on this theoretical approach). That is, the normalizing process happens through the discourse—the constant and indirect, elusive ways in which people talk and act regarding gender and sexuality. Online communication gives us as researchers and users a unique access to this discourse, as it is archived and accessible to all.

Once the conversations, questions and answers, articles, and literature of a community or worldview are "fossilized" online, we as researchers can decode and analyze them. In the case of this book, I examine the worldviews of Orthodox Jews who embrace digital technology and use it, perhaps unknowingly, to construct, maintain, and negotiate communal norms. I specifically focus on the construction and negotiation of gender and sexual norms as they are presented and discussed in this Orthodox digital discourse. Furthermore, in this discourse, I argue, we must consider not only the ways in which users talk (the discursive and linguistic components) but also the religious worldviews that inform them and the technological affordances that enable the discourse. To that end, I employed a three-layered critical discourse analysis model in order to highlight three elements that constitute this discourse. The model suggests an analysis of (1) technological affordance, (2) religious cultural context, and (3) discursive strategies.

This conclusion chapter details the key findings from the analysis, highlighting the ways gender and sexual norms are negotiated in the Orthodox digital discourse examined. These key findings are organized around four tensions that were implicitly highlighted throughout the book: traditional-neoliberal thinking; community-individual voice; rabbinical-communal regulation; and power resistance. These tensions inform each other and together structure the process of social norm regulation within this discourse. At the end of the chapter, I also discuss how these findings could be helpful for scholars in digital religion, digital media studies, and feminist or contemporary Judaism studies. I end by asking, what's next? How do we use this information and go beyond the pages of this book?

Key Findings: The Construction and Negotiation of Gender and Sexuality Online

The analysis of the Orthodox discourse offered in this book examined discourse related to both practice (Halachic rules) and meaning (narratives and explanations for these) as these relate to the different stages in a Jewish woman's life: dating, marriage, intimacy, and child raising. The findings highlight the fact that in these online sources, a traditional approach to gender and sexuality was preferred and maintained not only by the authors but also by the commenters and the users in general. Thus, the online media logic of participatory culture was found to maintain hierarchal and traditional approaches. In this concluding chapter, I bring together the findings from the four previous chapters, mix in a little theory, and present to you how the internet is used in mainstream Orthodox Jewish communities. To do so, I highlight four interrelated tensions that are noted throughout the book: traditional-neoliberal thinking; community-individual voice; rabbinical-communal regulation; and power resistance.

Traditional-Neoliberal Thinking

Contemporary Judaism (like other religions) lives in a world that combines traditional thinking with modern, neoliberal thinking. First, it is important to consider how the traditional religious worldview and language play into this online discourse. Here, I briefly summarize what role religious canonic texts (such as the Torah and Halachic texts), religious terms (such as religious denomination, for example), and, more generally, religious theology (such as messianic times or holiness) play in this discourse. Throughout the analysis chapters, the monosemic use of religious terms was noted, alongside the addition of modern terms and online sources. Because in Judaism religious language includes both theology and praxis, it was of special interest to examine how Halachic language plays out in this digital discourse. One of the key findings of the analysis chapters revealed the minimal use of Halachic language to support "legal" rulings. This finding supports previous research on Jewish online Q&A,[2] which argues that online Q&A are different from traditional Jewish Q&A. While traditional Q&A are often long and complex answer, online Q&A tend to be shorter and not supported by Halachic texts, and overall ascribe to the logics of the internet and not the logics of traditional Halachic Q&A. Alongside the minimal use of Halachic language, it was found that material discussed in the chapters included modern and online sources supporting or complementing the religious language, for example, using the concept of "sexual harassment" as a reason to maintain religious abstinence (*Shmirat Negiaa*) or modesty. This means that one of the ways traditional gender and sexual behaviors are normalized is by using secular or "commonsense" arguments. It also means that to some extent, the religious reasons and motivations themselves are not strong or convincing enough to maintain these norms, thus hinting at a religious worldview that combines religious culture with general secular Western modern culture. Separating the "religious" from the "cultural" is to an extent artificial, as religion both preserve cultures and are influenced by them. That being said, when this artificial separation is used, it can show how—in this case—the norms of a specific culture (internet culture) can impact and shift religious norms. At the same time, it is worth noting that religious worldviews were at times used to explain modern values, especially regarding feminism. For example, some Chabad authors and users talked about the feminist movement as a sign of messianic days. Furthermore, theology and spirituality were constantly used to explain gender roles. For example, it was argued by the websites' authors and users that women are more spiritually inclined, that their spirituality and "true self" are internal, and that they derive divine joy through nurturing and giving. These findings point to a use of religious cultural context focused on personal empowerment. That is, the religious language and worldview were themselves presented through a neoliberal perspective—providing meaning through self-empowerment and choice, rather than through commitment to the divine or to the tradition.

This neoliberal thinking was used to avoid discussing practical oppressive elements in these gender norms. In many of these online sources, we find authors presenting a positive view on gender and sexual relation while overlooking or downplaying the applied consequences of these norms. For example, discussing the joy and empowerment of domestic duties without mentioning how these norms might make financial independence less accessible to women. This strategy is noteworthy for two reasons. First, what is not said is as important to analyze as what is said. Silencing is in itself a discursive strategy that maintains certain knowledge as acceptable and other types of knowledge as invisible.[3] Second, in the case of this discourse, the meaning of gender roles has legal, Halachic, daily and practical consequences. Not mentioning these outcomes when discussing gender and sex norms is a silent acceptance of these outcomes, thus supporting the existing structures.

One of the ways neoliberal logic works is by dismantling structures and placing the burden of "success" on individuals. For example, not allowing workers to unionize and instead encouraging workers to "be their best self." In the Jewish online discourse examined in this book, there is a similar thread of thought that encourages readers to understand social patriarchal power structures as divinely inspired for the individual and as a source of joy and empowerment. One prominent example is in Aish's Tziporah Heller's article, in which she claims that "the Torah frees a woman to be herself with self-esteem and joy."[4] That is, the religious (patriarchal) Halachic structures ("the Torah") are framed as a matter of choice, freedom, and joy. This discursive strategy focuses on self-actualization and choice, making existing traditional structures into an issue of personal identity, growth, and individual preference. In reality, many of these "choices" have very real impact on women's lives—for example, as discussed in the chapter on motherhood, if a Jewish Orthodox woman chooses not to be mother (or can't), they become an outsider in their own society and feel that they have no place or meaning.

When gender and sexuality are framed in this neoliberal way, resisting on a macro social level is harder because it seems like a matter of personal choice (or failure) and not a shared societal or gendered struggle. In some ways, the Orthodox approach to gender and sexuality in the digital discourse examined in this book is similar to the theme demarcated by the term "vulnerable empowered woman" as coined and described by Tasha Dubriwny. According to Dubriwny, the vulnerable empowered woman "is one who appears to have some agency and power to shape her own life"[5] but, in reality, is limited by the constraints of the societal norms around her. By encouraging women (and men) to view their problems and solutions at the hands of "individual women, not society," this type of ideology avoids having to deal with societal changes. Thus, constructing a neoliberal discourse allows these religious authors and users to maintain the traditional, Halachic, religious societal norms by moving it from the level of society or community to the level of the individual. Furthermore, through individual narratives, these traditional norms become a source of empowerment and joy, of spiritual growth and meaning, and as such cannot be challenged.

In this online, neoliberal discourse, users are thus encouraged to *regulate themselves* (and others). Theorized as a form of governmentality, this online discourse operates on religious individuals in such a way that they are "ruled, mastered, held in check, administered, steered, guided, by means of which they are led by others or have come to direct or regulate their own actions."[6] The analysis provided in this book suggests that the Orthodox online discourse strengthens existing religious patriarchal structures of power by offloading them to the users and framing them in the language of meaning and agency, and it does so by focusing on the individual.

Communal-Individual Voice

The second tension noted throughout the book is the focus on individual agency rather than communal concerns. Judaism, like other religions, is very much a community-based religion. In fact, there are many religious practices in Judaism that cannot be done without a community. However, online, and in relation to gender and sexuality, the discourse seems to focus on the individual, not the community.

Throughout much of this material, the personal voice had a much greater emphasis than in traditional Jewish writing. For example, recommending users who had trouble maintaining the Orthodox gender and sex ideals seek professional therapy is a strategy that allows downplaying the need for changes at the social-cultural level. In many cases, users utilized personal experiences and stories to either explain or negotiate religious norms, making the private a tool to negotiate the social. This strategy was apparent in the online articles and social media when users asked questions about their specific situations; when authors related their personal stories to their main argument; and when commenters supported or resisted an article based on their personal experience. Using personal experience keeps the problem at the level of the individual and protects the religious systems from needing to change. It also adds to the overall self-focused, neoliberal approach underlining this discourse.

This focus on the self makes sense when considering the "media logic" of the internet. Media logics, as discussed in chapter 1, are "the various institutional, aesthetic, and technological *modus operandi* of the media, including the ways in which the media distribute material and symbolical resources, and operate with the help of formal and informal rules."[7] The internet has a lot of "media logics" and those are hard to pin down, but some that were found present in the Orthodox Jewish online discourse are its affective mode[8] and focus on identity.[9] This was exemplified in chapter 4, where emphasis was given to how motherhood (or lack thereof) makes women *feel*; women shared their fears and intimate emotions as a way of sharing, but also as a way of claiming expertise. In other words, the emotions shared online became a source for acting one way or another, even when those norms seem to contradict the official narratives. Online, in comment sections and on social media, opinions were formed not through expertise but by emotive, personal, affective reasoning. The digital media logic of affective, emotive communication seems to have become part of this religious sense-making discourse. While in traditional, offline, Jewish Orthodox texts expertise is gained through knowledge and interpretation of older religious texts, in the online discourse, emotive expression (both by authors and users) becomes part of the knowledge-production process, an integral part of the discourse itself. Similarly and in addition, in chapter 5 we saw how digital media is pivotal in the process of the construction of the self, especially in close-knit communities where the self and the many are often at odds. And in return, the focus on self, on identity, which is common to digital media, constructed the narratives around feminism not as an issue of social importance, but as an issue of personal importance. Using the media logic of personalization and self-focused content,[10] these religious websites and web spaces present a discourse where the self, not the community, is the main event. While both these media logics allow for a greater expression for the individual, they are, in this case, found to be used to support the communal, religious, norms. Through the self and the affective narratives, traditional opinions were framed as a matter of choice (as discussed above). As such, they can be presented and preserved in the twenty-first century mindset and in the media logics of the internet, and by doing so, they create the groundwork for peer regulation.

Rabbinical-Peer Regulation

Another important tension was brought to light by focusing on the digital media logic of participation. The online discourse examined in this book is by and large dependent on enabling community-based interactions, which it thrives on. This is obvious in the social media examples, but even in the more top-down mainstream websites, that seems to be the case. All three websites have sharing and commenting abilities, although these play out in different ways. For example, Aish permits commenting on general articles but does not offer this ability in the ask-the-rabbi section. Kipa allows for sharing and "liking" but only through Facebook, and not on any other social media platform. Chabad and Aish, by comparison, allow sharing on many more social media sites, using an "add this" button that gives the user the option to share an article or webpage through multiple social media platforms. While these differences are in themselves worthy of research, the important underlying notion emphasized in this book is that these Orthodox websites allow and encourage a *participatory* discourse, which is community based and tends to bend traditional hierarchies.

This is significant when considering religious discourse and power, because it means lay people have constant access to religious sources and religious leaders, thus making religious debates and conversations accessible to people who traditionally were left out, like women, uneducated men, or non-Jews. Preinternet Orthodox religious communication, especially theological and Halachic communication, has been traditionally controlled by the "religious elite"—educated men who took on religious authority roles, such as a rabbi or community leader.[11] With the advent of mass communication and digital communication, Orthodox theological and Halachic discussions became more widespread and accessible.[12] Some rabbis and Orthodox leaders view this as a challenge to their authority and try to ban or minimalize internet usage in their communities. Other Orthodox communities, perhaps ones that would be considered more embracing of modern values, accepted the internet early on. These religious communities, which are the focus of this book, still have a variety of choices in how they manage their digital communication. As highlighted by Oren Golan and Heidi Campbell, at least three website management strategies can be noted within the Orthodox world: control (intense regulation of both content and users), layering (creation of different layers with the website with varying regulation), and guiding (very moderate regulation by the website editors).[13] That is, website designers and editors could have chosen a stricter approach to participation, one that did not allow for feedback and, in that way, disabled verbal resistance ("talkback"). Indeed, the fact the Aish does not allow comments on the rabbis' answers could fall under the control strategy suggested by Golan and Campbell. Still, most of the communication options on these websites, judging by the websites' designs and affordances, seem to take a "guiding" or "lenient" strategy, allowing disagreements and encouraging discussion and participation. And this is, of course, true for the discourse in forums and social media, which is designed to be participatory—either a totally free zone or a moderated regulation of content by the forum or group leaders. The findings from this book suggest that even sensitive or "off-limits" issues, like masturbation, female sexuality, or divorce, are discussed in these mainstream online religious spaces. That is, the technological affordances expand the discourse so that what was once taboo, to be discussed not only behind closed doors, can now also be discussed on websites publicly accessible to all.

However, the interactive, participatory affordances of the online discourse have not necessarily led to a proliferation of opinions on topics related to gender and sexuality, or to a break from traditional authority, as shown throughout the book. As suggested by feminist scholars of technology, the use of these technologies is always already framed through an existing gendered worldview.[14] For example, in the three websites' online articles, the comment sections were mostly used to support traditional or strict religious interpretations of Halacha and the Torah. Aside from strengthening the rabbis' authority, users also utilized the comment section to enforce and regulate each other, by shaming or correcting users who resisted. In other words, more often than not, the participatory abilities of the online discourse were used for *peer regulation*. In many of the comment sections, forums, and social media groups, users corrected each other using shaming or Othering discursive tactics, thus enacting peer pressure. While the comment section was one of the areas where some resistance could be noted, it was also in the comment section that users most clearly enforced a strict religious approach to gender and sexuality on each other. Here, cosurveillance and peer regulation were enacted to correct and normalize certain concepts and norms regarding gender and sexuality. This is significant because it further highlights how this online religious discourse is not simply a top-down enforcement of rules and norms, but rather a more collaborative creation of norms. The peer regulation that takes place in this discourse is an important aspect in how gender and sexuality are negotiated.

Peer regulation happened in various ways. One obvious and common way was by disagreeing with resisting voices and correcting them. Expressing disagreement was enacted through either disputing the other person ("it's not so"), bringing forth arguments against their position ("but the Torah clearly says . . ."), or even shaming them ("how dare you!"). Expressing disagreement is exactly one of the ways in which a Foucauldian discourse operates—concepts or norms are discussed, and it is at the hands of "everyone" to decide what is right or wrong. There are always more powerful actors in such a discourse, for example, those to whom we ascribe authority—like doctors or, in this case, rabbis. The majority or "normal" position is also quite powerful, and online, it is easier to sense what is the majority opinion because of the quantitative nature of online discourse. What is interesting in an online Foucauldian discourse, like the one we examined throughout this book, is that the power of mass consensus—the agreement of the many—is clearly seen and can even be quantified. In that sense, peer regulation in these online religious communities is not just a part of a temporary conversation between peers, but becomes fossilized, a consent testimony to the agreement of "normal" people with a traditional stance. Overwhelmingly, the voices heard and repeated in this online participatory discourse were those who agreed and enforced traditional stances.

Aside from disagreement, peer regulation also happened through a practice of Othering. Othering occurs when users suggest that an opinion or author is not Jewish, Orthodox, or part of the "in-group," thus delegitimizing their stance. This strategy was noted throughout the book, but especially in the chapter on body and intimacy—for example, when suggesting that women who dress immodestly are not religious,[15] or that a certain approach to modesty is "not-Jewish."[16] Othering is a common strategy in creating in and out groups and in normalizing certain behaviors,[17] one that was noted throughout the book as a tool for both resistance and enforcement, but mostly enforcement. Namely, this strategy highlights the fact that there is an ongoing attempt to decide what and who is in or out, thus supporting the notion that concepts of gender and sexuality are currently negotiated and that gender and sexual norms play an important part in defining one's identity and community. This also highlights the important role of online peer regulation in this process of defining community and even individual identity. When one's offline practices (for example, wearing pants instead of a skirt, which is considered by some an immodest action) are described by others online as "not religious," the individual is confronted with their place in the community and their own self-definition. Notably, this was mostly done through peers, lay people, and not the rabbinical authority.

This tension shows that online, the construction of gender and sexuality is not simply a top-down process led by religious authority. Rather, the technological features suggest a discourse that is maintained by authors and users together—not an authoritative attempt to define gender and sexuality by rabbis but a more mutual and public creation of knowledge and norms. And, as was highlighted in the analysis chapters, the online areas for participation—the comment sections in all three websites, the forums, and the social media groups—were all used as a tool for peer regulation and correction, thus maintaining traditional religious gender and sexual norms. In other words, these online discursive practices tend to help maintain the existing structural norms, thus mostly contributing to traditional power structure and not partaking in resistance.

Power Resistance

Throughout this book, it was not simply contemporary Judaism that was examined but contemporary Orthodox Judaism as it is expressed online. One of my main claims in the book is that we use digital media like a window and a mirror—a way to examine society and ourselves. Online, we participate in various discourses related to our communities and identities. Our contribution via digital participation to these discourses shapes the norms and terms discussed in them, and in return, these discourses then shape how we understand the world and ourselves. In the case of the Orthodox discourse, the online environment becomes a space for both resistance and maintaining traditional power.

Digital affordances, as discussed in chapter 1, are the ways in which the design features of the websites request, demand, allow, encourage, discourage, and refuse users' interactions and engagement.[18] One of the digital affordances highlighted throughout the book is the participatory affordances of digital media. For example, in the case of dating, there is a push and pull between the forum communication and some of the content found in top-down, edited online material. While the official, traditional perspective conceptualizes marriage as an agreement between two different partners, in the forums, love is sought. Users share their heartbreak, their concerns, their ideas about dating and marriage, much of which seems to be focused on finding "the one." While the "official" online texts suggest a gendered, almost businesslike attitude toward marriage, a softer (yet still gendered) attitude that is focused on love is found in the forums. Similarly, regarding motherhood, as discussed in chapter 4, there is a tension between the "official" attitude, which tends to present motherhood as a divine, positive experience, and some of the comments, which push back and discuss the hardships related to the work of motherhood. And in chapter 3 regarding sexuality, women and sexual minorities use these online spaces to ask questions they might not have been able to ask offline. In short, the participatory affordances allow for a multiplicity of voices and highlight the tension between traditional views ("power") and those that oppose them ("resistance").

These varying, contradicting opinions can exist in the same internet space—within these websites or forums. The participatory affordances—commenting, sharing, posting—seem to be allowed, if not encouraged, by the editors and webmasters of this digital spaces. Why? I suggest this is because these opposing opinions are still considered part of the same community discourse. That is, religious *digital enclaves* allow for various people, with varying viewpoints, in the community to participate in the same space. While the resisting opinions might not be encouraged (as seen in the section on peer regulation), they are still counted as voices in the same community. Judaism throughout its history did not shy from debate and disagreement, but those usually happen at the level of rabbinical authority. Online, lay people can also partake in these debates.[19] And these debates are possible online for one reason: because they happen in what Campbell and Golan call "digital

Conclusions

enclaves"[20]—safe spaces, guarded by rabbinical approval, religious language, and web editors moderating the content. The combination of Jewish attitude and history toward the multiplicity of opinions and the creating of these internet spaces as space for the community together allow for a more open discourse. To a degree, the discourse can be open because it is happening in what feels like a closed space. Using digital media affordances like moderating content alongside religious norms, like having rabbinical authority as part of the website, creates web spaces that are specifically catered for these communities. The internet is sanctified by putting a "digital *eruv*"—a digital border—around specific web spaces that are than used for religious purposes.

Using both digital affordance and digital media logics, the internet became a sacred space in which issues of gender and sexuality can be discussed and debated. This was done by using participation, emotive language, focus on the self, and crafting digital enclaves to ensure the religious message is maintained and upheld. While some push and pull, some negotiation, does happen in this online discourse, what was becoming clear throughout this book is that technology can be used for religious purposes. By sanctifying the internet, using it for religious purposes, online discourse around even religious taboo matters (like masturbation, feminism, choosing not to be a mother) can find a voice. However, these taboo matters are discussed and then regulated—women's voices are heard and then hushed again—this digital online discourse is used to, mainly, keep women in their traditional place.

Summary

Throughout this book, we saw how religious uses of the internet frame and inform gendered norms and beliefs. Throughout this discourse, rabbis, female authors, and users create a discourse about gender that ascribes sacred meaning to traditional social-cultural gender norms. They do so by using religious language and metaphors to describe traditional gender roles and imbue them with *neoliberal* thinking, such as by claiming that women's bodies are holy and thus need to be covered more modestly than men's bodies, or claiming that women are closer to God than men are and thus need not participate in public prayer (as men do). By framing women as holier than men, religious gender norms become harder to resist or to negotiate, because these norms are portrayed as a positive thing. Furthermore, the "holy" position of women suggests that females who accept and act out their prescribed gendered roles will find joy and personal meaning and will be empowered. The internet is used like a mirror, to better understand the self. And the mirror offered in this Orthodox Jewish online discourse is one that is tinted with neoliberal thinking and spiritual obscuring of traditional practices.

Furthermore, throughout the book, I highlighted how important online *peer regulation* is for the preservation of these traditional norms and practices. It might be unsurprising to find leaders and official statements that uphold the traditional perspectives toward gender and sexual norms. But the promise of the internet is its democratizing power, that anyone and everyone can talk and participate in the discourse. Indeed, we find that many of the mainstream religious websites allow and encourage this participation—and that this participation tends to overwhelmingly support the traditional perspectives. The power of "everybody" can be as important as (if not more important than) the official authority, especially in a community-based religion like Judaism. The internet works here as a window, giving the user a view into what is considered normal in the street, in their community.

These findings demonstrate how religious use of the internet allows for the discussion of gender and sexual norms and how these norms, while openly discussed, are viewed through religious framing that enforces strict and traditional approaches. This also provides the basis for answering this book's core research questions: How are gender and sexuality negotiated and constructed in online Orthodox discourse? How does using the internet as a religious person influence one's conceptions of gender and sex?

Through the discourse in these Jewish mainstream Orthodox websites and other Orthodox online spaces, issues related to gender and sexuality, even those typically considered taboo within their communities, are discussed equally among users, rabbis, and lay people, men and women. While the websites are created by religious organizations and individuals and seek to serve religious users, it was found that religious language used to discuss issues of gender and sexuality in these websites is presented in a simplified fashion. Perhaps this is because the websites are accessible to many different people (and thus are kept at a lower complexity). By and large, religious language is used in a way that does not encourage a multiplicity of opinions. Furthermore, the rationale in these online sources for maintaining certain gender and sex behaviors was focused on the individual's needs, and less on the community or the Halacha. Online, it reads as if the reason you should keep a certain commandment or religious practice is because it is good for you. While the technological affordances and media logics allow for a more egalitarian religious discussion, the overall discourse presents a simplified Jewish view on gender and sexuality. This is further supported by the discursive strategies, which, by and large, present traditional gender and sexual norms as personal and spiritually beneficial. In this fashion, oppressive structural religious gender norms are maintained and enforced by websites' authors and users by framing these norms as empowering and joyful.

In this conclusion chapter, I reiterated the main findings and argument of the book: that digital media serves as a space for the active negotiation of gender and sexual norms in contemporary Judaism through discursive structure. This negotiation is complex. Religious women speak online in their own voices about their bodies, their aspirations, and their experiences; at the same time, these narratives are constructed through traditional understandings of gender and power, de facto strengthening patriarchal religious authority. Digital tools—through their anonymity, participatory affordances, and general media logic—allow silenced voices to be heard and shift the weight of authority. However, as this book shows, most of those participating in the religious discourse use the ability to comment, share, and to produce their own interpretations in order to support and reinforce traditional norms. As a result, women and minority voices, or liberal modern opinions at large, are heard and then *shut down* actively in these online spaces. The internet serves as a "space" for discourse, and through this discourse, power is enacted. In these ways, new communication tools help maintain and even create fundamental viewpoints within Judaism. I leave the reader, then, with this question: who is really empowered in this online participatory religious discourse?

… and Beyond

The observations gleaned from this interdisciplinary book offer a number of important insights for scholars in various fields. This book's findings contribute to general research and the specific area of study in several ways. First, it contributes to communication technology studies by discussing and articulating digital communication as a Foucauldian discourse and by specifying discursive strategies through which gender and sexual norms are maintained and resisted. Second, it contributes to the field of digital religion by operationalizing an analysis method that uniquely considers the sensibilities of researching religion and digital media. Last, it contributes to the study of contemporary Judaism, and specifically digital Judaism, by collecting and analyzing current Jewish attitudes toward gender and sexuality, as they are presented in Orthodox mainstream online media. I expand on each of these contributions in more detail below.

First, throughout this book I have insisted on conceptualizing digital media as a Foucauldian discourse. As discussed in chapter 1, digital media seem to both empower women and gender minorities and at the same time maintain gender binaries.[21] One way to understand this duality is to think of digital communication as a site of struggle different from other media because it reflects not only authoritative knowledge producers (as in rabbis, or more broadly, mass media producers) but the knowledge enacted by "everyone and no one in particular."[22] I suggest we think of digital media as a *discourse in the making*, in which we can see the push and pull between authoritative opinions, the concerns of lay people, the liberty to speak on taboo matters, and the correction and negotiation of gender and sexuality practices and concepts. In other words, digital media (conceptualized as a discourse) offer a visual, tangible, and constantly accessible discourse. As such, we as readers and researchers can more easily analyze digital discourses within a specific community or on a specific concept than we could in offline contexts.

Another contribution of this book that could be helpful for feminist scholars is in naming and noting the discursive strategies that are used to maintain and resist gender and sexual norms, especially those outlined in this chapter as neoliberal strategies. The various discursive strategies highlighted throughout this book as an answer to the question "How are gender and sex negotiated?" might resonate with other negotiations of power—for example, in examining other religious constructions and negotiations of gender and sex or in examining Jewish negotiation of other issues, for example racism or nationality. The analysis done in naming these practices is a helpful step for researchers of discourse or of feminist struggles. Some of these strategies seem to be especially useful for religious gendered discourse—for example, imbuing traditional restrictions or motherhood labor with spiritual meaning. But these strategies can be found even in nonreligious discourses. Therefore, I hope these are useful for other feminist scholars trying to understand or even deconstruct systems of power. While these specific strategies might need to be expanded on, having them described could be helpful for other researchers attempting to decipher the ways in which discursive power operates.

In addition, the type of three-layered critical discourse analysis developed in this book is especially suited for research in digital religion, as it takes into consideration the specific characteristics of studying religious discourse in digital environments. Scholars in this field are particularly aware of the need to examine both religion and media and how they work simultaneously to construct theology, ritual, religious norms, and lived religious experiences. The analysis offered in this book tries to consider these different elements of digital religion, specifically when it comes to the negotiation of gender. As briefly discussed in the literature review, the study of digital religion is at an intersectional moment, in which questions of race, gender, sex, nationality, ethnicity, and more are brought into conversation. My analysis, which combines reviewing religious history and norms alongside technological affordances and media logic to see how both forces are enacted as building blocks of a discourse, might be found useful for that type of study, which needs to consider religion, media, and a discourse concerning another element, such as gender, sexuality, race, or ethnicity.

That being said, it is possible that this type of three-layered critical discourse analysis could be useful in analyzing other forms of discourse, even those that are not religious or digital. This could be done by paying attention to whatever technological affordances through which the discourse takes place (printed books, for example, also have capacities and limitations) and by replacing a focus on "religious" with a focus on "cultural" terminology. In this way, communication researchers can pay attention to the "physical" elements that enable a certain discourse, the ideological tools or worldviews that inform it, and the discursive strategies that participants in the discourse employ for resistance, power, or both.

Finally, this study provides a description of current Orthodox attitudes toward gender and sexuality, at least as those are expressed online. While the study cannot be generalized to represent the entire Jewish or Orthodox world, it does highlight certain trends and attitudes within them. Scholars of Judaism, and more specifically those researching digital Judaism or feminism and Judaism, can find valuable information and multiple examples in this book regarding content in the mainstream websites Chabad, Aish, and Kipa as well as forums and social media, their attitudes toward digital media, and the presentation of gender and sexual norms in these websites. By reading this book, scholars of Judaism can explore current understandings of dating, marriage, intimacy, motherhood, and general attitudes toward feminism, gender, and sexuality in the Orthodox world.

This book sought to answer the question "How are Jewish concepts and norms regarding gender and sexuality negotiated and constructed via Orthodox digital discourse?" Put simply, it arrived at the following answer: The technological affordances of digital communication allow gender and sexuality to be negotiated on religious online spaces through a participatory discourse. Because these online spaces are operated as religious spaces, the negotiation of even sensitive topics can take place. These sensitive topics are constructed and negotiated through a personal perspective, which uses neoliberal self-empowerment as a strategy to maintain traditional norms. In this fashion, traditional and even strict approaches to gender and sexuality are maintained and reinforced by rabbis, website authors, and users. Namely, traditional patriarchal structures are reframed to have spiritual or personal meanings. Resistance to these traditional structures becomes more difficult as the discourse is at the level of the personal and not the social. Conceptualized as a Foucauldian discourse, it is noted that this online discourse maintains power through embracing subtle discursive strategies, such as the communication from of users as well as rabbis, peer regulation, and so on. The "work" of enforcing gender and sexual norms in the Orthodox community online is enacted by all participants of the discourse, not only the religious authority.

While the research question of this book is answered, the questions motivating this book can be further explored. Further research into this topic might include expanding the material that is included in "Orthodox digital discourse" to incorporate additional, less popular Jewish websites, social media groups, or forums. While this research aimed to examine mainstream Jewish discourse, scholarship would also benefit from exploring more peripheral discourses, for example, those about homosexuality or transsexuality. Another avenue that could further assess the findings of this research is to compare it to other religions online—to explore the construction and negotiation of gender and sex in other cultures and religions, such as Christianity, Islam, or in American teenage culture—and see if similar discursive behaviors can be traced in other discourses.

As I'm writing the last few pages of this book, I am patiently awaiting the birth of my first daughter, due in just a few days. She will be born as a Jewish female into twenty-first century's communication technology and twenty-first century's Judaism. I wonder what norms, paths, and conversations she will have. Will she, like me, understand herself through the study of culture, through being Jewish and being a woman? Will she use the internet as a mirror to explore her identity, her role, or as a window to understand her community, the norms? What tools can we as a society provide this unborn young one, so that she has a spiritual path that is not ruled by old patriarchal systems or new neoliberal technologies? In a way, this book began as a journey to answer these questions for myself, became a tool to offer some insight to my fellow peer feminists and scholars (or anyone who is interested), and ends as a wish for my daughter: may you never cease exploring, and know that in your exploration, you might need to break some windows and mirrors.

Notes

Introduction

1. Lövheim, *Media, Religion, and Gender*.
2. Bavli, Berachot 62a.
3. Dosick, *Living Judaism*.
4. Israeli Central Bureau of Statistics, "Israeli Population 1990–2009," Israeli Central Bureau of Statistics, 2010. http://www.cbs.gov.il/www/statistical/isr_pop_heb.pdf.
5. Cooperman et al., "Portrait of Jewish Americans."
6. Ibid.
7. Ibid., 10.
8. Paltiel et al., "Fifty Years Population Projections."
9. Dosick, *Living Judaism*.
10. Lövheim, *Media, Religion, and Gender*, 2.
11. Dosick, *Living Judaism*.
12. Schleicher, "Constructions of Sex and Gender."
13. Boyarin, *Unheroic Conduct*.
14. Ibid., 2.
15. Ibid., 184.
16. Ibid., 153.
17. Biale, *Women and Jewish Law*, 17. The brackets here signal my own omission, which was made to help the reader focus on the main message derived from this text. Throughout the book, I have omitted sections from quotes for the same reason.
18. Adler, *Engendering Judaism*, xx.
19. Irshai, "Toward a Gender Critical Approach."
20. Ibid., 75.
21. Biale, *Women and Jewish Law*.
22. Genesis, 1:28.
23. Mishna, Ketovot, 5:5–6.
24. Rambam, Mishne Torah, Issurei-Biah, 21:9.
25. Theobald, "It's a Tefillin Date."
26. Stadler, *Yeshiva Fundamentalism*.
27. Ibid.
28. Englander and Sagi, *New Discourse*.
29. See Englander and Sagi, *New Discourse*; Stadler, *Yeshiva Fundamentalism*; Theobald, "It's a Tefillin Date."
30. Stadler, *Yeshiva Fundamentalism*.
31. Katz, "Technology Use."
32. Ibid.
33. Fader, "Nonliberal Jewish Women's Audiocassette Lectures."
34. Campbell, *When Religion Meets New Media*.
35. Livio and Tenenboim Weinblatt, "Discursive Legitimation."
36. See Barzilai-Nahon, and Barzilai, "Cultured Technology"; Rosenthal and Ribak, "On Pomegranates and Etrogs."
37. See Raucher, "Yoatzot Halacha"; Lerner, "Internet Resources"; Lev-On and Shahar, "Forum of Their Own."
38. Campbell, *Digital Judaism*, 1.
39. See Campbell, *When Religion Meets New Media*; Campbell, *Digital Judaism*.
40. Barzilai-Nahon and Barzilai, "Cultured Technology."
41. Ibid.
42. This internet filter tool can be found at http://www.neto.net.il.
43. Campbell and Golan, "Creating Digital Enclaves."
44. Ibid.

45. Green, *Judaism on the Web*.

46. Naomi Elbinger, "The Top 11 Orthodox Jewish Websites in the World," *My Parnasa*, October 15, 2012, http://myparnasa.com/orthodox-jewish-websites/.

47. Rashi and McCombs, "Agenda Setting, Religion and New Media."

48. Ibid., 134.

49. Dovid Zaklikowski, "The Infancy and Growth of Judaism on the Web," Chabad.org, http://www.chabad.org/library/article_cdo/aid/784112/jewish/The-Infancy-and-Growth-of-Judaism-on-the-Web.htm.

50. Tapper, "'Cult' of *Aish Hatorah*."

51. Ibid.

52. Campbell and Bellar, "Sanctifying the Internet," 76.

53. Ibid.

54. Rosenthal and Ribak, "On Pomegranates and Etrogs."

55. Israeli Central Bureau of Statistics, "Israeli population 1990–2009."

56. Rosenthal and Ribak, "On Pomegranates and Etrogs," 156.

57. Golan and Campbell, "Strategic Management of Religious Websites," 479.

Chapter 1

1. Ruth Tsuria, "Power Online: The Internet as Discourse," *Society Pages*, September 26, 2018, https://thesocietypages.org/cyborgology/2018/09/26/power-online-the-internet-as-a-discourse/.

2. Foucault, *Archaeology of Knowledge*.

3. Taylor, Falconer, and Snowdon, "Queer Youth, Facebook and Faith."

4. Ibid.

5. Mills, *Discourse*.

6. Finnemann, "Mediatization Theory and Digital Media."

7. Ibid., 83.

8. Jenkins, *Fans, Bloggers, and Gamers*.

9. Plant, *Zeros and Ones*, 37.

10. Meyrowitz, *No Sense of Place*.

11. Haraway, *Simians, Cyborgs, and Women*, 177. My emphasis.

12. Banet-Weiser, *Empowered*.

13. Balsamo, *Technologies of the Gendered Body*, 159.

14. O'Brien, "Writing in the Body," 86.

15. Wallis, *Technomobility in China*, 88.

16. Ibid., 89.

17. Harrison, "Exorcising the 'Plague of Fantasies.'"

18. Pentzold and Seidenglanz, "Foucault@Wiki," 62.

19. Weedon, *Feminist Practice and Poststructuralist Theory*.

20. Jenkins, *Fans, Bloggers, and Gamers*.

21. Rainie and Wellman, *Networked*.

22. Hutchings, "Contemporary Religious Community."

23. Tsuria et al., "Approaches to Digital Methods."

24. Castells, *Rise of the Network Society*.

25. Aycock, "Technologies of the Self."

26. Stahl, "Whose Discourse?"

27. Pentzold and Seidenglanz, "Foucault@Wiki."

28. Harrison, "Exorcising the 'Plague of Fantasies.'"

29. Karaflogka, *E-Religion*.

30. Walby, "Theorising Patriarchy," 222.

31. See de Beauvoir, *Second Sex*; hooks, *Will to Change*.

32. Brown and Bohn, *Christianity, Patriarchy and Abuse*.

33. Weber, *Economy and Society*.

34. Foucault, *Technologies of the Self*.

35. Burchell, Gordon, and Miller, *Foucault Effect*.

36. Wallis, "Technology and/as Governmentality," 334.

37. Rose, "Governing the Enterprising Self," 142.

38. Ibid., 143.

39. Wallis, "Technology and/as Governmentality," 345.

40. Foucault, *Discipline and Punish*.

41. Williams et al., "Looking for Gender," 72.

42. Bartky, "Foucault."

43. Harrison, "Exorcising the 'Plague of Fantasies.'"

44. Campbell, "Introduction," 1.

45. Campbell and Lövheim, "Rethinking the Online-Offline Connection."

46. Wagner, "You Are What You Install."

47. See, for example, de Wildt and Aupers, "Pop Theology."

48. Bellar et al., "Reading Religion in Internet Memes."

49. Lundby, "Theoretical Frameworks."

50. Hjarvard, *Mediatization of Culture and Society*, 10.

51. Ibid., 17.

52. Ibid., 27.

53. Davis and Chouinard, "Theorizing Affordances."
54. Castells, *Rise of the Network Society*.
55. Gottesman, "New Direction."
56. Campbell, *When Religion Meets New Media*, 50.
57. Williams and Edge, "Social Shaping of Technology," 867.
58. Campbell, *When Religion Meets New Media*, 41–42.
59. Ibid., 59.
60. Lövheim, "Mediatization," 24.
61. For example, see Baumel-Schwartz, "Frum Surfing."
62. For example, see Livio and Tenenboim-Weinblatt, "Discursive Legitimation"; Barzilai-Nahon and Barzilai, "Cultured Technology."
63. See Baumel-Schwartz, "It Is Our Custom"; Pitkowsky, "Dear Rabbi."
64. See Gottesman, "New Direction"; Theobald, "It's a Tefillin Date."
65. Theobald, "It's a Tefillin Date."
66. Rosenthal, "Infertility, Blessings, and Head Coverings."
67. Fader, "Nonliberal Jewish Women's Audiocassette Lectures."
68. Lev-On and Shahar, "Forum of Their Own," paragraphs 3 and 4.
69. Theobald, "It's a Tefillin Date," 289.
70. Baumel-Schwartz, "It Is Our Custom"; Baumel-Schwartz, "Frum Surfing."
71. Baumel-Schwartz, "Frum Surfing," 25.
72. Baumel-Schwartz, "It Is Our Custom."
73. Ibid., 48. My emphasis.
74. Pitkowsky, "Dear Rabbi."

Chapter 2

1. Cooperman et al., *Portrait of Jewish Americans*.
2. Rubinstein, "Israelis under the Huppah."
3. Israeli bureau of Statistics, "Marriage in Israel in 2017," August 14, 2019, https://www.cbs.gov.il/he/mediarelease/pages/2019/לקט-נתונים-לרגל-טו-באב-תשעט.aspx.
4. Kiddushin, 2a.
5. Rockman, "Sexual Behavior."
6. Cohen and Tsuria, "Match Made in the Cloud," 188–89.
7. Taragin-Zeller and Kasstan, "'I Didn't Know How.'"
8. Zion-Waldoks, "Rescuing the Jewish Family."
9. A version of this data has been published in Cohen and Tsuria, "Match Made in the Cloud."
10. JDate, "About Us," https://about.jdate.com/about-us-en/.
11. Jewish Telegraphic Agency, "JDate Opens Up to Gay Searches," Jewish Telegraphic Agency, 2005, https://www.jta.org/2005/11/29/lifestyle/jdate-opens-up-to-gay-searches.
12. Aish, "Dating," https://aish.com/life/relationships/dating/.
13. Wandering Jew, forum comment on OKclarity, 2018, https://okclarity.com/forums/topic/lost-piece-of-heart/.
14. DefaultedForums, forum comment on Supertova, January 2012, https://www.supertova.com/forum/discussion/275/internet-dating-experiences-ive-had-mixed-reviews-of-it-what-has-yours-been-like/p1.
15. Tristan, forum comment on Supertova, December 2012, https://www.supertova.com/forum/discussion/275/internet-dating-experiences-ive-had-mixed-reviews-of-it-what-has-yours-been-like/p1.
16. Rahcahs, December 2012, forum comment on Supertova, https://www.supertova.com/forum/discussion/275/internet-dating-experiences-ive-had-mixed-reviews-of-it-what-has-yours-been-like/p1.
17. Sharabi and Caughlin, "Deception in Online Dating."
18. ANHPAM, forum comment on Supertova, July 2014, https://www.supertova.com/forum/discussion/comment/1412.
19. ZIK4u, forum comment on Supertova, July 2014, https://www.supertova.com/forum/discussion/comment/1412.
20. AnaBear3, forum comment on Supertova, July 2014, https://www.supertova.com/forum/discussion/comment/1412.
21. Ar58, forum comment on Kipa.co.il, February 2019, https://www.kipa.co.il/community/show/11806303#11806303/.
22. Forum comments on Kipa.co.il, https://www.kipa.co.il/community/show/11806303#11806303/.
23. StoryTeller, forum comment on Kipa.co.il, January 2019, https://www.kipa.co.il/community/show/11792632#11792632/.
24. Hummingbird, forum comment on Kipa.co.il, January 2019, https://www.kipa.co.il/community/show/11792632#11792632/.

25. OdiSedCredo, forum comment on Kipa.co.il, January 2019, https://www.kipa.co.il/community/show/11792632#11792632/.

26. Bungee, forum comment on Kipa.co.il, February 2019, https://www.kipa.co.il/community/show/11807280#11807280/.

27. Menteul, forum comment on Kipa.co.il, March 2019, https://www.kipa.co.il/community/show/11816574#11816574/.

28. Molli Grossman, "Myths Behind Marriage," Kipa.co.il, July 15, 2016, https://www.kipa.co.il/הורים-וילדים/אין-כניסה-כאן-בוני-ם-מיתוסים-בזוגיות-חל-2.

29. Netanel Kraus, "What Is the Solution to the Problem of Late Bachelorhood?," Kipa.co.il, November 26, 2019, https://www.kipa.co.il/יחסים/דייטים-950181/אז-מה-הפתרון-לבעיית-הרווקות.

30. Ibid.

31. Netanel Liefer, "Seker shel Banot Datiyot Ravekot" [Survey of religious single women: External looks matter but love wins], Kipa.co.il, March 26, 2015, http://www.kipa.co.il/family/173/61942.html.

32. "Bashert: What It Really Means," TorchWeb, accessed October 16, 2023, https://www.torchweb.org/torah_detail.php?id=129.

33. "Basheret—Jewish Dating," Apple Store, accessed October 16, 2023, https://apps.apple.com/us/app/basheret-jewish-dating/id1486274771.

34. Banana, forum comment on OKclarity, 2018, https://okclarity.com/forums/topic/lost-piece-of-heart/.

35. AsherL, forum comment on OKclarity, 2018, https://okclarity.com/forums/topic/lost-piece-of-heart/.

36. Odelia Maimon, "LeBaali Yesh Zogiut Niflaa Veli Lo" [My husband has a wonderful marriage but I don't], Kipa.co.il, August 14, 2014, https://www.kipa.co.il/יחסים/לבעלי-יש-זוגיות-נפלאה-ולי-לא/. My emphasis.

37. Comment on Maimon, "LeBaali Yesh Zogiut Niflaa Veli Lo."

38. Comment on Maimon, "LeBaali Yesh Zogiut Niflaa Veli Lo."

39. Merav Lavi, "Your Husband Doesn't Do Anything at Home?," Kipa.co.il, August 23, 2015, http://www.kipa.co.il/family/173/64168.html.

40. Ibid.

41. Comment on Lavi, "Your Husband Doesn't Do Anything at Home."

42. Comment on Lavi, "Your Husband Doesn't Do Anything at Home."

43. Comment on Lavi, "Your Husband Doesn't Do Anything at Home."

44. Sara Easther Crispe, "The Role of Women in Judaism," Chabad.org, http://www.chabad.org/theJewishWoman/article_cdo/aid/376141/jewish/TheRole-of-Women-in-Judaism.htm.

45. Ibid. My emphasis.

46. Comment on Crispe, "Role of Women in Judaism."

47. Comment on Crispe, "Role of Women in Judaism." My emphasis.

48. 7brachot, https://www.7brachot.co.il/.

49. 2Become1, "Main Page," accessed October 16, 2023, http://2become1.co.il.

50. Taltalim Edomim, forum comment on kipa.co.il, May 2019, https://www.kipa.co.il/community/show/11828241/.

51. See for example, users TovTovTov and EinLeeNick, forum comments on kipa.co.il, May 2019, https://www.kipa.co.il/community/show/11828241/.

52. Yehoshua Jacobs, forum comment on Supertova, January 2013, https://www.supertova.com/forum/discussion/2448/surprise-theres-no-such-thing-as-a-bashertand-6-other-dating-myths-debunked.

53. Sharonit, forum comment on Supertova, February 2013, https://www.supertova.com/forum/discussion/2448/surprise-theres-no-such-thing-as-a-bashertand-6-other-dating-myths-debunked.

54. Tovamode, forum comment on Supertova, January 2013, https://www.supertova.com/forum/discussion/2448/surprise-theres-no-such-thing-as-a-bashertand-6-other-dating-myths-debunked.

55. DOUH8D8NG2, forum comment on Supertova, February 2013, https://www.supertova.com/forum/discussion/2455/ deleted.

56. Elisheve39, forum comment on Kipa.co.il, June 11, 2019, https://www.kipa.co.il/community/show/11835401#11835401/.

57. WanderingJaw, forum comment on Okclarity, 2018, https://okclarity.com/forums/topic/lost-piece-of-heart/.

58. TaloyiBamatzavRoch, forum comment on kipa.co.il, January 2019, https://www.kipa.co.il/community/show/11796112#11796112/.

59. Emuna Braverman, "What Men Really Want," Aish.com, March 6, 2004, http://www.aish.com/f/m/48950326.html.
60. Emuna Braverman, "What Women Really Want," Aish.com, May 8, 2004, http://www.aish.com/f/m/48949236.html.
61. Tzvi Gluckin, "Marriage—For Women Only," video, Aish.com, February 9, 2008, http://www.aish.com/f/m/48959376.html.
62. Ibid.
63. Comment on Tzvi Gluckin, Marriage—For Men Only," video, Aish.com, February 2, 2008, http://www.aish.com/f/m/48958956.html.
64. Comment on Gluckin, "Marriage—For Women Only."
65. Comment on Gluckin, "Marriage—For Women Only."
66. Comment on Gluckin, "Marriage—For Women Only."
67. Gluckin, "Marriage—For Men Only."
68. Comment on Braverman, "What Women Really Want."
69. Comment on Gluckin, "Marriage—For Women Only."
70. See, for example, Yeal Mishalei, "Don't Get Divorced," Kipa.co.il, October 25, 2016, http://www.kipa.co.il/family/69305.html; Aron Moss, "Jewish View of Divorce," Chabad.org, http://www.chabad.org/library/article_cdo/aid/387647/jewish/Jewish-View-ofDivorce.htm.

Interlude 1

1. McLuhan and Fiore, *Medium Is the Message*.
2. Davis, *How Artifacts Afford*, 31.
3. Grapevine, accessed October 16, 2023, shiduch.hidabroot.org.
4. Tsuria and Campbell, "In My Own Opinion," 78.
5. Tsuria, "Jewish Q&A Online," 1.
6. Ibid., 8.

Chapter 3

1. For example, see Lövheim, *Media, Religion and Culture*; Pitkowsky, "Dear Rabbi"; Theobald, "It's a Tefillin Date."
2. Bavli, Beracheot 60a.
3. Bavli, Nedarim 20a.
4. Dosick, *Living Judaism*.

5. See Stadler, *Yeshiva Fundamentalism*; Tsuria, "Jewish Q&A Online."
6. Englander and Sagi, *Sexuality and the Body*.
7. Elor, "Veiled Winter."
8. Ibid.
9. Stadler, *Yeshiva Fundamentalism*.
10. Ibid.
11. Modlifashion, Facebook group, accessed September 2023, https://www.facebook.com/modlifashion.
12. Modest Jewish Fashion, Facebook group, https://www.facebook.com/modest.jewish.fashion/. My emphasis.
13. Shira Teichman, "Dating with Dignity," Aish.com, https://www.aish.com/d/w/Dating-with-Dignity.html.
14. Hanan Greenwed, "Mechar: Banot Datiyot Mitlabshot Besygnon Hilony Mitkashot Limtzo Hatan" [Research: Religious girls dressed in secular style will have difficulty finding a husband], Kipa.co.il, July 23, 2015, https://www.kipa.co.il/מחקר-דתיו/יחסים-ת.-שמתלבשות-בסגנון-חילוני-יתק. My Emphasis.
15. Comment on Greenwed, "Mechar."
16. Comment on Greenwed, "Mechar."
17. Comment on Greenwed, "Mechar."
18. Comment on Greenwed, "Mechar."
19. Chabad, "Modesty," Chabad.org, 2017, http://www.chabad.org/library/article_cdo/aid/1317275/jewish/Modesty.htm.
20. Ibid.
21. Shira Teichman, "Dating with Dignity," Aish.com, https://www.aish.com/d/w/Dating-with-Dignity.html.
22. Comment on Teichman, "Dating with Dignity."
23. Comment on Teichman, "Dating with Dignity."
24. Comment on Chabad, "Modesty."
25. Comment on Chabad, "Modesty."
26. Comment on Chabad, "Modesty."
27. Comment on Chabad, "Modesty."
28. Aron Moss, "Do Women Have Something to Hide?," Chabad.org, http://www.chabad.org/theJewishWoman/article_cdo/aid/650631/jewish/DoWomen-Have-Something-to-Hide.htm.
29. Ibid. My emphasis.
30. Taragin-Zeller, "Modesty for Heaven's Sake," 85.
31. Dina Bacharach, "Restrictions That Free," Chabad.org, http://www.chabad.org/theJewishWoman/article_cdo/aid/1547784

/jewish/Restrictions-That-Free.htm. My emphasis.

32. Comment on Bacharach, "Restrictions That Free."

33. Manis Friedman, "Doesn't Blush Anymore?," Chabad.org, https://www.chabad.org/library/article_cdo/aid/392720/jewish/Doesnt-Anyone-Blush-Anymore.htm.

34. Lori Palatnik, "General Petraeus & Us," Aish.com, https://aish.com/general-petraeus--us/.

35. Mendel Kaplan, "The Jewish Perspective on Love Intimacy," Chabad.org, https://www.chabad.org/multimedia/media_cdo/aid/594602/jewish/The-Jewish-Perspective-on-Love-Intimacy-1.htm. (03:00–03:08).

36. Ibid. (06:02–06:15). My emphasis.

37. Ibid. (46:43–46:50).

38. Maurice Lamm, "Jewish Sexuality," Chabad.org, https://www.chabad.org/library/article_cdo/aid/465153/jewish/The-Intimate-Component-in-Love-and-Marriage-in-Judaism.htm.

39. Manis Friedman, "An Intimate View on Intimacy," Chabad.org, https://www.chabad.org/library/article_cdo/aid/411652/jewish/An-Intimate-View-on-Intimacy.htm.

40. Ibid.

41. Lamm, "Jewish Sexuality."

42. Friedman, "Intimate View on Intimacy."

43. Lamm, "Jewish Sexuality."

44. Friedman, "Intimate View on Intimacy."

45. Comment on Lamm, "Jewish Sexuality."

46. Comment on Friedman, "Intimate View on Intimacy."

47. Comment on Friedman, "Intimate View on Intimacy."

48. Comment on Friedman, "Intimate View on Intimacy."

49. Comment on Friedman, "Intimate View on Intimacy."

50. Comment on Friedman, "Intimate View on Intimacy."

51. Anonymous, "The Touch of Two World," Chabad.org, https://www.chabad.org/theJewishWoman/article_cdo/aid/699739/jewish/The-Touch-of-Two-Worlds.htm.

52. Sarah Zadok, "The Love of Midnight," Chabad.org, https://www.chabad.org/theJewishWoman/article_cdo/aid/387256/jewish/The-Love-of-Midnight.htm.

53. Theobald, "It's a Tefillin Date."

54. Merkaz Yahel, "About," accessed October 20, 2023, https://merkazyahel.org.il/en/.

55. Michel Prince, "New Series in Kipa: Speaking Intimately," Kipa.co.il, August 17, 2016, http://www.kipa.co.il/women/68604.html.

56. Theobald, "It's a Tefillin Date."

57. Comment on Prince, "New Series in Kipa."

58. Comment on Prince, "New Series in Kipa."

59. Comment on Prince, "New Series in Kipa."

60. Comment on Prince, "New Series in Kipa."

61. Comment on Prince, "New Series in Kipa."

62. Comment on Prince, "New Series in Kipa."

63. Comment on Prince, "New Series in Kipa."

64. Comment on Aviva Stav, "Tedabro al ze" [Talk about it], video, Kipa.co.il, August 28, 2015, http://www.kipa.co.il/women/68713.html.

65. Comment on Yehudit Yeser-Weinstein, "Ze Beseder LiTzchuk" [It's OK to laugh], video, Kipa.co.il, August 15, 2016, http://www.kipa.co.il/family/68574.html.

66. Yeser-Weinstein, "Ze Beseder LiTzchuk."

67. Ibid.

68. Stav, "Tedabro al ze."

69. Ella Ben-Shitrit, "How to Prepare Correctly for the Night of Purity Washing," video, Kipa.co.il, August 21, 2016, http://www.kipa.co.il/women/68572.html.

70. Ella Ben-Shitrit, "How to Prepare Correctly."

71. Ma-Tov, "Halaylya harishon beyahad" [First night together], video, Kipa.co.il, 2016, August 23, http://www.kipa.co.il/women/68664.html.

72. Ibid. My emphasis.

73. Ibid. My emphasis.

74. Comment on Ma-Tov, "Halaylya harishon beyahad."

75. Comment on Ma-Tov, "Halaylya harishon beyahad."

76. Comment on Ma-Tov, "Halaylya harishon beyahad."

77. Comment on Ma-Tov, "Halaylya harishon beyahad."

78. Moria Tassan-Michaeli, "Lo lefachid lagaat" [Not afraid to touch], video, Kipa.

co.il, August 22, 2016, http://www.kipa.co.il/women/68653.html.
79. Ibid.
80. Comment on Tassan-Michaeli, "Lo lefachid lagaat."

Interlude 2

1. Jenkins, *Fans, Bloggers, and Gamers.*
2. Andrejevic, *iSpy.*
3. Cheong, "Authority."

Chapter 4

1. Cooperman et al., "Portrait of Jewish Americans."
2. Israeli Central Bureau of Statistics, "Live Births by Mother's Age," Israeli Central Bureau of Statistics, April 2018. https://old.cbs.gov.il/shnaton69/st03_15.pdf.
3. Dubriwny, *Vulnerable Empowered Woman.*
4. Habermas, "Public Sphere," 398.
5. Lehman, "Dressing and Undressing the High Priest."
6. Lehman, Kanarek, and Bronner, *Mothers in the Jewish Cultural Imagination.*
7. Ibid., 1.
8. Cooperman et al., "Portrait of Jewish Americans."
9. Berkovitch, "Motherhood as a National Mission."
10. Ibid.
11. Birenbaum-Carmeli et al., "Cryopreserving Jewish Motherhood," 346.
12. Lehman, Kanarek, and Bronner, *Mothers in the Jewish Cultural Imagination.*
13. Sered, "Introduction."
14. Bjorck and Lazar, "Religious Support."
15. Lehman, Kanarek, and Bronner, *Mothers in the Jewish Cultural Imagination.*
16. Feinstein, "Absent Fathers."
17. Sered, "Introduction."
18. Feinstein, "Absent Fathers."
19. See Stoler-Liss, "Mothers Birth the Nation"; Yuval-Davis, "National Reproduction."
20. Steinfeld, "Wars of the Wombs."
21. Kriger and Kroes, "Child-Rearing Attitudes."
22. Chiswick, "Labor Supply," 703.
23. Winston-Macauley, "*Yiddishe Mamas*," 1.
24. Antler, *You Never Call!*
25. Ibid.
26. Cantor, *Jewish Women/Jewish Men.*
27. Emuna Braverman, "Men's Rights," Aish.com, February 4, 2006, http://www.aish.com/f/mom/48906777.html.
28. Comment on Braverman, "Men's Rights."
29. MOMentum, "The Journey Begins," accessed October 20, 2023, https://momentumunlimited.org/journey/.
30. Alexandra Lukesh, "The Mother of the Mothers in the Diaspora Will Light a Beacon," Ynet.co.il, April 20, 2020, https://www.ynet.co.il/articles/0,7340,L-5721629,00.html.
31. Ibid.
32. Ibid.
33. MOMentum, "Journey Begins."
34. Ibid.
35. Tzvi Freeman, "Eight Great Things About Jewish Mothers," Chabad.org, https://www.chabad.org/library/article_cdo/aid/3976582/jewish/Eight-Great-Things-About-Jewish-Mothers-Really.htm.
36. Chana Weisberg, "No, I'm Not Satisfied with Women's Role in Judaism," Chabad.org, http://www.chabad.org/theJewishWoman/article_cdo/aid/926500/jewish/NotSatisfied-with-Womens-Role-in-Judaism.htm. My emphasis.
37. Ibid.
38. Rachel Bergman, "Freezing My Eggs," Aish.com, https://www.aish.com/ci/w/Freezing-My-Eggs.html.
39. Sarah Hofstetter, "Why Being and Orthodox Jewish Mom Makes Me a Better CEO," Aish.com, https://www.aish.com/ci/w/Why-Being-an-Orthodox-Jewish-Mom-Makes-Me-a-Better-CEO.html.
40. See Siri Rimon, "Being a Working Mom or a Present Mom?," Kipa.co.il, June 2018, https://www.kipa.co.il/הבחיר/יוקר/הורים-וילדים/ה-להיות-אמא-עובדת-או-אמא-נוכחת/; Avisag Adari, "It's Impossible to Be a Prefect Mom with a Glorious Career," Kipa.co.il, March 2019, https://www.kipa.co.il/נשים/יחסים-גם-היום-מצופה-מהאישה---לוותר-על-קריירה-למען-המשפחה.
41. Sara Eshter Crispe, "The Role of Women in Judaism," Chabad.org, http://www.chabad.org/theJewishWoman/article_cdo/aid/376141/jewish/TheRole-of-Women-in-Judaism.htm.
42. Comment on Crispe's article, "The Role of Women in Judaism."

43. Imamother, "Taking Care of Children—A Spiritual Activity?," forum thread on Imamother.com, https://www.imamother.com/forum/viewtopic.php?t=11211.

44. Shalhevet, "Taking Care of Children—A Spiritual Activity?," forum comment on Imamother.com, https://www.imamother.com/forum/viewtopic.php?t=11211. My emphasis.

45. JewishMOM, "Moms Are Like the Sun," Jewishmom.com, May 28, 2019, http://jewishmom.com/2019/05/28/moms-are-like-the-sun/.

46. JewishMom Facebook Group, Facebook, accessed October 22, 2023, https://www.facebook.com/JewishMOMcom/photos/pb.100044428059767.-2207520000./10157706495348336/?type=3.

47. JewishMOM, "HeroMoms," Jewishmom.com, May 13, 2019, http://jewishmom.com/2019/05/13/heromoms/.

48. Ibid.

49. Motek, forum comment on "Taking Care of Children—A Spiritual Activity?," Imamother.com, https://www.imamother.com/forum/viewtopic.php?t=11211.

50. Ibid.

51. Ibid.

52. Chayi Hanfling, "Staying at Home with the Kids on Rosh Hashanah While My Husband Prays in Shul," Aish.com, September 2, 2017, https://www.aish.com/ci/w/Staying-at-Home-with-the-Kids-on-Rosh-Hashanah-while-My-Husband-Prays-in-Shul.html.

53. Comment on Hanfling, "Staying at Home with the Kids."

54. JewishMOM, "Pesach Cleaning is Spiritual," Jewishmom.com, March 23, 2017, http://jewishmom.com/2017/03/23/why-i-think-pesach-cleaning-is-spiritual/.

55. Comment on Emuna Braverman, "What Men Really Want," Aish.com, March 6, 2004, http://www.aish.com/f/m/48950326.html.

56. Sara Esther Crispe, "If Women Were Men," Chabad.org, http://www.chabad.org/theJewishWoman/article_cdo/aid/632330/jewish/IfWomen-Were-Men.htm.

57. Comment on Crispe, "If Women Were Men."

58. Yehudit Oliver, "Parenthood and Partnership—7 Common Myths That Need to Be Re-examined" (Hebrew, my translation), Kipa.co.il, July 8, 2020, https://www.kipa.co.il/יחסים-1095460-הורות-וזוגיות-7---מיתוסים-נפוצים-שצריך-לבחון-מחדש-.

59. Tzvi Freeman, "10 Tips the Parenting Books Won't Tell You," Chabad.org, https://www.chabad.org/library/article_cdo/aid/3389828/jewish/10-Tips-the-Parenting-Books-Wont-Tell-You.htm.

60. Tzippora Price, "Dad's Way," Chabad.org, April 22, 2008, https://www.chabad.org/blogs/blog_cdo/aid/665516/jewish/Dads-Way.htm.

61. Ibid.

62. LoRakIma, comment on Kipa.co.il, September 2018, https://www.kipa.co.il/community/show/11746338#11747392.

63. Kegefen, comment on Kipa.co.il, September 2018, https://www.kipa.co.il/community/show/11746338#11747392.

64. LoRakIma, comment on Kipa.co.il., September 2018, https://www.kipa.co.il/community/show/11746338#11747392.

65. Dikla90, comment on Kipa.co.il, September 2018, https://www.kipa.co.il/community/show/11746338#11747392.

66. Sallam and Sallam, "Religious Aspects of Assisted Reproduction."

67. Silber, "Judaism and Reproductive Technology."

68. For example, see RMA, "Fertility Treatments Religion," MRANY.com, August 5, 2019, https://www.rmany.com/blog/fertility-treatments-religion-how-rma-of-new-york-provides-care-for-the-jewish-community.

69. Rachel C., "Infertility Won't Stop Me from Bringing Life to the World," Chabad.org, https://www.chabad.org/theJewishWoman/article_cdo/aid/4779162/jewish/Infertility-Wont-Stop-Me-From-Bringing-Life-to-the-World.htm.

70. JewishMOM, "The Miracle Working Washerwoman," Jewishmom.com, July 5, 2018, http://jewishmom.com/2018/07/05/the-miracle-working-washerwoman-miriam/.

71. JewishMOM, "The Children I will Never Have," Jewishmom.com, March 14, 2016, http://jewishmom.com/2016/03/14/mourn-with-me-for-the-children-i-will-never-have-by-tamar/.

72. Ibid.

73. Donna Halper, "A Feminist's Quest for a Place in Jewish Life," Chabad.org, http://www.chabad.org/therebbe/article_cdo

/aid/921935/jewish/A-FeministsQuest-for-a-Place-in-Jewish-Life.htm.

74. Chabad.org, "The Rebbe's Letter." Chabad.org, 2017, http://www.chabad.org/therebbe/letters/default_cdo/aid/887542/jewish/TheChildless-Womans-Role-in-Judaism.htm.

75. Comment on Chabad.org, "Rebbe's Letter."

76. Comment on Chabad.org, "Rebbe's Letter."

77. Yarden Yerchi, "Horim? Lama Tzrich Yaladim?" [Parents? Why Do We Need to Have Children?], Kipa.co.il, January 1, 2015, http://www.kipa.co.il/women/60313.html.

78. Comment on Yerchi's article.

79. Comment on Yerchi's article.

80. Comment on Yerchi's article.

81. Comment on Crispe, "The Role of Women in Judaism," Chabad.org, http://www.chabad.org/theJewishWoman/article_cdo/aid/376141/jewish/TheRole-of-Women-in-Judaism.htm. My emphasis.

82. Rivka Slonim, "Chassidic Feminism," Chabad.org, http://www.chabad.org/theJewishWoman/article_cdo/aid/1335/jewish/ChassidicFeminist.htm.

83. Comment on Slonim, "Chassidic Feminism."

84. Comment on Slonim, "Chassidic Feminism."

85. Comment on Slonim, "Chassidic Feminism."

86. Comment on Slonim, "Chassidic Feminism."

87. Ibid.

88. Yvette Alt Miller, "5 Ways Judaism Honors Mothers," Aish.com, https://www.aish.com/f/p/5-Ways-Judaism-Honors-Mothers.html.

89. Chana Weisberg, "No, I'm Not Satisfied with Women's Role in Judaism," Chabad.org, http://www.chabad.org/theJewishWoman/article_cdo/aid/926500/jewish/NotSatisfied-with-Womens-Role-in-Judaism.htm.

Interlude 3

1. Lim, "Clicks, Cabs, and Coffee Houses."

2. Juris, "Reflections on #Occupy Everywhere."

3. Chiluwa, "Social Media Networks," 217.

4. Mihailidis and Viotty, "Spreadable Spectacle in Digital Culture."

5. Ringrose and Harvey, "Digital Mediation."

6. Juris, "Reflections on #Occupy Everywhere."

7. Gill, "Post-Postfeminism?"

8. Cheong, "Authority."

9. For example, see Nas, "'Women in Mosques'"; Kassler and Hinderaker, "To God, I Was Visible"; Tsuria, "Discourse of Practice."

10. Peterson, *Unruly Souls*, 127.

11. See Kassler and Hinderaker, "To God, I Was Visible."

12. Sara Esther Crispe, "The Role of Women in Judaism," Chabad.org. http://www.chabad.org/theJewishWoman/article_cdo/aid/376141/jewish/TheRole-of-Women-in-Judaism.htm.

Chapter 5

1. Irshai and Zion-Waldoks, "Modern-Orthodox Feminism in Israel."

2. Adler, *Engendering Judaism*.

3. Plaskow, "Jewish Feminist Thought."

4. Plaskow, "Jewish Feminist Thought"; Adler, "Jew Who Wasn't There"; Irshai and Zion-Waldoks, "Modern-Orthodox Feminism in Israel."

5. Adler, "Jew Who Wasn't There."

6. Schleicher, "Constructions of Sex and Gender."

7. Avrohom Gordimer, "Ordaining Women and the Role of Mesorah," *Cross-currents*, June 3, 2013, https://cross-currents.com/2013/06/03/what-about-mesorah-do-you-not-understand/.

8. Irshai, "Toward a Gender Critical Approach," 75.

9. Biale, *Women and Jewish Law*.

10. Burman, "Experience, Identities and Alliances."

11. Robinson, "Cyberself"; Tosun, "Motives for Facebook Use."

12. Davidman, "Accommodation and Resistance to Modernity."

13. Israel-Cohen, *Between Feminism and Orthodox Judaism*.

14. Halpern and Safrai, *Jewish Legal Writings by Women*.

15. Hartman, *Feminism Encounters Traditional Judaism*.

16. Sara Esther Crispe, "If Women Were Men," http://www.chabad.org/theJewish Woman/article_cdo/aid/632330/jewish/If-Women-Were-Men.htm.

17. Emuna Braverman, "Men's Rights," Aish.com, February 4, 2006, http://www.aish.com/f/mom/48906777.html.

18. Emuna Braverman, "Post-Feminism Discontent," Aish.com, https://www.aish.com/f/mom/48907517.html.

19. Debbie Gutfreund, "Revisiting Betty Friedan," Aish.com, https://www.aish.com/ci/w/Revisiting-Betty-Friedan.html.

20. Moses Vistoch, "We Are Not Contained by the Disease of Feminism," Kipa.co.il, January 2, 2018, https://www.kipa.co.il/חדשות/רבנית-איצקוביץ-אנחנו-לא-נגועות-במחלת-הפמיניזם/.

21. Baruch Efrati, "Don't Surrender to Feminism," Kipa.co.il, January 20, 2015, https://www.kipa.co.il/חדשות/דעות/הרב-ברוך-אפרתי-לא-לכניעה-לפמיניזם-רעשנ-.

22. Tziporah Heller, "Men and Women: Jewish View of Gender Differences," Aish.com, January 30, 2000, http://www.aish.com/ci/w/48955181.html.

23. Ibid. My emphasis.

24. Wallis, "Technology and/as Governmentality."

25. Comment on Heller, "Men and Women."

26. Comment on Heller, "Men and Women."

27. Comment on Heller, "Men and Women."

28. Comment on Heller, "Men and Women."

29. Imale1, forum comment on Kipa.co.il, June 2017, https://www.kipa.co.il/community/show/11583817#11584638.

30. Bungee, forum comment on Kipa.co.il, November 2018, https://www.kipa.co.il/community/show/11768263#11771502.

31. Anonymous, forum comment on Kipa.co.il, October 2018, https://www.kipa.co.il/community/show/11768263#11771502.

32. Koalee, forum comment on Kipa.co.il, November 2018, https://www.kipa.co.il/community/show/11768263#11771502.

33. Bungee, forum comment on Kipa.co.il, November 2018, https://www.kipa.co.il/community/show/11768263#11771502.

34. Gurrieri and Drenten, "Feminist Politics of Choice."

35. Sommers, *Who Stole Feminism?*; Flew, *How to Think Straight*.

36. Yaakov Rosenblatt, "The Feminist Rabbi," Aish.com, https://www.aish.com/ci/w/The-Feminist-Rabbi.html.

37. Ibid.

38. Sara Esther Crispe, "The Role of Women in Judaism," Chabad.org, http://www.chabad.org/theJewishWoman/article_cdo/aid/376141/jewish/The-Role-of-Women-in-Judaism.htm.

39. Ibid.

40. Comment on Crispe, "Role of Women in Judaism."

41. Comment on Crispe, "Role of Women in Judaism."

42. Comment on Crispe, "Role of Women in Judaism."

43. Rivkah Slonim, "Chassidic Feminism," Chabad.org, http://www.chabad.org/theJewishWoman/article_cdo/aid/1335/jewish/Chassidic-Feminist.htm. My emphasis.

44. Comments on Slonim, "Chassidic Feminism."

45. Comment on Slonim, "Chassidic Feminism." My emphasis.

46. Heilman and Friedman, *Rebbe*.

47. LeOran, "About," leoran.org.il, http://www.leoran.org.il/אודות.

48. LeOran Facebook, "Righteous Actions," Facebook group, accessed May 5, 2020, https://www.facebook.com/leoran.nelech/posts/1089787214699851.

49. See Banet-Weiser, *Empowered*.

50. Mariam Adler, "And You Should Tell Your Daughter," Kipa.co.il, April 21, 2016, http://www.kipa.co.il/women/67368.html.

51. Ibid.

52. Comment on Adler, "And You Should Tell Your Daughter."

53. Comment on Adler, "And You Should Tell Your Daughter."

54. Comment on Adler, "And You Should Tell Your Daughter."

55. Comment on Adler, "And You Should Tell Your Daughter."

56. Melissa Klapper, "Adventures of an Orthodox Feminist in Academia," *NYJewishWeek*, May 5, 2020, https://jewishweek.timesofisrael.com/adventures-of-an-orthodox-feminist-in-academia/.

57. Zeo Lang, "The Journeys of Ruth and Naomi," *NYJewishWeek*, May 21, 2020, https://jewishweek.timesofisrael.com/the-journeys-of-ruth-and-naomi/.

58. Carolyn Hochstadter Dicker, "The Values and Strengths that Orthodox Jewish

Women Bring to the Workplace," *NYJewishWeek*, May 5, 2020, https://www.jta.org/2020/05/05/ny/the-values-and-strengths-that-orthodox-jewish-women-bring-to-the-workplace

59. JOFA, "Shabbaton," Jofa.org, https://www.jofa.org/shabbaton.

60. Jewish Women's Archives, "About," Jwa.org, https://jwa.org/aboutjwa.

61. Kolech, "About Us," Kolech.org.il, https://www.kolech.org.il/he/about-us.html.

62. Hagbah, Facebook group, https://www.facebook.com/groups/hagbah/.

63. Seat at the Table—a Forum for Orthodox Feminism, Facebook group, https://www.facebook.com/groups/1175731335772287/.

64. Teenage Orthodox Feminists, Facebook group, https://www.facebook.com/groups/114029888748700.

65. I'm a religious feminist and I too lack a sense of humor, Facebook group, https://www.facebook.com/groups/352850698102983.

66. FlatbushGirl, "Urgent appeal," Facebook, https://www.facebook.com/flatbushgirl/posts/2665905990205710:0.

Conclusions

1. See Haraway, *Simians, Cyborgs, and Women*; Theobald, "It's a Tefillin Date."

2. See Nachtstern, "Yehdot 2.0 hahaspaa"; Gottesman, "New Direction"; Steinitz, "Responsa 2.0."

3. Alcoff and Gray, "Survivor Discourse."

4. Tziporah Heller, "Men and Women: Jewish View of Gender Differences," Aish.com, January 30, 2000, http://www.aish.com/ci/w/48955181.html.

5. Dubriwny, *Vulnerable Empowered Woman*, 7.

6. Rose, "Governing the Enterprising Self," 143.

7. Ibid., 17.

8. Van Dijck and Poell, "Understanding Social Media Logic."

9. For example, see Pan et al., "Who Do You Think You Are?"; Duffy and Pooley, "'Facebook for Academics.'"

10. Bennett and Segerberg, "Logic of Connective Action."

11. Gottesman, "New Direction."

12. Pitkowsky, "Dear Rabbi."

13. Golan and Campbell, "Strategic Management of Religious Websites."

14. Balsamo, *Technologies of the Gendered Body*.

15. Hanan Greenwed, "Mechar: Banot datiyot mitlabshot besygnon hilony mitkashot limtzo hatan" [Research: Religious girls dressed in secular style will have difficulty finding a husband], Kipa.co.il, July 23, 2015, https://www.kipa.co.il/דתיות/מחקר-דתיות/יחסים-שמתלבשות-בסגנון-חילוני-יתק.

16. Chabad, "Modesty," Chabad.org, 2017, http://www.chabad.org/library/article_cdo/aid/1317275/jewish/Modesty.htm.

17. Johnson et al., "Othering and Being Othered."

18. Davis and Chouinard, "Theorizing Affordances."

19. Pitkowsky, "Dear Rabbi"; Steinitz, "Responsa 2.0."

20. Campbell and Golan, "Creating Digital Enclaves."

21. Haraway, *Simians, Cyborgs, and Women*.

22. Bartky, "Foucault."

Bibliography

Adler, Rachel. *Engendering Judaism: An Inclusive Theology and Ethics.* Boston: Beacon Press, 1999.

———. "The Jew Who Wasn't There: Halacha and the Jewish Woman." *Response: A Contemporary Jewish Review* (Summer 1973): 16–17.

Alcoff, Linda, and Laura Gray. "Survivor Discourse: Transgression or Recuperation?" *Signs: Journal of Women in Culture and Society* 18, no. 2 (1993): 260–90. https://doi.org/10.1086/494793.

Andrejevic, Mark. *iSpy: Surveillance and Power in the Interactive Era.* Lawrence: University Press of Kansas, 2007.

Antler, Joyce. *You Never Call! You Never Write! A History of the Jewish Mother.* Oxford: Oxford University Press, 2008.

Aycock, Alan. "'Technologies of the Self': Foucault and Internet Discourse." *Journal of Computer-Mediated Communication* 1, no. 2 (2006): 0–0. https://doi.org/10.1111/j.1083-6101.1995.tb00328.x.

Balsamo, Anne Marie. *Technologies of the Gendered Body: Reading Cyborg Women.* Durham, NC: Duke University Press, 1996.

Banet-Weiser, Sarah. *Empowered: Popular Feminism and Popular Misogyny.* Durham, NC: Duke University Press, 2018.

Bartky, Sandra Lee. "Foucault, Femininity, and the Modernization of Patriarchal Power." In *Writing on the Body: Female Embodiment and Feminist Theory,* edited by Katie Conboy, Nadia Medina, and Sarah Stanbury, 129–54. New York: Columbia University Press, 1997.

Barzilai-Nahon, Karine, and Gad Barzilai. "Cultured Technology: The Internet and Religious Fundamentalism." *Information Society* 21, no. 1 (2005): 25–40. https://doi.org/10.1080/01972240590895892.

Baumel-Schwartz, Judy Tydor. "Frum Surfing: Orthodox Jewish Women's Internet Forums as a Historical and Cultural Phenomenon." *Journal of Jewish Identities* 2, no. 1 (2009): 1–30. https://doi.org/10.1353/jji.0.0007.

———. "'It Is Our Custom from *Der Alter Heim*': The Role of Orthodox Jewish Women's Internet Forums in Reinventing and Transmitting Historical and Religious Tradition." *Journal of Jewish Identities* 6, no. 1 (2013): 23–56. https://doi.org/10.1353/jji.2013.0003.

Beauvoir, Simone de. *The Second Sex.* New York: Vintage Books, 1974.

Bellar, Wendi, Heidi A. Campbell, Kyong James Cho, Andrea Terry, Ruth Tsuria, Aya Yadlin-Segal, and Jordan Ziemer. "Reading Religion in Internet Memes." *Journal of Religion, Media* and *Digital Culture* 2, no. 2 (2013): 1–39. https://doi.org/10.1163/21659214-90000031.

Bennett, W. Lance, and Alexandra Segerberg. "The Logic of Connective Action: Digital Media and the Personalization of Contentious Politics." *Information, Communication and Society* 15, no. 5 (2012): 739–68. https://doi.org/10.1080/1369118X.2012.670661.

Berkovitch, Nitza. "Motherhood as a National Mission: The Construction of Womanhood in the Legal Discourse in Israel." *Women's Studies International Forum* 20, nos. 5–6 (1997): 605–19. https://doi.org/10.1016/S0277-5395(97)00055-1.

Biale, Rachel. *Women and Jewish Law: An Exploration of Women's Issues in Halakhic Sources*. New York: Schocken Books, 1984.

Birenbaum-Carmeli, Daphna, Marcia C. Inhorn, Mira D. Vale, and Pasquale Patrizio. "Cryopreserving Jewish Motherhood: Egg Freezing in Israel and the United States." *Medical Anthropology Quarterly* 35, no. 3 (2021): 346–63. https://doi.org/10.1111/maq.12643.

Bjorck, Jeffery P., and Aryeh Lazar. "Religious Support, Motives for Having Large Families, and Psychological Functioning Among Religious Jewish Mothers." *Journal of Religion and Health* 50, no. 1 (2011): 177–94. https://doi.org/10.1007/s10943-009-9294-2.

Boteach, Shmuel. *Kosher Sex: A Recipe for Passion and Intimacy*. New York: Broadway Books, 2001.

Boyarin, Daniel. *Unheroic Conduct: The Rise of Heterosexuality and the Invention of the Jewish Man*. Contraversions 8. Berkeley: University of California Press, 1997.

Brown, Joanne Carlson, and Carole R. Bohn, eds. *Christianity, Patriarchy, and Abuse: A Feminist Critique*. New York: Pilgrim Press, 1989.

Burchell, Graham, Colin Gordon, and Peter Miller, eds. *The Foucault Effect: Studies in Governmentality; With Two Lectures by and an Interview with Michel Foucault*. Chicago: University of Chicago Press, 1991.

Burman, Erica. "Experience, Identities and Alliances: Jewish Feminism and Feminist Psychology." *Feminism and Psychology* 4, no. 1 (1994): 155–78. https://doi.org/10.1177/0959353594041009.

Campbell, Heidi, ed. *Digital Judaism: Jewish Negotiations with Digital Media and Culture*. Routledge Studies in Religion and Digital Culture. New York: Routledge, 2017.

———. Introduction to *Digital Religion: Understanding Religious Practice in New Media Worlds*, edited by Heidi A. Campbell, 1–30. Abingdon, UK: Routledge, 2013.

———. *When Religion Meets New Media*. London: Routledge, 2010.

Campbell, Heidi A., and Wendi Bellar. "Sanctifying the Internet." In *Digital Judaism: Jewish Negotiations with Digital Media and Culture*, edited by Heidi A. Campbell, 74–90. New York: Routledge, 2015.

Campbell, Heidi A., and Oren Golan. "Creating Digital Enclaves: Negotiation of the Internet Among Bounded Religious Communities." *Media, Culture and Society* 33, no. 5 (2011): 709–24. https://doi.org/10.1177/0163443711404464.

Campbell, Heidi A., and Mia Lövheim. "Rethinking the Online-Offline Connection in the Study of Religion Online." *Information, Communication and Society* 14, no. 8 (2011): 1083–96. https://doi.org/10.1080/1369118X.2011.597416.

Cantor, Aviva. *Jewish Women/Jewish Men: The Legacy of Patriarchy in Jewish Life*. San Francisco: HarperCollins, 1995.

Castells, Manuel. *The Rise of the Network Society*. Vol. 1, *The Information Age: Economy, Society, and Culture*. 2nd ed., with a new preface. Oxford: Wiley-Blackwell, 2010.

Cheong, Pauline Hope. "Authority." In *Digital Religion: Understanding Religious Practice in Digital Media*, 2nd ed., edited by Heidi A. Campbell and Ruth Tsuria, 87–102. Abingdon, UK: Routledge, 2022.

Chiluwa, Innocent. "Social Media Networks and the Discourse of Resistance: A Sociolinguistic CDA of *Biafra* Online

Discourses." *Discourse and Society* 23, no. 3 (2012): 217–44. https://doi.org/10.1177/0957926511433478.

Chiswick, Barry R. "Labor Supply and Investment in Child Quality: A Study of Jewish and Non-Jewish Women." *Review of Economics and Statistics* 68, no. 4 (1986): 700-703. https://doi.org/10.2307/1924532.

Cohen, Yoel, and Ruth Tsuria. "A Match Made in the Cloud: Jews, Rabbis, and Online Dating Sites." In *It Happened on Tinder: Reflections and Studies on Internet-Infused Dating*, edited by Amir Hetsroni and Meric Tincez, 177–90. Amsterdam: Institute of Network Cultures, 2019.

Cooperman, Alan, Luis Logu, Gregory A. Smith, Erin O'Connell, and Sandra Stencel. "A Portrait of Jewish Americans: Findings from a Pew Research Center Survey of US Jews." Washington, DC: Pew Research Center, 2013. https://www.pewresearch.org/religion/2013/10/01/jewish-american-beliefs-attitudes-culture-survey/.

Davidman, Lynn. "Accommodation and Resistance to Modernity: A Comparison of Two Contemporary Orthodox Jewish Groups." *Sociological Analysis* 51, no. 1 (1990): 35-51. https://doi.org/10.2307/3711339.

Davis, Jenny L. *How Artifacts Afford: The Power and Politics of Everyday Things*. Design Thinking, Design Theory. Cambridge, MA: MIT Press, 2020.

Davis, Jenny L., and James B. Chouinard. "Theorizing Affordances: From Request to Refuse." *Bulletin of Science, Technology and Society* 36, no. 4 (2016): 241–48. https://doi.org/10.1177/0270467617714944.

Dosick, Wayne D. *Living Judaism: The Complete Guide to Jewish Belief, Tradition, and Practice*. San Francisco: HarperSanFrancisco, 1995.

Dubriwny, Tasha N. *The Vulnerable Empowered Woman: Feminism, Postfeminism, and Women's Health*. Critical Issues in Health and Medicine. New Brunswick, NJ: Rutgers University Press, 2013.

Duffy, Brooke Erin, and Jefferson D. Pooley. "'Facebook for Academics': The Convergence of Self-Branding and Social Media Logic on Academia.edu." *Social Media and Society* 3, no. 1 (2017). https://doi.org/10.1177/2056305117696523.

Elor, Tamar. "A Veiled Winter." [Hebrew] *Theory and Criticism* 37 (2010). https://theory-and-criticism.vanleer.org.il/product/החורף-של-הרעולות-כיסוי-וגילוי-ב-20078.

Englander, Yakir, and Avi Sagi. *The New Discourse in Religious Zionist Law on Sexuality and the Body*. Jerusalem: Shalom Hartman Institute, 2013.

———. *Sexuality and the Body in the New Religious Zionist Discourse*. Translated by Batya Stein. Israel: Society, Culture and History; Boston: Academic Studies Press, 2015.

Fader, Ayala. "Nonliberal Jewish Women's Audiocassette Lectures in Brooklyn: A Crisis of Faith and the Morality of Media." *American Anthropologist* 115, no. 1 (2013): 72–84. https://doi.org/10.1111/j.1548-1433.2012.01536.x.

Feinstein, Margarete Myers. "Absent Fathers, Present Mothers: Images of Parenthood in Holocaust Survivor Narratives." *Nashim: A Journal of Jewish Women's Studies and Gender Issues*, no. 13 (2007): 155–82. https://doi.org/10.2979/nas.2007.-.13.155.

Finnemann, Niels Ole. "Mediatization Theory and Digital Media." *Communications* 36, no. 1 (2011). https://doi.org/10.1515/comm.2011.004.

Flew, Antony. *How to Think Straight: An Introduction to Critical Reasoning*. 2nd ed. Amherst, NY: Prometheus Books, 1998.

Foucault, Michel. *The Archaeology of Knowledge*. New York: Vintage Books, 2010.

———. *Discipline and Punish: The Birth of the Prison*. 2nd ed. New York: Vintage Books, 1995.

———. *Technologies of the Self: A Seminar with Michel Foucault*. Edited by Luther H. Martin, Huck Gutman, and Patrick H. Hutton. Amherst: University of Massachusetts Press, 1988.

Gill, Rosalind. "Post-Postfeminism? New Feminist Visibilities in Postfeminist Times." *Feminist Media Studies* 16, no. 4 (2016): 610–30. https://doi.org/10.1080/14680777.2016.1193293.

Golan, Oren, and Heidi A. Campbell. "Strategic Management of Religious Websites: The Case of Israel's Orthodox Communities." *Journal of Computer-Mediated Communication* 20, no. 4 (2015): 467–86. https://doi.org/10.1111/jcc4.12118.

Gottesman, Yael. "A New Direction to Halachic Questions and Answers: The Compatibility of Responsa Topics to the Internet Medium, Regarding Sexuality and Attitudes Towards the Internet." Master's thesis, Bar-Ilan University, 2011. https://www.nli.org.il/he/dissertations/NNL_ALEPH990032541960205171/NLI.

Green, Irving. *Judaism on the Web*. New York: MIS Press, 1997.

Gurrieri, Lauren, and Jenna Drenten. "The Feminist Politics of Choice: Lipstick as a Marketplace Icon." *Consumption Markets and Culture* 24, no. 3 (2021): 225–40. https://doi.org/10.1080/10253866.2019.1670649.

Habermas, Jürgen. "The Public Sphere." In *Rethinking Popular Culture: Contemporary Perspectives in Cultural Studies*, edited by Chandra Mukerji and Michael Schudson, 398–404. Berkeley: University of California Press, 1991.

Halpern, Micah D., and Chana Safrai, eds. *Jewish Legal Writings by Women*. Jerusalem: Urim; New York: Distributed outside of Israel by Lambda, 1998.

Haraway, Donna Jeanne. *Simians, Cyborgs, and Women: The Reinvention of Nature*. New York: Routledge, 1991.

Harrison, Rodney. "Exorcising the 'Plague of Fantasies': Mass Media and Archaeology's Role in the Present; or, Why We Need an Archaeology of 'Now.'" *World Archaeology* 42, no. 3 (2010): 328–40. https://doi.org/10.1080/00438243.2010.497339.

Hartman, Tova. *Feminism Encounters Traditional Judaism: Resistance and Accommodation*. HBI Series on Jewish Women. Waltham, MA: Brandeis University Press; Lebanon, NH: University Press of New England, 2007.

Heilman, Samuel C., and Menaḥem Friedman. *The Rebbe: The Life and Afterlife of Menachem Mendel Schneerson*. 1st paperback ed. Princeton: Princeton University Press, 2012.

Hjarvard, Stig. *The Mediatization of Culture and Society*. New York: Routledge, 2013.

hooks, bell. *The Will to Change: Men, Masculinity, and Love*. 1st paperback ed. New York: Washington Square Press, 2004.

Hunt, Stephen, and Andrew Kam-Tuck Yip. *The Ashgate Research Companion to Contemporary Religion and Sexuality*. London: Routledge, 2016.

Hutchings, Tim. "Contemporary Religious Community and the Online Church." *Information, Communication and Society* 14, no. 8 (2011): 1118–35. https://doi.org/10.1080/1369118X.2011.591410.

Irshai, Ronit. "Toward a Gender Critical Approach to the Philosophy of Jewish Law (Halakhah)." *Journal of Feminist Studies in Religion* 26, no. 2 (2010): 55-77. https://doi.org/10.2979/fsr.2010.26.2.55.

Irshai, Ronit, and Tanya Zion-Waldoks. "Modern-Orthodox Feminism in Israel: Between Nomos and Narrative." *Mishpat U'Mimshal* [Law and Governance] 15 (2013): 233–327.

Israel-Cohen, Yael. *Between Feminism and Orthodox Judaism: Resistance, Identity, and Religious Change in Israel*. Jewish Identities in a Changing World 20. Leiden: Brill, 2015.

Jenkins, Henry. *Convergence Culture: Where Old and New Media Collide*. New York: New York University Press, 2006.

———. *Fans, Bloggers, and Gamers: Exploring Participatory Culture*. New York: New York University Press, 2006.

Johnson, Joy L., Joan L. Bottorff, Annette J. Browne, Sukhdev Grewal, B. Ann Hilton, and Heather Clarke. "Othering and Being Othered in the Context of Health Care Services." *Health Communication* 16, no. 2 (2004): 255–71. https://doi.org/10.1207/S15327027HC1602_7.

Juris, Jeffery. "Reflections On #Occupy Everywhere: Social Media, Public Space, and Emerging Logics of Aggregation." In *Youth, Space and Time*, edited by Charles Feixa, Carmen Leccardi, and Pam Nilan, 385–414. The Hague: Brill, 2016.

Karaflogka, Anastasia. *E-Religion: A Critical Appraisal of Religious Discourse on the World Wide Web*. London: Equinox, 2006.

Kassler, Katie, and Amorette Hinderaker. "'To God, I Was Visible, and I Was Beautiful': Parody and Religious Organizational Resisting Within (UN)CHANGED Online Narratives." *Communication Quarterly* 70, no. 3 (2022): 250–69. https://doi.org/10.1080/01463373.2022.2046622.

Katz, Yaron. "Technology Use in the Religious Communities in Israel: Combining Traditional Society and Advanced Communications." *Journal of Religion, Media and Digital Culture* 1, no. 2 (2012): 1–30. https://doi.org/10.1163/21659214-90000014.

Kriger, Sara Finn, and William H. Kroes. "Child-Rearing Attitudes of Chinese, Jewish, and Protestant Mothers." *Journal of Social Psychology* 86, no. 2 (1972): 205–10. https://doi.org/10.1080/00224545.1972.9918618.

Lehman, Marjorie. "Dressing and Undressing the High Priest: A View of Talmudic Mothers." *Nashim: A Journal of Jewish Women's Studies and Gender Issues*, no. 26 (2014): 52. https://doi.org/10.2979/nashim.26.52.

Lehman, Marjorie, Jane L. Kanarek, and Simon J. Bronner, eds. *Mothers in the Jewish Cultural Imagination*. Jewish Cultural Studies. Liverpool: The Littman Library of Jewish Civilization, 2017.

Lerner, Heidi G. "Internet Resources for Researching Orthodox Judaism." *Journal of Religious and Theological Information* 7, nos. 3–4 (2009): 161–69. https://doi.org/10.1080/10477840902783028.

Lev-On, Azi, and Rivka Neriya-Ben Shahar. "A Forum of Their Own: Views About the Internet Among Ultra-Orthodox Jewish Women Who Browse Designated Closed Fora." *First Monday* 16, no. 4 (2011). https://doi.org/10.5210/fm.v16i4.3228.

Lim, Merlyna. "Clicks, Cabs, and Coffee Houses: Social Media and Oppositional Movements in Egypt, 2004–2011." *Journal of Communication* 62, no. 2 (2012): 231–48. https://doi.org/10.1111/j.1460-2466.2012.01628.x.

Livio, Oren, and Keren Tenenboim Weinblatt. "Discursive Legitimation of a Controversial Technology: Ultra-Orthodox Jewish Women in Israel and the Internet." *Communication Review* 10, no. 1 (2007): 29–56. https://doi.org/10.1080/10714420601168467.

Lövheim, Mia, ed. *Media, Religion, and Gender: Key Issues and New Challenges*. Media, Religion and Gender. London: Routledge, 2013.

———. "Mediatization: Analyzing Transformations of Religion from a Gender Perspective." *Media, Culture and Society* 38, no. 1 (2016): 18–27. https://doi.org/10.1177/0163443715615411.

Lundby, Kunt. "Theoretical Frameworks for Approaching Religion and New Media." In *Digital Religion: Understanding Religious Practice in New Media Worlds*, edited by Heidi A. Campbell, 225–37. Abingdon, UK: Routledge, 2013.

McLuhan, Marshall, and Quentin Fiore. *The Medium Is the Message: An Inventory of Effects*. Berkeley, CA: Gingko Press, 2001.

Meyrowitz, Joshua. *No Sense of Place: The Impact of Electronic Media on Social Behavior*. 1st paperback ed. New York: Oxford University Press, 1986.

Mihailidis, Paul, and Samantha Viotty. "Spreadable Spectacle in Digital Culture: Civic Expression, Fake News, and the Role of Media Literacies in 'Post-Fact' Society." *American Behavioral Scientist* 61, no. 4 (April 2017): 441–54. https://doi.org/10.1177/0002764217701217.

Mills, Sara. *Discourse*. New Critical Idiom. London: Routledge, 2004.

Nachtstern, Boaz. "Yehdot 2.0 hahaspaa she haineternet al. hahevrah hadtit" [Judaism 2.0: The Influence of the Internet on the Religious Society in the 21st Century]. In *Yehaud VeTiksoret* [Judaism and Media], edited by Tsurial Rashi and Motti Zepth, 195–208. Israel: Golden Crown Press, 2008.

Nas, Alparslan. "'Women in Mosques': Mapping the Gendered Religious Space Through Online Activism." *Feminist Media Studies* 22, no. 5 (2022): 1163–78. https://doi.org/10.1080/14680777.2021.1878547.

O'Brien, Jodi. "Writing in the Body, Gender (Re)Production in Online Interaction." In *Communities in Cyberspace*, edited by Peter Kollock and Marc Smith, 76–105. London: Routledge, 1999.

Paltiel, Ari, Michel Sepulchre, Irene Kornilenko, and Martin Maldonado. "Fifty Years Population Projections for Israel: 2009–2059." Israel Demography and Census Department, November 30, 2011. http://www.news1.co.il/uploadFiles/659603297710419.pdf.

Pan, Zhao, Yaobin Lu, Bin Wang, and Patrick Y. K. Chau. "Who Do You Think You Are? Common and Differential Effects of Social Self-Identity on Social Media Usage." *Journal of Management Information Systems* 34, no. 1 (2017): 71–101. https://doi.org/10.1080/07421222.2017.1296747.

Pentzold, Christian, and Sebastian Seidenglanz. "Foucault@Wiki: First Steps Towards a Conceptual Framework for the Analysis of Wiki Discourses." In *Proceedings of the 2006 International Symposium on Wikis*, 59–68. Odense, Denmark: ACM, 2006. https://doi.org/10.1145/1149453.1149468.

Peterson, Kristin M. *Unruly Souls: The Digital Activism of Muslim and Christian Feminists*. New Brunswick, NJ: Rutgers University Press, 2022.

Pitkowsky, Michael. "'Dear Rabbi, I Am a Woman Who . . .': Women Asking Rabbis Questions, from Rabbi Moshe Feinstein to the Internet." *Nashim: A Journal of Jewish Women's Studies and Gender Issues* 21, no. 1 (2011): 134–59.

Plant, Sadie. *Zeros and Ones: Digital Women and the New Technoculture*. New York: Doubleday, 1997.

Plaskow, Judith. "Jewish Feminist Thought." In *History of Jewish Philosophy*, edited by Daniel Frank and Oliver Leaman, 885–95. New York: Routledge, 2003.

Rainie, Harrison, and Barry Wellman. *Networked: The New Social Operating System*. Cambridge, MA: MIT Press, 2012.

Rashi, Tsuriel, and Maxwell McCombs. "Agenda Setting, Religion and New Media: The Chabad Case Study." *Journal of Religion, Media and Digital Culture* 4, no. 1 (2015): 126–45. https://doi.org/10.1163/21659214-90000103.

Raucher, Michal. "Yoatzot Halacha: Ruling the Internet, One Question at a Time." In *Digital Judaism: Jewish Negotiations with Digital Media and Culture*, edited by Heidi A. Campbell, 57–73. New York: Routledge, 2015.

Ringrose, Jessica, and Laura Harvey. "Digital Mediation, Connectivity, and Networked Teens." In *Routledge Handbook of Physical Cultural Studies*, edited by Michael Silk, David Andrews, and Holly Thorpe, 451–64. London: Routledge, 2019.

Robinson, Laura. "The Cyberself: The Self-Ing Project Goes Online, Symbolic Interaction in the Digital Age." *New Media and Society* 9, no. 1 (2007): 93–110. https://doi.org/10.1177/1461444807072216.

Rockman, Hannah. "Sexual Behavior Among Ultra-Orthodox Jews." In *Jewish Explorations of Sexuality*, edited by Jonathan Magonet, 191–204. New York: Berghahn Books 1995.

Rose, Nikolas. "Governing the Enterprising Self." In *The Values of the Enterprise Culture: The Moral Debate*, edited by Paul Heelas and Paul Morris, 141–64. London: Routledge, 1992.

Rosenthal, Michele. "Infertility, Blessings, and Head Coverings: Mediated Practices of Jewish Repentance." In *Media, Religion and Gender: Key Issues and New Challenges*, edited by Mia Lövheim, 111–24. London: Routledge, 2013.

Rosenthal, Michele, and Rivka Ribak. "On Pomegranates and Etrogs: Internet Filters as Practices of Media Ambivalence Among National Religious Jews in Israel." In *Digital

Judaism: Jewish Negotiations with Digital Media and Culture, edited by Heidi A. Campbell, 153–68. New York: Routledge, 2015.

Rubinstein, Roee. "Israelis Under the Huppah: Age of Marriage Is Down, Number of Bachelors Is Up." Ynet, August 14, 2019. https://www.ynet.co.il/articles/0,7340,L-5569097,00.html.

Sallam, Hassan Nooman, and N. H. Sallam. "Religious Aspects of Assisted Reproduction." Facts, Views and Vision in ObGyn 8, no. 1 (2016): 33–48.

Schleicher, Marianne. "Constructions of Sex and Gender: Attending to Androgynes and Tumtumim Through Jewish Scriptural Use." Literature and Theology 25, no. 4 (2011): 422–35. https://doi.org/10.1093/litthe/frr051.

Sered, Susan. "Introduction: Mothers and Icons." Nashim: A Journal of Jewish Women's Studies and Gender Issues, no. 3 (2000): 5–14.

Sharabi, Liesel L., and John P. Caughlin. "Deception in Online Dating: Significance and Implications for the First Offline Date." New Media and Society 21, no. 1 (2019): 229–47. https://doi.org/10.1177/1461444818792425.

Silber, Sherman J. "Judaism and Reproductive Technology." In Oncofertility, edited by Teresa K. Woodruff, Laurie Zoloth, Lisa Campo-Engelstein, and Sarah Rodriguez, 71–80. Cancer Treatment and Research. Boston: Springer, 2010. https://doi.org/10.1007/978-1-4419-6518-9_38.

Sommers, Christina Hoff. Who Stole Feminism? How Women Have Betrayed Women. New York: Touchstone, 1995.

Stadler, Nurit. Yeshiva Fundamentalism: Piety, Gender, and Resistance in the Ultra-Orthodox World. New York: New York University Press, 2009.

Stahl, Carsten Bernd. "Whose Discourse? A Comparison of the Foucauldian and Habermasian Concepts of Discourse in Critical IS Research." In Proceedings of the 10th Americas Conference on Information Systems, 4239–336. New York: AMC, 2004.

Steinfeld. "Wars of the Wombs: Struggles Over Abortion Policies in Israel." Israel Studies 20, no. 2 (2015): 1–26. https://doi.org/10.2979/israelstudies.20.2.1.

Steinitz, O. Z. "Responsa 2.0: Are Q&A Websites Creating a New Type of Halachic Discourse?" Modern Judaism 31, no. 1 (2011): 85–102. https://doi.org/10.1093/mj/kjq034.

Stoler-Liss, Sachlav. "'Mothers Birth the Nation': The Social Construction of Zionist Motherhood in Wartime in Israeli Parents' Manuals." Nashim: A Journal of Jewish Women's Studies and Gender Issues 6, no. 1 (2003): 104–18. https://doi.org/10.1353/nsh.2004.0012.

Tapper, Aaron Joshua. "The 'Cult' of Aish Hatorah: Ba'alei Teshuva and the New Religious Movement Phenomenon." Jewish Journal of Sociology 44, nos. 1–2 (2002): 5–29.

Taragin-Zeller, Lea. "Modesty for Heaven's Sake: Authority and Creativity Among Female Ultra-Orthodox Teenagers in Israel." Nashim: A Journal of Jewish Women's Studies and Gender Issues, no. 26 (2014): 75–96. https://doi.org/10.2979/nashim.26.75.

Taragin-Zeller, Lea, and Ben Kasstan. "'I Didn't Know How to Be with My Husband': State-Religion Struggles over Sex Education in Israel and England." Anthropology and Education Quarterly 52, no. 1 (2021): 5–20. https://doi.org/10.1111/aeq.12358.

Taylor, Yvette, Emily Falconer, and Ria Snowdon. "Queer Youth, Facebook and Faith: Facebook Methodologies and Online Identities." New Media and Society 16, no. 7 (2014): 1138–53. https://doi.org/10.1177/1461444814544000.

Theobald, Simon. "'It's a Tefillin Date': Alternative Narratives of Orthodox Jewish Sexuality in the Digital Age." In The Ashgate Research Companion to Contemporary Religion and Sexuality, edited by Andrew Kam-Tuck Yip and Stephen Hunt, 289–304. London: Routledge, 2012.

Tosun, Leman Pınar. "Motives for Facebook Use and Expressing 'True Self' on the Internet." Computers in Human Behavior 28, no. 4 (2012): 1510–17. https://doi.org/10.1016/j.chb.2012.03.018.

Tsuria, Ruth. "Discourse of Practice: The Negotiation of Sexual Norms Via Online Religious Discourse." *International Journal of Communication* 14 (2020): 3595–613.

———. "Jewish Q&A Online and the Regulation of Sexuality: Using Foucault to Read Technology." *Social Media and Society* 2, no. 3 (2016): 205630511666217. https://doi.org/10.1177/2056305116662176.

Tsuria, Ruth, and Heidi A. Campbell. "'In My Own Opinion': Negotiation of Rabbinical Authority Online in Responsa Within *Kipa.Co.Il*." *Journal of Communication Inquiry* 45, no. 1 (2021): 65–84. https://doi.org/10.1177/0196859920924384.

Tsuria, Ruth, Aya Yadlin-Segal, Alessandra Vitullo, and Heidi A. Campbell. "Approaches to Digital Methods in Studies of Digital Religion." *Communication Review* 20, no. 2 (2017): 73–97. https://doi.org/10.1080/10714421.2017.1304137.

Van Dijck, José, and Thomas Poell. "Understanding Social Media Logic." *Media and Communication* 1, no. 1 (2013): 2–14. https://doi.org/10.17645/mac.v1i1.70.

Wagner, Rachel. "You Are What You Install: Religious Authenticity and Identity in Mobile Apps." In *Digital Religion: Understanding Religious Practice in New Media Worlds*, edited by Heidi A. Campbell, 199–206. Abingdon, UK: Routledge, 2013.

Walby, Sylvia. "Theorising Patriarchy." *Sociology* 23, no. 2 (1989): 213–34. https://doi.org/10.1177/0038038589023002004.

Wallis, Cara. "Technology and/as Governmentality: The Production of Young Rural Women as Low-Tech Laboring Subjects in China." *Communication and Critical/Cultural Studies* 10, no. 4 (2013): 341–58. https://doi.org/10.1080/14791420.2013.840386.

———. *Technomobility in China: Young Migrant Women and Mobile Phones*. Critical Cultural Communication. New York: New York University, 2013.

Weber, Max. *Economy and Society: An Outline of Interpretive Sociology*. 2 vols. Edited by Guenther Roth and Claus Wittich. With a New Foreword by Guenther Roth. Berkeley: University of California Press, 2013.

Weedon, Chris. *Feminist Practice and Poststructuralist Theory*. 2nd ed. Cambridge, MA: Blackwell, 1997.

Whitmer, Jennifer M. "You Are Your Brand: Self-Branding and the Marketization of Self." *Sociology Compass* 13, no. 3 (2019): e12662. https://doi.org/10.1111/soc4.12662.

Wildt, Lars de, and Stef Aupers. "Pop Theology: Forum Discussions on Religion in Videogames." *Information, Communication and Society* 23, no. 10 (2020): 1444–62. https://doi.org/10.1080/1369118X.2019.1577476.

Williams, Dmitri, Mia Consalvo, Scott Caplan, and Nick Yee. "Looking for Gender: Gender Roles and Behaviors Among Online Gamers." *Journal of Communication* 59, no. 4 (2009): 700–725. https://doi.org/10.1111/j.1460-2466.2009.01453.x.

Williams, Robin, and David Edge. "The Social Shaping of Technology." *Research Policy* 25, no. 6 (September 1996): 865–99. https://doi.org/10.1016/0048-7333(96)00885-2.

Winston-Macauley, Marnie. *"Yiddishe Mamas": The Truth About the Jewish Mother*. Kansas City, MO: Andrews McMeel, 2007.

Yuval-Davis, Nira. "National Reproduction and 'the Demographic Race' in Israel." In *Woman-Nation-State*, edited by Nira Yuval-Davis, Floya Anthias, and Jo Campling, 92–109. London: Palgrave Macmillan, 1989.

Zion-Waldoks, Tanya. "Rescuing the Jewish Family, One Divorce at a Time: An Israeli Take on the 'Jewish Continuity Crisis' Debates." *Contemporary Jewry* 42, no. 1 (2022): 61–84. https://doi.org/10.1007/s12397-022-09419-0.

Index

activities, spiritual, 110, 112
Adler, Rachel, 9, 131
affordances, technology, 25, 32, 34–36, 41, 54, 61, 68–70, 158, 161–62
Aish HaTorah
    organization, 15–16, 117
    website, 48, 63, 65, 80–81, 115, 157–58
age, 43, 71, 102, 109, 117
agency, 28, 45, 125, 155–56
applications, 30, 32, 55, 133

Balsamo, Anne, 24
Baumel-Schwartz, Judith 39
Biale, Rachel, 8–9, 133
Bible, 55, 74, 94, 104, 147–8
birth, 32, 102, 108, 117, 132, 140, 148
blog, 89, 110, 113, 118, 147
bodies, 19, 24, 29, 71, 73, 75–77, 80–82, 90, 94–96, 160, 162
boys, 45, 73–74, 91, 127–28

Campbell, Heidi, A., 12–13, 16–17, 34, 70, 158, 161
Chabad
    movement, 12–15, 140–41, 143
    website 6, 46–47, 52, 58–59, 80–81, 84–85, 103, 107–9, 115, 119–22, 154, 157
children, 57, 59–60, 86, 91, 99, 102, 105–6, 108–12, 114–23, 126
communication technologies, 22, 30–31, 34, 40–41
communities
    boundaries, 79–80, 99–100
    dating, 45–49, 54–55
    feminist, 147–50

Jewish communities and Halacha, 4–5, 9
    online, 30, 33–38, 93, 123, 126, 152
    respect and belonging, 116, 118, 120–24
contemporary Judaism, 7–8, 152–53, 160, 164
culture, participatory, 23, 26, 80, 153

dating websites, 46–47, 54–55, 60–61, 67, 69
digital discourse, 9, 12, 35, 66, 103–4, 133–34, 145, 150, 153, 165
digital enclaves, 13, 38, 161–62

education, 14, 26, 103, 108, 128, 134, 144
emotions, 51, 137–38, 156–57
empowerment, 103, 133, 136, 142, 167
    negotiation online, 37
    personal, 56, 77, 83, 149–50, 154–55
    self, 56, 67, 88, 108
Englander, Yakir, 10–11
ethnicity, 6, 8, 32, 166

Facebook, 22, 68–69, 93, 96, 110, 144, 150
    group, 14, 84, 89, 107, 148–50
    sharing, 77–78, 137, 142, 157
family purity, 7, 53, 74, 76, 86–87, 94–95, 105
fathers, 68, 104–5, 111, 115–16, 129
female sexuality, 72–73, 158
feminine, 7, 58–59, 82, 133, 135, 137–45
femininity, 23, 26, 29, 138, 140–43
Feminism, 11, 17, 19, 66, 110, 122–23, 127–50, 157, 162, 166
    Feminism, religious, 9, 130, 133, 145–46
    Feminist Movement, 131,134,136, 142–43, 145, 149, 154
    Feminist Scholars, 23, 25, 158, 165
forums, 70, 77, 100, 104, 116, 125–26, 166–67

comments, 110–11, 138, 158–61
dating, 46–52, 61–63
ultra-Orthodox, 37, 39–40
Foucault, Michel, 9, 26, 28–29, 40, 132
Foucauldian Discourse, 21, 25, 27, 152, 159, 164–65, 167

gender differences, 56, 135–36, 138–39, 142
girls, 17, 45, 51, 73, 79, 86, 103, 120, 127–29, 144, 147
God, 54–55, 59, 109–10, 113, 116, 121–23, 133–35, 140, 162
governmentality, technology and/as, 28–29, 137, 155

Halacha, 4–6, 8–10, 27, 82, 97, 136, 146, 148, 159, 163
Halachic rulings, 73, 75–76, 93–95, 108, 131–34, 153
texts, 79, 128, 153
Hashem, 55, 59, 110, 113
Hebrew, 6, 15, 47–48, 143, 148
hegemonic, 3, 9, 23, 25, 29, 132–3
heterosexual, 38, 66, 73, 87, 90, 137
Hjarvard, Stig, 33–35
holidays, 105, 113, 119, 147
holy, 80, 86, 110, 113, 116, 122, 162
homosexuality, 10, 37, 48, 86, 167

identity, 22, 133, 155–56
digital, 21, 26, 130–31, 145, 157
gendered, 6, 23, 123, 136–39, 146–49
Jewish, 7, 45, 60, 78, 80, 121
sexual, 38, 81, 160
ideology, 15, 28, 39, 45–47, 111, 130, 133, 146, 155
infertility, 118–19
institutions, 12, 16–17, 26–28, 33, 105–6, 129, 148, 156
Instagram, 2, 14
intimacy, 10–11, 72–76, 107
discussion, 53, 83–87, 89
healthy, 90–91, 94–98
See also sexuality
Israel (state), 4–6, 14–18, 43, 51, 70, 74–76, 78, 82, 102, 105–6, 108, 128
Israeli Orthodox. *See* National Religious

Jewish culture, 8, 14, 105–6, 108
Jewish feminism, 9, 130–32, 134, 140–41, 147, 149
Jewish identity, 7, 121
Jewish motherhood, 105–6, 110–11, 123
Jewish Orthodox Feminist Alliance (JOFA), 132, 147–48

Jewish Women's Archives (JWA), 147–48

Kabbalah, 14, 82
kids, 44, 48, 61, 91–92, 108–11, 114–16
See also children
kiruv, 15–16
Kolech, 132, 145, 147–48
Kosher Sexuality, 77, 83–88, 92

masculinity, 7–8, 23, 26, 138, 140
media logics, 34–36, 41–42, 156–57, 162–63
mediatization, 32–33, 35, 41
mediatization of religion, 22, 32–33, 35

National Religious, 5, 10, 16–18, 45–46, 53, 74, 78, 89, 128–29
neoliberal, 54, 59, 67, 77, 83, 88, 97, 103, 139, 145, 150, 153–56
Networked Society, 26
newspaper, 11–12, 15, 57
niddah, 7, 94

offline, 15, 21, 32, 39, 52, 61, 76–77, 101, 147, 157, 160–61
OKClarity, 14, 47–48, 55, 63
online Q&A, 39, 46, 70, 153
opposition, 18, 125, 136
oppression, 36, 133, 136–37, 139, 154, 164
Orthodox (Jewish Denomination), 4–7, 53, 102, 105, 152, 155–58, 161, 163, 166
community, 9–17, 43, 45–46, 74–75, 89–91, 119
discourse, 35, 37–38, 71–72, 77, 100
othering, 71, 146, 159–60

panopticon, 28–29
parenting, 45, 49, 60, 87, 103–9, 114–6
participatory affordances, 19, 25, 72, 158, 161, 164
Passover, 17, 112–13
peer regulation, 70, 100, 157, 159–61, 163, 167
Pitkowsky, Michelle, 39–40
Plant, Sadie, 23
power, 27–31, 40–41, 99–101, 152, 160–62, 163–67
patriarchal, 12, 155–6
religious, 9, 58–59, 131–32, 158–9
online discourse, 2–3, 18–25, 72, 123–26
prayer, 7, 114, 116, 131–33, 135–36, 139, 147
public sphere, 42, 99–101, 103–4, 123
purity, 11, 53, 72, 74–76, 79, 86–87, 94–95, 105

Q&A, *see* Online Q&A
Queer (including LGBTQIA+), 11, 38, 125

rabbis, 4, 69–70, 115, 128, 157–60, 162
    rabbinical texts and logic, 8, 10, 29–30, 74, 76
    reactions to digital media, 12, 46, 60
    rabbinical authority, 17, 37, 39, 52, 83, 88, 146
Rebbe, the (Menachem Mendel Schneerson), 14–15, 119, 143
religious authority, 37, 149, 158, 160, 167
    patriarchal, 19, 164
    online, 30–31, 99, 125
Religious Social Shaping of Technology (RSST), 21, 32–35, 41
religious texts, 55, 73, 128, 157
Reform (Jewish denomination), 4–5, 95, 132, 146
regulation, 25, 37, 54, 81
    rabbinical, 12, 152, 157–60
    self-regulation, 29, 40, 103, 137
    peer-regulation, 70, 100, 157–60, 163, 167
restrictions, 10, 76–77, 81–83, 86, 88, 165
rights, 8, 10, 45, 54, 107, 114, 132, 134, 139, 143, 146, 150
romantic, 44, 47–50, 52–55, 62

Sabbath, 47, 61, 111
Sacred, 33, 82, 85–88, 90, 110, 162
sexuality, 6–11, 37–38, 73–77, 81–83, 84–88, 155–56, 159, 163
    harassment, 85, 154
    premarital, 47, 86, 100
    sex education, 46, 75, 90

schools, 11, 28, 45, 74–75, 103, 115, 128–29
secular, 4–6, 11, 15, 17, 27, 66, 75, 78, 80, 122, 131, 142, 154
Social Shaping of Technology (SST), 34
Stadler, Nurit, 10–11, 75–76
SuperTova, 47–50, 62

taboo, 34, 70–72, 84, 87–93, 96, 158, 162–63, 165
Talmud, 3, 73, 104, 128, 131, 134
technological determinism, 33
technology, cultured, 13, 92
temple, 4, 74, 112, 123
Twitter, 22, 68–69

Ultra-Orthodox, 4–7, 10–13, 37–39, 43, 74, 76, 82, 128
United States, 4, 14, 16, 74, 102, 106, 131, 147

video(s), 32, 48, 63–65, 67, 84, 89–96, 103–4, 107, 126

website editor(s), 88, 91, 93, 125–26, 158
wedding, 45–46, 52, 56, 73–74, 94–96

Yahel Center, 89–92, 96–97, 126

www.ingramcontent.com/pod-product-compliance
Lightning Source LLC
LaVergne TN
LVHW041634060526
838200LV00040B/1562